Factor Analysis
and Related Methods

FACTOR ANALYSIS AND RELATED METHODS

RODERICK P. MCDONALD
Macquarie University
New South Wales, Australia

LAWRENCE ERLBAUM ASSOCIATES, PUBLISHERS
1985   Hillsdale, New Jersey   London

Lawrence Erlbaum Associates, Inc., Publishers
365 Broadway
Hillsdale, New Jersey 07642

Library of Congress Cataloging in Publication Data

McDonald, Roderick P.
  Factor analysis and related methods.

  Bibliography: p.
  Includes index.
  1. Social sciences—Statistical methods.   2. Factor
analysis.   I. Title.
HA29.M4385 1985   300'.28   84-21157
ISBN 0-89859-388-3

Printed in the United States of America
10   9   8   7   6   5   4   3   2   1

Contents

TO AVIS
PETER, CHRISTINE, AND STEPHANIE
AND IN MEMORY OF MY PARENTS

Preface

This book is a revision and expansion of a set of chapters on factor analysis written in 1975 while I was on study leave in the Department of Psychology, University College, London. These chapters have been used as course notes for postgraduate classes in factor analysis at the Ontario Institute for Studies in Education over a number of years, and the reactions of my students have helped to guide the process of revising and completing the text.

It is hoped that the book will serve both as a textbook for postgraduate and advanced undergraduate students in the social sciences and as a reference book.

In writing the book, I have tried to imagine, as the reader, a student or worker in one of the social sciences who wishes to be able to read studies using factor analysis and perhaps to do research using factor-analytic methods, with technical advice, but who does not wish to learn the mathematics of factor theory. (The term *social science* is here interpreted widely to include economics, behavioral science, and education.) Specifically, I disciplined myself not to use any matrix algebra or multivariate statistical theory in the body of the text. An account of the elements of matrix algebra (in the appendix and in the mathematical notes at the ends of the chapters) can be skipped without any sense of discontinuity or loss, but they would be helpful to the reader who wishes to make a transition to more advanced treatments of these topics and could also deepen understanding of the account in the main text. An attempt has been made to use verbal expressions to describe what are basically mathematical concepts in such a way that they will have an intuitive meaning for the nonmathematical reader, while not appearing to be shamefully lacking in rigor from the point of view of a mathematician. Others may judge the success of this attempt.

It has to be admitted frankly that in contrast to some other areas of research method (e.g., the main body of univariate statistical methods) factor analysis, in its broadest sense, is open to a wide variety of opinion, both as to which methods are to be preferred and how and to what purpose they should be applied. There are some who would hold that the common factor model is best fitted by maximum likelihood and others who hold that it should never be fitted by maximum likelihood. There are some who would hold that factors are principles of classification, and others who would hold that they are underlying causes. There are those who prefer common factors to components, and those who prefer components to common factors. Other contrasting views on important issues could be added to this list. Although recognizing often the cogency of arguments on both sides of questions such as these, I have chosen to recommend what I consider to be a set of opinions that is both internally consistent and reasonably consistent with the eighty-year history of the topic as I interpret it. There is virtually nothing in the book that can be considered an original contribution. Any material that is not fully referenced is a restatement of very well-known facts. The references are of two sharply contrasting kinds: namely, those that would be suitable for further reading, and those (possibly very technical) that constitute original sources of ideas.

The question of acknowledgments is a difficult one. I taught myself factor analysis from Thomson's classical text book and therefore cannot resist recommending it, although it is both out-of-date and, I presume, long out-of-print. My thinking has been about equally influenced by three papers of D. N. Lawley and many more by Louis Guttman, though the results of these influences might not be recognizable in this book. A more personal influence is that of Professor John Keats. Thanks are due to Professor Drew and Professor Audley for the hospitality of the Department of Psychology, University College, London, where six of the chapters were first drafted. I am also indebted to my students at O.I.S.E. and especially to members of the G.R.O.U.P. (General Research On Understanding Psychometrics) who detected some of the errors in earlier drafts. I am grateful to Mr. Colin Fraser for a large part of the computer programming and numerical work, and I thank Mr. David Cairns and Mr. John Breen for obtaining some further numbers for me when I needed them. Much of the computer programming was supported by a Canadian National Research Grant No. A6346. I wish to thank Mrs. Gloria Powell and Mrs. Lucia Kelly who at different stages typed the manuscript. Helpful comments on some of the chapters have been provided by Dr. Stanley Mulaik, Dr. George Cooney, Dr. Jack McArdle, and Professor Glen Evans. Professor Max Deutscher provided a philosopher's comments on Section 4.1 on causal relations. Of course I also thank my wife, Avis, for her loving encouragement. After all these acknowledgments, I alone accept responsibility for such errors of omission and commission as may yet come to light.

R. P. McDonald
Macquarie University

Factor Analysis
and Related Methods

1 Introduction

1.1. AIMS OF THE BOOK

Factor analysis is a generic term for a somewhat vaguely delimited set of techniques for data processing, mainly applicable to the social and biological sciences. These techniques have been developed for the analysis of mutual relationships among a number of measurements made on a number of measurable entities. It may be convenient to be rather more concrete than this and to imagine a typical application in which the measures are scores on tests and the measurable entities are human subjects to whom the tests have been given. When, to fix ideas, we speak of subjects, and occasionally of tests, the reader should bear in mind that any other measurable quantities and anything whatsoever on which the measurements are made could be substituted, if we have reason to do so, for test scores and for subjects.

Factor analysis in the broad sense comprises both a number of statistical models, which yield testable hypotheses (i.e., hypotheses that we may confirm or disconfirm in terms of the usual statistical procedures for making tests of significance), and also a number of simplifying procedures for the approximate description of data, which do not in any sense constitute disconfirmable hypotheses, except in the loose sense that they supply approximations to the data, and sometimes we can say that the approximations are very bad. In the literature, the two types of analysis have often been confused.

The following account of factor analysis is intended to be as elementary as possible. It is hoped that the reader will be able to understand applications of factor analysis in the literature and, up to a point, be able to evaluate them critically. It is hoped that the reader will also be able to undertake a study applying factor analysis to the area of empirical research in which he or she engages, given the availability of a computer center that has up-to-date programs for the purpose and someone to advise on how to prepare and submit the data to the available programs.

Because of the aspects of the subject that this book is not in the slightest degree attempting to cover, a number of general warnings must be issued. The mathematical theory of factor analysis is relatively complex. To come to grips with the deeper literature on the subject, the reader must have reasonable grounding in both mathematical statistics (the mathematical theory of statistical inference as opposed to elementary accounts of statistical techniques for the user) and in linear algebra (the algebra of vectors and matrices). It is an area of inquiry in which, to quote Pope's couplet fully:

A little learning is a dangerous thing,
Drink deep, or taste not the Pierian spring.

It is also an area beset by confusion and disagreement. The full extent of the confusion and disagreement will not be reflected in this book. The attempt will be made to present a view of the subject that is internally consistent and tenable as far as it goes. Others may judge the success of that attempt. Bibliographical notes are appended to the chapters, some of which amount to suggestions for further reading, but the temptation, in the course of writing to add remarks pointing outside the area actually covered has been suppressed to avoid distracting complications.

We turn next to the delicate question of what the reader is assumed to know. The simplest statement is that the reader is assumed to know basic univariate and bivariate statistics—sample versus population, the computation and use of sample means, variances and correlation coefficients, the testing of simple statistical hypotheses about population means, variances and correlation coefficients, using the normal curve, chi-square and F tables, and typical applications of these to research problems in social science, especially psychological or educational research. Implicit in this assumption are other assumptions, of course (viz., that the reader is familiar with the devices from elementary algebra—subscripting, summation notation, elementary algebraic manipulations—that accompany the teaching of statistical methods to the user). He or she should also have acquired some working intuitions, not too far from those of the mathematician, about probability and statistical distributions. An appendix summarizes some results in matrix algebra, and these are used in mathematical notes at the ends of the chapters. The reader can choose to omit all this material but is encouraged to work with it to see if it is helpful.

From one point of view, the task here is to come to understand the numerical input and the numerical output supplied to and obtained from factor-analytic computer programs. It is particularly true of factor analysis that contemplating or working with the computational formulas will not help us with this task at all. Surely this is fortunate. On the other hand, it seems desirable that understanding of factor-analytic input/output be firmly based on the statistical concepts— multiple regression and partial and multiple correlation—of which factor analysis is only a slight extension. The following section is therefore offered as a review of basic concepts, and the next section thereafter is devoted to multiple regression theory.

1.2.   REVIEW OF BASIC CONCEPTS

(a) Modes of Inquiry

Students of the social and biological sciences gradually acquire, through the whole course of their training, a general sense of the nature of scientific inquiry as well as notions as to how to inquire into specific problems in specific fields. The reader will know how to supply suitable qualifications and corrections to the broad and perhaps wild generalizations that will now be offered as a way of getting started. Let us agree quickly, virtually without thinking, that the objectives of science are the explanation, prediction, and control of events in nature and that the tools of science are empirical observation and abstract thought.

In mathematical statistics, the word *experiment* is used very broadly to mean any systematic procedure for making observations (for which statistical analysis can, in principle, be performed). But, generally, we want to distinguish between two modes of empirical observation that may be called the *experimental* mode and the *survey* mode.

In the prototypical experiment, we take a given number of subjects (experimental units, objects of some kind) and assign them to two or more distinct and contrastable experimental conditions (treatments). We choose some property or behavior of the subjects, commonly a measurable quantity, that we are going to regard as the *response* to the *treatment*. We follow an elaborate tradition of experimental design, yielding an analysis of variance, in which the statistical question is whether the variation of the mean responses from one experimental condition to another is greater than we should expect from the particular assignment of the subjects to the treatments. The logical justification of our statistical inference rests in part on making the assignment of our subjects to the different treatments by a random process. The process of randomly assigning our subjects to our treatments is supposed to have randomized and spread out into random, estimable variability all the effects that might otherwise be confounded with (confused with) the treatment effects that we hope to find. These other effects are of a number of kinds, including variations in the properties of the subjects (individual differences between the subjects in the experiment), errors of measurement of the response, and perhaps (though random assignment does not necessarily cover this) failure to keep each treatment condition as uniform as we would wish. Typically, we do not care how much of the random, within-treatment variability is due to treatment variation, individual differences, or errors of measurement, just so long as we have successfully randomized it. What we do care about is to be able to say that a difference in the mean response to two treatments cannot reasonably be thought due to chance aspects of what we did. Once we can say this, what we say next depends on certain vexed questions in philosophy.

Broadly, we usually want to say that the treatment has an effect on the subjects; that the treatment, in part, determines the response; or that the response is affected by, or dependent on, the treatment. In short, we edge up to an admission that we are trying to tease out cause-and-effect relations. However, there seems to be an argument among philosophers that can be expected to last for some centuries yet as to whether we can make sense of statements such as: "X (in part) causes Y," whereas "Y varies with X but does not (in part) cause X." So usually social scientists, out of embarrassment, restrict themselves to ambiguous language rather than risking a confrontation with the philosophers who regard *causal* talk as absurd. One clever way to do this is to use the word *determine* in both of its meanings at once. In the mathematical sense of the word, to say that Y is determined by X is to say that Y is a function of X (i.e., there is a numerical correspondence of a value of Y to a value of X, so given a value of X we know the value of Y). In that case, conversely, in just the same sense, X is usually determined by Y. But, in speaking of treatments and responses, the truth is that we usually want to say that the response is determined by the treatment in a sense in which the treatment is not determined by the response. Surely, here *determined* is *caused* in disguise.

Whatever the next centuries of philosophical analysis may reveal, for the moment it will here be asserted that there does seem to be a difference between a causal relationship and a merely concomitant relationship and that the experimental method is the best way known to us to tease out cause–effect relationships. At the very least, the notion of a causal relation may mean no more than the possibility of control. As a rule, the prediction of X from Y should be *as good as* the prediction of Y from X. But from success in manipulating X to control Y we do not ordinarily expect to manipulate Y to control X.

Experimental control is obviously the basis of applied science and our applied technologies. It is also a major part of the process of advancing "pure" scientific knowledge. The question, therefore, that we shall leave to the philosophers is whether the distinction between empirical relations that enable us to control events and empirical relations that do not has a fundamental character. For the present, we seem free to believe in an important difference between causal relations, which are best teased out by experiments and at least some of which enable control as well as prediction, and empirical relations that offer prediction only.

In contrast to the experimental mode of empirical inquiry, we consider now the survey mode. In the prototypical survey, we draw a number of subjects from a population of subjects "of the same kind" and choose one or more properties or behaviors of the subjects that we measure. The measurements are often made under (stated or unstated) standard conditions of observation, which resemble a single treatment condition, without any contrasting conditions. In the totally dull type of study, we simply want to know the basic statistics of each property measured, usually summarized in means and standard deviations, with perhaps some further information about the shape of the distribution. Knowledge of this sort—number of children per family, to the second decimal place; average income; how abnormal the distribution of income is; and so on—tends to be acquired by the keepers of state records, the original "statisticians," rather than by social and biological scientists.

Typically a survey becomes interesting to the extent that it yields information about the relationships between distinct observed properties of the subjects studied and to the extent that we can draw inferences from these about relationships in the population from which the subjects were drawn. The basic tools of such an inquiry tend to be correlational statistics, in contrast to the analysis of variance as developed for experimental designs.

The logical justification of inferences about the population from the sample rests on the very, very difficult, not to say unrealizable, ideal of random sampling from the population, in contrast to the very, very easy process of random assignment of a (commonly small) number of subjects to a few experimental treatment conditions.

It seems easier to be clear about the nature and objectives of experiments than to be clear about the nature and objectives of multivariate data-getting, that is, of surveys in which we measure a number of properties on each member of a sample of subjects, which we regard as representative of a population. Historical considerations seem relevant here. The foundations of the theory of correlation were laid in the last quarter of the nineteenth century. Mathematicians, mainly working on the theory of errors in physical science, had developed remarkably sophisticated probability and statistical theory from the seventeenth century through the nineteenth, but although they often came close to the concept of correlation, they kept missing it primarily because the covariation of measures really only becomes interesting in biological and social science material. Galton, the founder of correlational concepts, was primarily a psychologist and biologist, interested in questions of human genetics. The framework of his thinking was provided by Darwin's theory of evolution on the basis of natural variation and selection by survival of more adaptive variations. For example, to Galton, a key question was whether human stature, human intelligence, and so on were stable from generation to generation in respect to general level (mean) and general variability (variance). He was led to the key concepts of correlation theory by meditating on the conditions that would make these characteristics stable.

Pearson, working in the 1890s, completed the basic mathematics of Galton's theory. It is barely an exaggeration to say that the discovery of correlational methods formed the initial foundation of biometric methods, as literally embodied in Pearson's journal *Biometrika*. In the first decades of this century, the study of the covariation of properties of organisms, in both biology and psychology, had the general character of an inquiry, motivated by Darwinism, into interindividual (intraspecies) variations in adaptive traits and the interaction of these with environment.

After the first wave of specifically Darwinian enthusiasm for correlational methods had passed, no clear idea emerged as to what correlational methods are for, comparable to the use of contrasted-treatment experimental designs to establish control over effects. Indeed, it seems rather as though we cannot point to one general method of use or to one general aim.

Consider the question: Why are two variables correlated? We shall suggest five possible responses to this question, and the reader is encouraged to think of as many others as possible.

1. We can reasonably deny that the question has meaning. If, in a given species, there is a correlation between height and weight or hair color and eye color, we can say that such *natural* covariation in the distribution of individuals of this species is just a fact about the species. It may be an interesting fact, and it may be a fact that we use in turn in our explanation of other facts or in our practical dealings with the world. In psychology, in particular, we might choose to regard individual variations in cognitive performances, in personality traits, or in attitudes, as just the raw givens about individuals, including information about covariation of these characteristics. A refusal to answer the question can indeed be reasonable when the only kinds of answer that come to mind are tenuous, or untestable, or tautological in character.

2. We may give a theoretical answer. For example, a physicist might argue that height and weight covary in the population of adult human beings (to state our finding carefully) because (a) bone and other tissue make on the whole a relatively constant density, (b) the volume of the body is just obviously correlated with height, and (c) mass is equal to density times volume. To take another example, the covariation of hair color and eye color may be attributed to the determination (that ambiguous word again) of each characteristic by linked genes. In the early stages of genetic theory, this would have been almost a tautology in an elaborate framework of descriptions of covariations (viz., hair color and eye color are linked characters because they are linked characters). Later genetic theory has acquired a very substantial biochemical basis in which the statement that two genes are linked means that two sets of molecules are to be found on the same chromosome. We could consider other examples. It is not

clear whether we can or should look for a complete classification of kinds of theoretical answer to the question: Why are two variables correlated? The remaining three responses to be considered may be regarded as particular types of theoretical answer.

3. We may say that one variable (say x) determines the other (say y), and we do not mean that the converse is also true. In spite of all the misgivings we have about the uncertainty of causal inferences from *mere* correlations, in the social sciences at least we often feel impelled to substitute a correlational study for the experiment that we are unable for practical or ethical reasons to carry out. In economics, the aim is to find variables outside an economic system (exogenous variables, e.g., cost of imported raw materials) that determine variables inside an economic system (endogenous variables, e.g., market prices of manufactured goods). To the extent that we can find economic systems that are passive, isolated receivers of goods, etc., causal inferences will become plausible. The plausibility of any specific causal interpretation of a specific correlation between variables will depend on the entire body of related knowledge. Sometimes it may be obvious that covariation *given by natural events* has substituted effectively for an experiment. For example, we could heat a metal bar through a sequence of temperatures and measure its consequent expansion, or we could measure its length, and the day temperature, over a period of time, and plot the relationship on a graph. At the other extreme, it is currently the hope of a number of social scientists that the elaboration of correlational methods into the *analysis of linear structural relations* (Chapter 4) will enable a plausible teasing out of paths of causal determination from complex sociological or economic data.

4. We may say that the correlated measures are correlated effects of a common cause. (One interpretation of linked genes would put them under this heading.) An obvious case in point is the covariation of prices of various market commodities in response to factors affecting an economy. To the extent that we feel we understand both effects as effects of a given third variable, we feel that we understand the covariation of these effects. The statistical methods of partial correlation (Section 1.3) are relevant here. If we find that the correlation between two variables would become zero if a third variable is held constant, this is an indication that we might consider the third variable as a *common cause* of these effects. (It may be a third effect of an unknown common cause or some quite other explanation may obtain.)

5. We may say the two measures are correlated because they measure something in common. This can be literally true. For example, some personality tests consist of items that can be scored for more than one trait, so the correlation between the traits is a correlation between sum scores that contain identical part scores (i.e., scores on the items that are included in both trait measures). But, generally, by ''measuring something in common'' we mean something less literal and more subtle. For example, we may say that the height of the column in a mercury thermometer, the resistance in the wire in a resistance thermometer,

and the voltage in a thermocouple thermometer are all correlated because they all measure the same thing, namely temperature. We say they are three indicators or three operations for measuring a common (abstract) attribute of objects—temperature.

This is a very deep philosophical issue, but we should be able to accept that we often use one property of objects as a measure of another (empirical or abstract) property. Clearly, for example, we use the length of a mercury column as an indicator of temperature (some would say as a definition of temperature, but that view has its problems). As soon as we see that one property can be used as a measure of another, we see that we can say that two distinct properties measure *the same thing*—at least in part. Hence, we can say that two variables, with nothing so literal as a part score in common, are correlated because they *measure* something in common.

We shall see later that this is the standard explanation of correlation offered by common factor analysis. In general, provided that we name the "something," the explanation can be nontrivial and nontautological.

Consider some examples:- Height and weight are correlated because they measure body size in common. Scores on addition items and subtraction items are correlated because they both measure arithmetic ability.

We might suggest that practicing psychometricians have acquired the habit of supposing that the higher the correlation between two variables, the more they have in common. The correlation coefficient is thought of as a measure of conceptual similarity of the variables. It is not always obvious how to work this rule—that conceptual similarity is measured by correlation coefficients. For example, if height and weight are correlated 0.8 and length of nose and length of big toe are correlated only 0.4, should we say that height and weight are more alike than length in noses and length in big toes? The social scientists have not thought these questions through, it seems, nor have the philosophers of science.

Let us now sum up the matter of explanations for correlations. We are given a correlation between two variables x and y. (1) we regard this as just a given general property of the subjects under study, which we can use for prediction or take into account in our description of individuals. (2) We may find a theoretical explanation of the relationship, deducing it from other known facts or accepted theory. (3) We may assert, cautiously, a causal direction to the relationship, in effect believing that if we could gain experimental control over x, we could thereby vary y as a material consequence of manipulating x. If "good" teachers get "good" results, and we can see how to put the particular "good" properties into teachers by training, we expect to control the "good" results. But if the teachers were "good" because their good classes made them happy, we would be working in the wrong direction. In contrast, we don't dream of blonding someone's hair in order to turn their eyes from brown to blue. (4) We assert that x and y are related effects of some third variable, which in principle we can imagine manipulating to control both x and y. (5) We assert that x and y are indicators of, or measures of, the same property of the things measured.

Whatever else we may say, it is easy to find instances of all five of these positions in the literature of social and biological science. It is not however easy to find any consistency of choice between or even within the work of the investigators in the adoption of these five positions. For example, in studies of behavior ''as a function of'' personality, it often seems to be a totally arbitrary matter which measures the investigator regards as indicators of the *prior* person- ality structure and which he regards as the *consequent* behavior. Thus, one investigator might use the time a subject persists at a task set for him as a measure of an *enduring trait* of persistence and ask whether the ability to persist at a task lowers the subject's test anxiety, whereas another might study per- sistence as a piece of behavior (not, somehow, a trait) that is causally dependent on the subject's enduring trait of test anxiety. The only recommendation that comes to mind is that the reader practice an analysis of the correlational literature in terms of these five positions, sharpening any ambiguous remarks in the work with the aid of the rest of the argument, and then with an open mind he should consider the plausibility of the cause–effect, effect–effect, elements-in-com- mon, or other explanation offered. The view taken here is that any of these explanations can be plausible, and sometimes almost compelling, but social scientists can sometimes just follow habit in their choice of explanation and thereby miss the obvious.

(b) Measurement and Scaling

To offer yet another broad and perhaps wild generalization, we might claim that there are essentially two kinds of property or behavior of subjects that we can observe and employ in multivariate analysis. The first is what we shall call *measurable observations,* meaning that we can find sufficient reason to assign a number to each subject we observe as a measure of the property. Height in inches; weight in pounds; number of teeth, of items correctly answered in a mental test, or of responses scored in a given direction in an attitude question- naire; all these are measurable observations. The second is what we shall call *multicategory observations,* meaning that we have a scheme for classifying the property or behavior into one of a fixed number of mutually exclusive and exhaustive categories. Hair color or eye color might be treated as multicategory observations, and the response to a multiple-choice item can obviously be treated this way. There is a special kind of observation, *binary* or *dichotomous* observa- tions, which we can treat as measured data or multicategory data at will, namely, a property or response that has just two alternative states, such as present or absent, right or wrong, yes or no. Such a property or response can certainly be recorded as multicategory data. But by scoring one of the two states as zero and the other as unity, we make it a primitive form of measured data. Multicategory data, generally, are outside the scope of this book. Binary data, especially from psychological questionnaire items, are discussed in Chapter 7, but for the most part we suppose that we are working with measured data obtained by a reasonable scoring procedure for measurable observations.

Generally, in social science data, there is no absolute meaning to the numbers we assign to measurable observations to create measured data (or, more simply, measurements). In particular, we are free as a rule to transform the data to make the distribution of measurements in a given sample have a nice shape (e.g., to make it resemble the normal distribution or to make the relation between two variables linear). There are limits to this process. If we have two samples, the one transformation of scale will generally not make both distributions normal, or the relations between variables linear. Also, if we have n variables, we have $n(n - 1)/2$ relations between them (by the theory of combinations), so we cannot make all the relations linear by transforming the n sets of measurements, as there are more relations than transformations at our disposal (if n is greater than 2). Hence the assumption, in multivariate data, that the statistical distribution of our variables is normal and the assumptions that all the relations between variables are linear are indeed assumptions, which may be incorrect. There is a strange kind of comfort to be found in the reflection that social science data are so extremely prone to error and instability that our samples are seldom large enough to enable us to detect that our assumptions of normality or linearity of relationship are false.

A very useful simplification of thought about multivariate statistics, and factor analysis in particular, follows from the recognition that the zero point (the origin) of our scale of measurement and the unit of measurement can always be chosen, in imagination or in practice, in a way that is convenient for the thinking in which we are engaged. For the purpose of this book, we can regard the infinite population from which our sample is drawn as a limit and an analog of the sample (i.e., like an infinitely large sample). For deeper purposes, this would not be adequate. We can compute, by the usual working formulas in the textbooks, the sample mean and standard deviation of a variable x and the sample mean and standard deviation of a variable y, measured on the subjects in our sample, and the correlation in the sample between x and y. We recognize that the parameters of the population from which our sample was drawn (i.e., the corresponding population mean, standard deviation, and correlation coefficient) are almost certainly different from the sample values we have computed and that the population values will remain forever unknown to us (though we may estimate them fairly accurately). But, at least for the purposes of developing an argument, we can always imagine a change of scale of our measures that consists in subtracting the (unknown) population mean, yielding measures that are *deviations from the mean,* or simply *deviation scores* in the population. By definition, the deviation scores have a population mean of zero. Further, we can imagine dividing each deviation score by the population standard deviation to yield *standard measures* or *standard scores* in the population.

By definition, standard scores have a mean of zero and a standard deviation of unity in the population. Both in imagination and in practice, we can perform the counterpart operations on the observations in a sample, using the sample mean and sample standard deviation, to give sample deviation scores and sample standard scores. It is important to remember that if we standardize scores in the sample, they are not standardized in the population, and conversely. Some writings on factor analysis fail to distinguish between the population, about which factor-analytic statements can be true, and the sample, about which these statements are never true. Such accounts are generally misleading and often erroneous.

(c) Correlation, Regression, and the Analysis of Variance

The assumption that the distribution of measures in a population is normal is extremely powerful for the development of theory. In the case of a univariate distribution (i.e., the distribution of one measure) the entire distribution is specified by just two parameters, namely the mean and the standard deviation. In the case of a bivariate distribution (i.e., the joint distribution of two measures) five parameters describe it completely, namely the two means, the two standard deviations, and the correlation coefficient. More generally, if n variables have a (multivariate) normal distribution, it is completely specified by the n means, the n standard deviations, and the $n(n - 1)/2$ correlations between pairs of variables. Further, under this assumption, the correlation coefficient is a direct index of the degree of association in probability of the values of the two measures. Without a strong distributional assumption, the correlation coefficient is not, strictly speaking, interpretable as an index of statistical association. In particular, under normal theory, if two measures are uncorrelated, they are completely statistically independent; whereas otherwise two variables could be uncorrelated, and one might be a perfect (nonlinear) function of the other.

The assumption that all relations between varibles are linear is less strict than the assumption of normality. Pearson, in the 1890s, worked out normal correlation theory, and almost immediately his student, Yule, reworked the theory on the assumption of linear relations. In normal theory, we study the behavior of the mean of one variable, the dependent variable, as a function of selected values of the other, the independent variable, and find that as a matter of fact it is a linear function. For the moment we shall call it the *line of conditional means.*

In *linear least-squares* theory, as developed by Yule, we ask for the straight line of best fit. If as a matter of fact the distribution is normal, the straight line of best fit turns out to be the same as the line of conditional means. The straight line of best fit is chosen by the principle of least squares, a widely used principle according to which one list of numbers is as alike another list as possible, when the sum of the squares of the differences between paired numbers is as small as possible. For quite accidental and absurd historical reasons, the line on which we find the mean of the dependent variable y, say, corresponding to each value of the independent variable x, say, is known as the regression line of y on x. (Galton thought the line indicated a real tendency for the values of the dependent variable to regress toward the mean.) The same name is applied to the line of least squares best fit relating y to x, because in normal theory these coincide. In other distributions the mean of y for given x might possibly lie on a curved line, but even in a nonnormal distribution the line of such means and the straight line of best fit may coincide. This fact and the fact that the mathematics of least squares theory is easier to teach than normal theory has led to a strong tradition of presenting Yule's theory as the foundation of correlation and regression theory rather than the theory of Galton and Pearson.

In more detail, the problem in linear regression theory is this: Given a dependent variable y and an independent variable x, the mathematician is asked to find an expression for the straight line

$$\hat{y} = bx + a \tag{1.2.1}$$

(where b is the slope of the line and a is its intercept) that gives the smallest value to the variance of the discrepancy $y - \hat{y}$. We call this discrepancy the *residual* about the regression line. Let us denote it by e, (i.e., write the following):

$$e = y - \hat{y}. \tag{1.2.2}$$

If we denote the mean and variance of x by μ_x and σ_x^2, the mean and variance of y by μ_y and σ_y^2, and the correlation between x and y by ρ_{xy}, then the mathematician shows us that the constants a and b in (1.2.1) are given by

$$b = \rho_{xy}\frac{\sigma_y}{\sigma_x} \tag{1.2.3}$$

$$a = \mu_y - b\mu_x . \tag{1.2.4}$$

The mathematician also shows us that the residual e is uncorrelated with $\hat{y}$, the part of y that is *due to the regression on* x, as we say. This is a fundamental result in statistical theory and is true even if $\hat{y}$ is a nonlinear function of x, just as long as it is chosen to give a minimum variance to the residual e. That is, if we express a dependent variable y as the sum of a least-squares best-fitted function $\hat{y}$ of an independent variable (or of a number of independent variables) and a residual part, then the fitted function $\hat{y}$ and the residual $e = y - \hat{y}$ are uncorrelated. The mathematician then points out another fundamental result in statistical theory, namely that the variance of the sum of uncorrelated variables is the sum of their separate variances. That is, extending our notation in the obvious way,

$$\sigma_y^2 = \sigma_{\hat{y}}^2 + \sigma_e^2. \tag{1.2.5}$$

We thus have an *analysis of variance* of the dependent variable into the variance of the fitted values—the *variance due to the regression*—and the variance of the residuals about the fitted values—the *residual variance*. In our present case of a linear regression of one dependent variable on one independent variable, with the best-fit line given by (1.2.1) with (1.2.3) and (1.2.4), the analysis of variance is contained in the expressions

$$\sigma_{\hat{y}}^2 = \rho_{xy}^2 \sigma_y^2 \tag{1.2.6}$$

and

$$\sigma_e^2 = (1 - \rho_{xy}^2)\sigma_y^2. \tag{1.2.7}$$

From this, we see that the square of the correlation, ρ_{xy}^2, which is traditionally known as the *coefficient of determination* (of y by x), is the proportion of the variance of the dependent variable that is due to the regression. The index $1 - \rho_{xy}^2$, once known as the coefficient of alienation but now less picturesquely termed the *coefficient of nondetermination*, is the proportion of the variance of the dependent variable that is not due to the regression.

Notice that if we assume deviation measure, the constant a in (1.2.4) becomes zero. If we further assume standard measure, the *regression coefficient* b becomes the same as the correlation coefficient, and we have an analysis of the *unit* variance of y, $\sigma_y^2 = 1$, into

$$1 = \sigma_{\hat{y}}^2 + \sigma_e^2$$
$$= \rho_{xy}^2 + (1 - \rho_{xy}^2). \tag{1.2.8}$$

A major part of the strategy of social science research is to attempt to partition the variance of one or more "dependent" variables into parts due to their covariation with one or more independent variables. We think of this as a major basis of prediction and in some cases a major pointer to experimental or practical control. We also see in it one of the main meanings of the word *explanation* in statistical work, when we "explain" part of the variability of a dependent variable by its covariation with a given independent variable.

A virtue, and a danger, associated with least squares theory, unlike normal theory, is that it applies equally to a population or a sample. The remarks from (1.2.1) to this point can all be interpreted in terms of population or sample. As a result, least squares theory provides one of the main mathematical tools in statistics for estimating population parameters from sample statistics. The danger, however, that we must try to avoid is of applying concepts to the sample that only have meaning in reference to the population from which the sample has been drawn. Thus, the square of the population correlation coefficient is, indeed, the proportion of variance of the dependent variable predictable from the independent variable. But the square of the sample correlation is not the proportion of the variance of the list of y values in the sample that is "predictable" from knowing the list of x values in the sample.

We can leave to mathematicians, computers, and computer programs all questions of computing formulas for the methods discussed in this book. The output of a factor analysis will consist essentially of correlation coefficients and regression coefficients. The art of interpreting the data rests on judgments of magnitude of correlations and slopes of regression. It will be more important to build up experience in the art of making such comparative judgments than to know computing formulas.

1.3. MULTIPLE REGRESSION THEORY: THE FOUNDATION OF FACTOR ANALYSIS

Factor analysis is a direct extension, though perhaps at first sight a strange one, of the well-known statistical concepts of regression theory and partial correlation theory. A specialized language has been adopted by factor analysts, a fact that seems regrettable, because virtually none of the words in their special vocabulary is necessary, given the existing technical language of statistics. In this book we shall use both standard statistical language and the language of the factor analysts.

The concepts involved in multiple regression theory and partial correlation theory are fundamental and simple. The mathematics and the computational arithmetic associated with them are not so simple and will be glossed over as far as possible.

We begin with the simplest case. Suppose we have three measures x_1, x_2, and y, obtainable from each subject in an infinite population. For example, x_1, x_2 might be, respectively, accepted measures of "intelligence" and of "effectiveness of study habits," whereas y is a measure of achievement in an academic examination. We are told that the correlation between x_1 and y, ρ_{y1}, is .58; the correlation between x_2 and y, ρ_{y2}, is .50; and the correlation between x_1 and x_2, ρ_{12}, is .20. We want to combine the information about an individual supplied by his x_1 measure and his x_2 measure to give a best possible prediction of his y measure. The simplest way to combine two measures to form a composite measure is to form a *weighted sum*. For the present purpose, we can suppose that all the variables are in standard measure. We want to choose two numbers, which we refer to as *weights*, w_1 and w_2, to combine x_1 and x_2 in a single number s given by

$$s = w_1 x_1 + w_2 x_2. \tag{1.3.1}$$

We can think of the weights as yielding a "mixture" of x_1 and x_2, which would be open to our choice in terms of the relative *proportion* of w_1 and w_2, determining the proportional presence of each ingredient in the mixture, and open to choice in terms of the general numerical size of both weights. If we took two given weights and multiplied them by the same number, we would just be multiplying s by that number to yield an arbitrary rescaling of s. Intuitively, therefore, we feel that what matters most in the choice is the proportionate values of the weights rather than their absolute magnitudes. There are at least two obvious ways to choose "best" weights in such a combination. One is to invoke the least squares principle. That is, we would choose weights so that the discrepancies between the predictive values s and the predicted values y have a mean square as small as possible. The other is to choose weights so that the correlation between the predictive values s and the predicted values y is as large as possible. It turns out that the first of these choices also satisfies the requirement of the second (and conversely, except for a rescaling of s that is usually unimportant).

For our example, Table 1.3.1 gives the value of the correlation between y and s and the variance of the difference between y and s for a number of choices of the weights. Among these, the choice $w_1 = .50$, $w_2 = .40$ gives the highest correlation and the smallest variance of discrepancies. The best possible weights are calculated, according to a well-known formula, as functions of the given correlations. It is important and sufficient to accept that, given the correlations between a dependent variable and two or more independent variables and the correlations of the independent variables with each other as input to a computer program, the program can perform some tedious but well-known arithmetic and then output for us the best weights to give to the independent variables. It is unnecessary, and unimportant for our purposes, to contemplate the computing formulas used. As indicated already, it is the relative proportions of the weights that count in determining the maximum correlation between s and y. Multiplying the weights by a common constant just multiplies s by that constant, giving a rescaling of s that leaves its correlation with y unchanged, of course. But the choice of weights to minimize the variance of the residual $(y - s)$ fixes the magnitudes of the weights absolutely and makes, as it happens, the variance of s equal to the square of the correlation of s and y. With *this* choice, we have, strictly speaking, multiple regression theory as it is usually developed. It then turns out that the discrepancy $(y - s)$ is uncorrelated with the predictive quantity s, and we have an analysis of the variance of y into s, the part *due to the regression* on x_1 and x_2, in traditional language, and $(y - s)$, the *residual about the regression*. Let us write $\hat{y}$ for the value of s given when we choose weights in this fashion and write $w_1 = b_1$, $w_2 = b_2$ for the *multiple regression weights* (i.e., the weights so chosen). Then we have the expression

TABLE 1.3.1

w_1	.50	.40	.58	1.0	.0	1.0	1.0
w_2	.40	.50	.50	.0	1.0	1.0	-1.0
Correlation between y and s	.700	.688	.699	.580	.500	.648	.063
Variance ($y - s$)	.510	.526	.512	.664	.750	.514	.996

$$\hat{y} = b_1 x_1 + b_2 x_2 \tag{1.3.2}$$

replacing (1.3.1), and if we define the residual part of y by e, in the expression

$$e = y - \hat{y} \tag{1.3.3}$$

then we have a partition of y into two parts

$$y = \hat{y} + e \tag{1.3.4}$$

that are known to be uncorrelated. The correlation $\rho_{y\hat{y}}$ between y and $\hat{y}$ is known as the *multiple correlation* between y and x_1, x_2 thought of as a pair of (predictive) independent variables. The variance of y (unity in our chosen scaling) is analyzed into the part due to the regression on x_1 and x_2 and the variance of the residual e about the regression. That is, we may write

$$\sigma_y^2 = \sigma_{\hat{y}}^2 + \sigma_e^2 \tag{1.3.5}$$

or

$$\sigma_y^2 = 1 = \rho_{y\hat{y}}^2 + (1 - \rho_{y\hat{y}}^2) \tag{1.3.6}$$

as in the simpler case of bivariate relationships, (1.2.8), and regard $\rho_{y\hat{y}}^2$ as the coefficient of determination of y from both x_1 and x_2 and $1 - \rho_{y\hat{y}}^2$ as the coefficient of nondetermination.

It is important to recognize that if the independent variables are correlated with each other, we cannot carry the analysis of variance any further, at least in terms of neat, separated sources of variation. In more detail, what we are given, by well-known formulas, is

$$\sigma_y^2 = b_1^2 + b_2^2 + 2b_1 b_2 \rho_{12} + \sigma_e^2. \tag{1.3.7}$$

If the correlation between x_1 and x_2 were zero, this would reduce, not merely to

$$\sigma_y^2 = b_1^2 + b_2^2 + \sigma_e^2 \tag{1.3.8}$$

but even to

$$\sigma_y^2 = \rho_{y1}^2 + \rho_{y2}^2 + \sigma_e^2 \tag{1.3.9}$$

because the expressions (omitted) for the regression weights then reduce to the correlations themselves. In such a case, we would be in the happy position of being able to make simple and, usually, convincing assertions about the relative contributions of the separate independent variables to the explanation of the variance of the dependent variable. But if the independent variables are correlated, we have to consider them to be hopelessly tangled sources of variance, and any assertions we make about their relative importance as explainers of variance must be considered to be conjecture rather than truism. One gets the impression that some users of multiple regression computer programs think that they can draw clearer inferences about the relative contribution to variance of independent variables from their regression weights than from their correlations with the dependent variable. There is no mathematical foundation for such a belief. Perhaps it arises naively from the impression that regression weights are output from a computer program to which correlations are input and should therefore be more refined (less crude) because they have been processed by the computer. In practice, of course, we accept the necessity, together with the risks involved, of making guesses as to the relative importance of independent variables in a regression. The risks are mild when the correlations among the independent variables are low and become severe to the extent that these correlations are high.

Now let us suppose, more generally, that we have a dependent variable y, and n (usually correlated) independent variables $x_1, \ldots, x_n$. It is not necessary to repeat the discussion given so far in this section in order to treat this more general case. It is sufficient to recognize that the computer would now obtain for us n regression weights $b_1, \ldots, b_n$ in

$$\hat{y} = b_1 x_1 + b_2 x_2 + \cdots + b_n x_n \qquad (1.3.10)$$

to yield a minimum variance of $y - \hat{y}$ and that almost all the previous statements apply still, except that the expressions in (1.3.7) through (1.3.9) yield more extensive counterparts, which we have no need to consider. Broadly, we expect that the computer programs on which we must rely will be receiving large samples of measurements on three or more variables. They will be computing the sample correlations between the variables, and from these they will be obtaining, by further processing, multiple correlations between variables regarded as *dependent* and groups of variables regarded as independent. We shall be in a position to study and compare a list of correlations between any dependent variable and the given independent variables, together with a list of regression weights, and also the table of correlations between the independent variables. From these, we hope to draw conclusions about the corresponding quantities in the population from which the sample has been drawn. With experience, we hope to be able, at least when the correlations among the independent variables are low, to draw inferences about their relative importance as sources of variation. Table 1.3.2 gives a constructed example to illustrate how conclusions based on correlations and on regression coefficients might disagree.

The arithmetic procedure for obtaining regression weights can break down. The procedure fails if there are variables in the set of independent variables that have multiple correlations of unity or almost unity with other independent variables. In such a case, there is a redundancy of information among the independent variables (some are just functions of others), and variables have to be eliminated until each independent variable contributes something of its own to prediction of the dependent variable. This case commonly occurs when the investigator mistakenly includes part scores and their sum in the list of independent variables.

TABLE 1.3.2

$$\begin{bmatrix} \rho_{y1} = .000 \\ \rho_{y1} = .350 \end{bmatrix} \rho_{12} = .707 \qquad \begin{bmatrix} b_1 & -.4949 \\ b_2 = .7000 \end{bmatrix} \rho_{ys} = .4949$$

We turn now to the second major topic of this section, that of partial correlation. As in the introduction of multiple regression, we suppose that we have just three measures made on each subject in a population, but this time we have two dependent variables and one independent variable, respectively y_1, y_2, and x, say. For example, y_1 and y_2 might be measures of achievement in two distinct academic examinations, say English and mathematics, and x might be an accepted measure of "intelligence." We imagine choosing out of the population of subjects a subset of them, all of whom have a fixed common value of x. For example, if x were in the typical "Intelligence Quotient" form, we choose all those subjects who have x equal to 100 IQ points. We imagine computing the correlation between y_1 and y_2 for this subset of examinees. The correlation so obtained is the *partial correlation* between y_1 and y_2. We imagine repeating this procedure for various values of x: $x = 120$, $x = 80$, $x = \ldots$, as many values as we care to choose. In general, the partial correlation between the two dependent variables could vary according to the value of the independent variable at which we select our subpopulation. However, it is the basic assumption of almost all work on partial correlation that it will have the same value whatever the value of the independent variable; hence typically we speak as though there is just one value for partial correlation. That is, in a subpopulation selected to have a single value of x, although the correlation between y_1 and y_2 is in general different from that in the *parent* population, we assume that it is the same whether the subpopulation is selected to have a high, low, or intermediate value of x. (If x, y_1, and y_2 have a joint normal distribution, then this is certainly true.) In general, the partial correlation can be lower or higher than the unconditional correlation. In the example mentioned, we would expect that the correlation between two achievement tests would be lowered in a subpopulation selected to have intelligence fixed. This is because we think of individual differences in intelligence as partly determining individual differences in both the achievements; hence these covary with each other (mainly) as a consequence of their covariation with intelligence.

These last remarks serve to introduce a second way in which we use the word *explain* in statistical work. The notion is that if y_1 and y_2 are uncorrelated in any subpopulation in which x assumes a fixed value, then y_1 and y_2 are correlated *because* each is correlated with x. We say that the correlation between y_1 and y_2 is explained by the correlations of y_1 and of y_2 with x. Previously, we have "explained" part of the variance of a variable by its regression on (and correlation with) other variables. Here we propose to explain the correlation of two variables by their correlations with (and regression on) other variables. As we might expect, the two explanations are closely linked; yet they are also quite distinct. If, instead of assuming that our variables are normally distributed, we assume that all the regressions are linear, we find that the partial correlation between two dependent variables is the same as the correlation between their separate residuals about their separate regressions on the independent variable(s). It seems to be an accident of history that the explanation of the variance of a variable is dealt with as regression theory and that the explanation of the correlation of two variables is dealt with as partial correlation theory. It is really better to discuss all this material as "conditional statistics." The regression functions are the conditional means of the dependent variables, the variances of the residuals are their conditional variances, and the partial correlations are the conditional correlations of distinct dependent variables, all conditional on fixed values of independent variables.

At the same time, we should note that although partial correlation and regression are intimately connected, they do explain quite different things, namely correlation on the one hand and variance on the other, and the same variable does not do both equally well. It can be shown that the partial correlation between y_1 and y_2 "with x partialled out," is given by

$$\rho_{12.x} = \frac{\rho_{12} - \rho_{1x}\rho_{2x}}{\sqrt{(1 - \rho_{1x}^2)(1 - \rho_{2x}^2)}} \tag{1.3.11}$$

with fairly obvious notation. If in a special case we were able to find a variable x that explains the correlation between y_1 and y_2 entirely (i.e., that makes $\rho_{12.x}$ equal to zero), we would have

$$\rho_{12} = \rho_{1x}\rho_{2x}. \tag{1.3.12}$$

The variable x explains the correlation between y_1 and y_2 perfectly if (1.3.12) is satisfied, but to explain the variance of y_1 or of y_2 perfectly we would need to have ρ_{1x} or ρ_{2x} equal to unity.

It is tempting to offer a sweeping generalization to the effect that all the work with which we deal in the remainder of this book rests either on the partial correlation aspect of regression theory, to explain covariation, or on the multiple correlation aspect of regression theory, to explain variability. The first aspect leads us into common factor analysis and the analysis of covariance structures. The second leads us into component theory. The first type of theory yields testable statistical hypotheses, because a relation like (1.3.12) can hold or not hold, so we can ask whether the relation between y_1 and y_2 is indeed entirely explained by their separate relations with x. The second type does not, in our applications of it, yield testable statistical hypotheses, as it can virtually never be true that a correlation coefficient attains the value of unity, so we can only find out just how much of the variance we can explain. (In the usual applications of the analysis of variance we test whether any part at all of the variance of y can be explained by a relation with x. Here that question is seldom interesting.)

1.4. SOME BASIC MULTIVARIATE HYPOTHESES

In this section we list four basic statistical hypotheses with which the user of factor-analytic methods should be familiar and indicate how they are tested. Surprisingly, although the mathematical theory of all four was well known by the end of the 1930s, not everyone working with factor analysis seems to be acquainted with the last three.

(a) The Hypothesis that a Correlation Is Zero in the Population[1]

We draw a sample of size N from a population and calculate the sample correlation coefficient r_{xy} between two measures x and y. Does the size of r_{xy} constitute evidence that the correlation in the population ρ_{xy}, say, is not zero? The answer to this question is well known, and most textbooks of statistical methods give a table of the magnitude that r_{xy} must exceed, as a function of sample size, for us to reject the null hypothesis that $\rho_{xy} = 0$, at our favorite level of significance, either 5%, if we are anxious to publish a lot, or 1%, if we are anxious to be right in the long run. In the literature, we often find tables of sample correlations obtained between more than two measures on each member of a sample, sprinkled with stars (asterisks), with a footnote explaining that one star means that the correlation is significant at the 5% level; two stars, that it reaches the 1% level; and three stars, that it reaches the 0.1% level. This rather resembles gradings of hotels in guidebooks. The trouble is that the gradings in such a set of correlations are not statistically independent of each other and cannot be taken seriously as separate indicators of the individual significance of each correlation. Further, if we have enough correlations in the set, we can expect that some of them will reach the required level of significance by chance (i.e., even if every counterpart

[1]The hypothesis that an individual regression weight in a multiple regression is zero in the population also has a well-known test statistic, namely Student's (Gossett's) t, which is usually printed out, on request, by modern package computer programs for regression. The test is useful, provided the user bears in mind that (a) the t-values from a data set will not be independent of each other; (b) some will be significant "by chance" if a number of them are tested; and (c) the theory of the t-test assumes the independent variables are fixed quantities controlled by the experimenter, not measured properties of randomly drawn examinees, as in a survey. The theory is not, strictly speaking, applicable to survey data but becomes a better approximation as the sample size becomes larger.

correlation is zero in the population). We sometimes find social science studies in which some multivariate data have been treated in this way, purely because the data happen to be available and the investigator is simply hunting for relationships without any a priori expectations as to where the real associations should be. It is then no surprise when the best correlations found seem to disappear in follow-up or "cross-validation" samples, a phenomenon known in the literature as *attenuation*. A better word for it would be *recovery* (from delusion). The next two hypotheses to be discussed provide better ways to proceed when faced with a number of correlations from the same sample, and we want to ask if any of the corresponding population values are nonzero.

(b) The Hypothesis that all the Variables in a Set Are Mutually Uncorrelated

We draw a sample of size N from a population and obtain n measurements y_1, . . . , y_n from each member of the sample. We compute all the intercorrelations between distinct measures in the sample. We shall write r_{jk} for the sample correlation between y_j and y_k and ρ_{jk} for the corresponding population value. From the theory of combinations we know that we can choose $n(n-1)/2$ distinct pairs of objects out of n given objects. We apply that result here to remark that there are $n(n-1)/2$ correlations to calculate between n variables. We illustrate this in Table 1.4.1 with an example in which $n = 5$. The earliest studies using correlation methods commonly presented their results thus. How-

TABLE 1.4.1

Description First term vs. second term		Amount (Correlations)
(1) Classics	- (2) French	.83
(1) Classics	- (3) English	.78
(1) Classics	- (4) Mathematics	.70
(1) Classics	- (5) Music	.63
(2) French	- (3) English	.67
(2) French	- (4) Mathematics	.67
(2) French	- (5) Music	.57
(3) English	- (4) Mathematics	.64
(3) English	- (5) Music	.51
(4) Mathematics	- (5) Music	.51

ever, a much better representation of the results is the two-dimensional array of numbers given in Table 1.4.2.

In this book (except for the optional mathematical notes) we shall use only the format and some of the terminology of matrix algebra. We use representations of results that follow conventions whose inner logic stems from the advanced theory of linear algebra (the algebra of matrices and vectors). These conventions will simply have to be accepted on trust. Table 1.4.2 illustrates the first of these. By convention, the correlations between n variables are presented in a table with n rows by n columns. The correlation between the jth variable and the kth variable in our list of variables is at the intersection of the jth row (reading down from the top) and the kth column (reading from left to right). If we have a list of the measures (tests or whatever) in an accepted order and are given just the n by n arrangement of correlations without row labels or column labels, we can find the correlation between two named measures by finding the coefficient in the row and the column whose number corresponds to the position of each named measure in the list. In reading multivariate results, we expect to work with output on the basis of row order and column order and to rely comparatively little on supplied row and column labels.

We shall define a *matrix* as any two-dimensional table of numbers (or symbols representing numbers) whose entries, which we shall hereafter call *elements*, are identified by their row number (counting from the top down) and column number (counting from left to right). The symbol for an element of a matrix will always be a lowercase letter with two subscripts, of which the first is the row index and the second is the column index. In the present case, r_{jk} is the sample correlation in the jth row and kth column of the n (rows) by n (columns) *correlation matrix*, illustrated for $n = 5$, in Table 1.4.2. Note that the correlation matrix includes a set of n unities that by definition are the correlations of each variable y with itself. (We could have written r_{jj} in place of these with the knowledge that every $r_{jj} = 1$.)

TABLE 1.4.2

	(a)			
1	r_{12}	r_{13}	r_{14}	r_{15}
r_{21}	1	r_{23}	r_{24}	r_{25}
r_{31}	r_{32}	1	r_{34}	r_{35}
r_{41}	r_{42}	r_{43}	1	r_{45}
r_{51}	r_{52}	r_{53}	r_{54}	1

	(b)			
1.00	.83	.78	.70	.63
.83	1.00	.67	.67	.57
.78	.67	1.00	.64	.51
.70	.67	.64	1.00	.51
.63	.57	.51	.51	1.00

In any *square* matrix, that is, in any table that has the same number of rows and of columns, the elements whose row index and column index are the same are said to *lie on,* or to *form,* the *principal diagonal* of that matrix. Visually, this just means that of the two diagonals we can draw through the elements of the matrix, as in Table 1.4.2, the one that goes from top left to bottom right is the *principal diagonal.* Note also that by definition, the correlation between y_j and y_k is the same as the correlation between y_k and y_j. We still choose to *write* r_{jk} versus r_{kj} in Table 1.4.2a, but the equality of these *numbers* is, of course, open to inspection in Table 1.4.2b. We say that a matrix whose (j, k)th element is equal to its (k, j)th element is *symmetric.* This *symmetry,* about the principal diagonal, is immediately recognizable in Table 1.4.2b. Among other things, this means there is some redundancy of information in a symmetric matrix. Given all the numbers in and below the principal diagonal, we can immediately write in the remaining numbers by finding the (j, k)th number and copying it into the kth row and the jth column. In the case of a correlation matrix, we do not even need the principal diagonal, because this is just a set of unities. Some writers capitalize on symmetry by presenting two sets of correlations in one table, one set in the lower triangle (excluding the diagonal) and the other in the upper triangle (excluding the diagonal). The two sets might be sample correlations versus fitted theoretical values, or correlations from two samples. Some computer programs expect the user to enter the entire correlation matrix, whereas others expect only the numbers in the lower triangle (perhaps with, perhaps without, the diagonal unities). The first is more work; the second is more prone to undetected errors of entry or arrangement. We shall use the symbol **R** for the entire n by n matrix of correlations.

We return from the long excursus of the last three paragraphs to the following problem. Given the $n \times n$ sample correlation matrix from a sample of size N, can we reasonably reject the hypothesis that all $n(n - 1)/2$ values of the corresponding correlations in the population are zero? This null hypothesis is illustrated in Table 1.4.3. A matrix with unities in the diagonal and zeros for all its

TABLE 1.4.3
Ho: $R = 1$

$$
\begin{bmatrix}
1 & r_{12} & r_{13} & r_{14} & r_{15} \\
r_{21} & 1 & r_{23} & r_{24} & r_{25} \\
r_{31} & r_{32} & 1 & r_{34} & r_{35} \\
r_{41} & r_{42} & r_{43} & 1 & r_{45} \\
r_{51} & r_{52} & r_{53} & r_{54} & 1
\end{bmatrix}
=
\begin{bmatrix}
1 & 0 & 0 & 0 & 0 \\
0 & 1 & 0 & 0 & 0 \\
0 & 0 & 1 & 0 & 0 \\
0 & 0 & 0 & 1 & 0 \\
0 & 0 & 0 & 0 & 1
\end{bmatrix}
$$

other elements is called an identity matrix and is symbolized by **I**. We know how to sprinkle stars on a sample correlation matrix as discussed previously, but the presence of individually "significant" correlations will not prove that at least some correlations are nonzero in the population. We have one hypothesis, so we want just one sufficient and proper test of it. A general test is available, applicable to large samples, assuming normality. We get a computer program that calculates a single function of all the sample correlations, which is distributed like chi-square if the sample is large enough, with degrees of freedom given by

$$df = \frac{n(n-1)}{2} \qquad (1.4.1)$$

[Technically, the quantity is $(-2N)$ times the log likelihood ratio, which in this case is the natural logarithm of the determinant of the correlation matrix.]

We shall just think of the quantity as "the chi-square for testing $\mathbf{R} = \mathbf{I}$," which is a shorthand for "the chi-square for testing if all the elements in the $(n \times n)$ matrix of correlations are zero in the population except, of course, the self-correlations." Table 1.4.4 gives a (10×10) correlation matrix that was generated artificially, with $N = 100$, using random numbers from a population in which all correlations are zero. Note that one individual correlation reaches the 5% level. It will be shown later that if we factor analyze this matrix by one of the old-fashioned methods that are still in use, we obtain plausible and very silly results. We could protect ourselves from such foolishness by first calculating the chi-square for $R = I$. This turns out to be 49.0895, with 45 df; hence we could obtain our sample matrix, or one further removed from the identity matrix, by pure chance with a probability of .69. Obviously we cannot reject the hypothesis that all correlations are zero in the population. Although this test is very old, it does not seem well known to social scientists. It is the obvious test to use as a general protection against foolish optimism when hunting for relations in a mass of data.

(c) The Hypothesis that Two Groups of Variables Are Uncorrelated

We may have a sample from which we are prepared to classify the measurements into two groups (viz., n dependent variables $y_1, \ldots, y_n$ and m independent variables $x_1, \ldots, x_m$). Possibly some notions equivalent to cause-and-effect thinking will govern our classification with "causal" variables independent and "effect" variables dependent. On the other hand, some forms of prediction or "diagnosis" would allow us to regress causes on effects or not to care about or believe in the distinction. As the first step in its operation, we can expect the computer program we employ to receive the $(n + m)$ measures from each of the N subjects in the sample and to compute and print out the sample correlations. We might obtain three separate matrices: the symmetric $(n \times n)$ matrix of cor-

TABLE 1.4.4

$$
\begin{bmatrix}
1.000 & .088 & .024 & .076 & -.099 & -.110 & -.089 & -.028 & -.006 & .095 \\
.088 & 1.000 & .057 & .073 & -.030 & .082 & -.096 & .072 & -.183 & .009 \\
.024 & .057 & 1.000 & .046 & .147 & -.023 & -.024 & .066 & .006 & .014 \\
.076 & .073 & .046 & 1.000 & .099 & .179 & -.018 & .076 & -.047 & .114 \\
-.099 & -.030 & .147 & .099 & 1.000 & -.101 & -.154 & -.230 & -.091 & .020 \\
-.110 & .082 & -.023 & .179 & -.101 & 1.000 & .034 & .161 & .90 & -.104 \\
-.089 & -.096 & -.024 & -.018 & -.154 & .034 & 1.000 & -.020 & -.026 & -.126 \\
-.028 & .072 & .066 & .076 & -.230 & .161 & -.020 & 1.000 & .037 & -.108 \\
-.006 & -.183 & .006 & -.047 & -.091 & .190 & -.026 & .037 & 1.000 & .176 \\
.095 & .009 & .014 & .114 & .020 & -.104 & -.126 & -.108 & .176 & 1.000
\end{bmatrix}
$$

TABLE 1.4.5

$n = 3$ $m = 6$

$$
\begin{array}{c}
y_1 \\ y_2 \\ y_3
\end{array}
\begin{bmatrix}
1.000 & .828 & .776 \\
.828 & 1.000 & .779 \\
.776 & .779 & 1.000
\end{bmatrix}
\qquad
\begin{array}{c}
x_1 \\ x_2 \\ x_3 \\ x_4 \\ x_5 \\ x_6
\end{array}
\begin{bmatrix}
1.000 & .674 & .590 & .381 & .350 & .424 \\
.674 & 1.000 & .541 & .402 & .367 & .446 \\
.590 & .541 & 1.000 & .288 & .320 & .325 \\
.381 & .402 & .288 & 1.000 & .555 & .598 \\
.350 & .367 & .320 & .555 & 1.000 & .452 \\
.424 & .446 & .325 & .598 & .452 & 1.000
\end{bmatrix}
$$

Cross-correlation matrix

$$
\begin{array}{c}
y_1 \\ y_2 \\ y_3
\end{array}
\begin{bmatrix}
.439 & .432 & .447 & .447 & .541 & .380 \\
.493 & .464 & .489 & .432 & .537 & .358 \\
.460 & .425 & .443 & .401 & .534 & .359
\end{bmatrix}
$$

relations of the dependent variables, the symmetric ($m \times m$) matrix of correlations of the independent variables, and then in addition a matrix of mn correlations between each dependent and each independent variable. This could be arranged as n rows by m columns or m rows by n columns. See Table 1.4.5. The decision is arbitrary. Alternatively, we can present the information in the form of the entire ($n + m$) $\times$ ($n + m$) matrix of correlations shown in Table 1.4.6. Dotted lines indicate that the matrix is *partitioned* into four *submatrices*, as the four parts are called. The upper left submatrix is the correlation matrix of the independent variables. The lower right submatrix is the correlation matrix of the dependent variables. The upper right and lower left submatrices are two different representations of the cross-correlation matrix of independent and dependent variables. The two symmetric matrices ''lie on'' the diagonal of the entire matrix in a visually obvious sense and are called *diagonal* submatrices. The other two

TABLE 1.4.6

x_1	1.000	.674	.590	.381	.350	.424	.439	.493	.460
x_2	.674	1.000	.541	.402	.367	.446	.432	.464	.425
x_3	.590	.541	1.000	.288	.320	.325	.447	.489	.443
x_4	.381	.402	.288	1.000	.555	.598	.447	.432	.401
x_5	.350	.367	.320	.555	1.000	.452	.541	.537	.534
x_6	.424	.446	.325	.598	.452	1.000	.380	.358	.359
y_1	.439	.432	.447	.447	.541	.380	1.000	.828	.776
y_2	.439	.464	.489	.432	.537	.358	.828	1.000	.779
y_3	.460	.425	.443	.401	.534	.359	.776	.779	1.000

do not lie on the diagonal and are called *nondiagonal* or *off-diagonal* submatrices.

Using the information in the three (or, redundantly, four) submatrices of the entire correlation matrix, the computer program could perform further arithmetic on these numbers and obtain *n* regression equations, one for each dependent variable, each containing *m* terms, and the *n* corresponding multiple correlations. That is, we would have *n* best weighted combinations of the *m* independent variables, each of which has a maximum correlation with its appropriate dependent variable, in the sample. We could obtain also an *F*-ratio test of the significance of each of the *n* multiple correlations by a widely known procedure. But, again, these *n* multiple correlations are not independent of each other, and some of them may be "significant" by chance. We would like a single test of significance for the single hypothesis that all the cross-correlations in the matrix (i.e., all *mn* correlations between independent variables and dependent variables) are zero in the population. In the preferred language of matrix algebra, if all the elements of the nondiagonal submatrices of a matrix are zero, it is described as a *diagonal block* matrix. The hypothesis can be described by the shorthand expression: *The correlation matrix is diagonal block*. Again, a general test is available, applicable to large samples, assuming normality. Again, the computer program calculates a single quantity, a function of all the sample correlations in the $(n + m) \times (n + m)$ matrix, which is distributed like chi-square if the sample is large enough, with degrees of freedom given by

$$\text{df} = nm \qquad (1.4.2)$$

(Technically, the quantity is a log function of the determinant of the entire matrix divided by the product of the determinants of the diagonal submatrices.) We shall just think of this quantity as "the chi-square for testing if **R** is diagonal block."

(d) The Hypothesis that all the Partial Correlations Between the Variables in a Set Are Zero

This case contains logical features of the previous two. Suppose we have data like those of the last problem, already reduced to the form of an $(n + m) \times (n + m)$ sample correlation matrix. Instead of choosing independent variables that we hope will explain much of the variance of our dependent variables, we have chosen independent variables that we hope will explain their correlations. The computer program carries out only a very slight extension of the arithmetic that it performs to get multiple regression weights and multiple correlations. After all, as pointed out earlier, the partial correlations of the dependent variables are the correlations of their residual parts about their regressions on the independent variables. However, there is certainly no reason to believe, for example, that if the multiple correlations are high, the partial correlations will be low; so we are concerned now with a quite separate problem. The answer turns out to require no new work, except for the actual computation of the partial correlation matrix, which we leave to the computer program. Suppose then that the program yields the $(n \times n)$ sample correlation matrix of $y_1, \ldots , y_n$, when $x_1, \ldots , x_m$ are all partialled out. This matrix contains the sample counterpart of the correlations we expect to find in a subpopulation of subjects selected to have a fixed value of x_1, of $x_2, \ldots ,$ of x_m. We shall denote it by $\mathbf{R}_{y \cdot x}$. It turns out that the chi-square for $\mathbf{R} = \mathbf{I}$ applies also to the hypothesis that $\mathbf{R}_{y \cdot x} = \mathbf{I}$, with the same degrees of freedom. That is, we compute the same function of the sample partial correlations to test whether their population values are zero as we compute from correlations with nothing partialled out, to test whether their population values are zero.

As we see in Section 1.5, the hypotheses of common factor analysis form an immediate development from partial correlation theory. We test, on sample correlation matrices, whether the (population) partial correlations are zero if a number of unobserved variables, called *common factors*, are partialled out.

1.5.   THE KEY CONCEPTS OF COMMON FACTOR ANALYSIS

Consider the correlation matrix given in Table 1.5.1. It is to be thought of as the correlation matrix of five dependent variables, $y_j, j = 1, \ldots , 5$, bordered at the top and to the left by their correlations with a single independent variable x. Using the formula for partial correlation

$$r_{jk \cdot x} = \frac{r_{jk} - r_{jx} r_{kx}}{\sqrt{(1 - r_{jx}^2)(1 - r_{kx}^2)}} \tag{1.5.1}$$

we calculate the matrix of partial correlations between the five dependent variables when the independent variable x is partialled out and find that every partial correlation is zero. For example, we compute

TABLE 1.5.1

	x	y_1	y_2	y_3	y_4	y_5
x	1.00	.90	.80	.70	.60	.50
y_1	.90	1.00	.72	.63	.54	.45
y_2	.80	.72	1.00	.56	.48	.40
y_3	.70	.63	.56	1.00	.42	.35
y_4	.60	.54	.48	.42	1.00	.30
y_5	.50	.45	.40	.35	.30	1.00

$$r_{35 \cdot x} = \frac{.35 - .7 \times .5}{\sqrt{(1 - .7^2)(1 - .5^2)}} = 0.$$

That is, we have a single independent variable that explains (in the partial correlation sense) all the correlations in the matrix of correlations of the dependent variables.

Now suppose we had measured $y_1, \ldots, y_5$ but had not chosen to measure x. We just have the (5×5) submatrix in Table 1.5.1. We recognize in this table an obvious regularity, which can be described in a number of different ways. Except for the unities in the diagonal, the numbers in the columns (or rows) are proportional. For example, taking columns 1 and 2, we see that

$$\frac{.63}{.56} = \frac{.54}{.48} = \frac{.45}{.40} = \frac{.9}{.8} .$$

Taking columns 2 and 5, we have

$$\frac{.72}{.45} = \frac{.56}{.35} = \frac{.48}{.30} = \frac{.8}{.5} .$$

The reader can check the remaining columns similarly. Alternatively, we can say that every correlation in the matrix can be expressed as the product of two numbers chosen out of a set of five (actually, the correlations with the independent variable, but we are pretending we know nothing about it). That is, by sheer inspection of the table, we can see that if we choose the numbers .9, .8, .7, .6, .5, each correlation in the table is a product of two of these (e.g., $r_{12} = .9 \times .8$, $r_{35} = .7 \times .5$).

This observation, whichever way we express it, indicates a restrictive law of formation obeyed by the correlation matrix. There are 10 distinct correlations in the matrix, and each can be derived from just five basic numbers, as the product of two of them. This will not be true of just any (5×5) correlation matrix we happen to find. If we just change one correlation in the matrix a little bit—say we make $r_{12} = .60$ instead of .72—the law of formation no longer holds. We can no longer express the 10 correlations as products of pairs of five numbers.

Just from knowing the (5×5) correlation (sub)matrix of (dependent) variables in Table 1.5.1, we can deduce from the regularity of its formation that there may exist an independent variable, which we have not observed, that would make all the partial correlations zero if we partialled it out. We can also deduce the correlations of the given variables with such a variable. More generally, given a correlation matrix of at least three variables, it is a restrictive, falsifiable hypothesis that all the correlations in the matrix could be explained by the correlations of the given variables with an unknown variable. (With three variables or less, the "law" fits any correlation matrix at all, so it is trivial.) Common factor theory started from the recognition of empirical correlation matrices that look as if their correlations could be explained in this way.

Once we have a correlation matrix with this special structure, it might seem natural to go back to the source of our data and start trying to find the "missing," crucial variable (i.e., the test or measurement of whatever kind that will give us the empirical zero partial correlations that we now expect from theory). In fact, we are unlikely to find such a measurement. We shall probably succeed in finding more variables that can be added to our set, which can also have their correlations explained by x, but we shall almost certainly not happen upon x itself. Remember that the partial correlations of our variables are the correlations of their residuals about their regressions on x. Our search for "pure x" is most likely to yield just further measures that can be regressed on x but with nonzero residuals of their own. At the very least, any fresh variables we measure will consist in part of an error of measurement. By the usual notions about error in psychometric theory, the error part of a measurement should be uncorrelated with all other variables and so would make an irreducible part of the residual of the variable in its regression on another. Hence, at the very best we can only find an empirical measure of pure x + error of measurement, and probably it will contain also some "impurity"—something apart from error of measurement— that is also not pure x.

For these reasons, instead of taking the interesting, lawful structure of a matrix such as that of Table 1.5.1, as a cue to search for the explaining variable in further empirical measurements, we accord to the pure x that would explain our empirical correlations the status of an unobserved, hypothetical term. We call it a *common factor*, and all the inferences we make about it are based on the given observed variables. The notion is that each observed variable consists of two parts, namely its regression on the common factor and its residual about the regression. The common factor is what the variables "have in common," in the sense that it supplies their correlated parts; for if we partial out the common factor, the residuals of the variables are uncorrelated. It is not important whether the common factor explains a lot, or a little, of the variances of the variables. What is important is that it explains their correlations completely. Alongside the purely statistical notion of a regression part versus residual part of each variable, we are putting a logical classification notion. The notion is that the common factor part of each variable is its generic part (i.e., the general "whatever" that any one of the variables, interchangeably, measures) and the residual part of each variable is its specific part (i.e., the specific "whatever" that only the given variable measures and no other variable in the set measures).

At this point, it may help to recall the discussion of "why" variables are correlated. Here, we are applying the notion that two variables are correlated "because they measure (in part) the same thing." We say that the variables in our set are correlated, with the given law of formation, because they all measure just one thing in common (and also each measures something of its own).

Perhaps we should consider a concrete example. Suppose that the five variables in Table 1.5.1 are measures on students in (1) classics, (2) French, (3)

English, (4) mathematics, (5) music. (If the example has a quaintly old-fashioned appearance, this is because it is slightly modified from Spearman, 1904.) We believe that there is some property x of the students, which we have not measured, and perhaps shall never directly measure, that explains all the observed correlations. If, hypothetically, we selected students having a fixed value of x, then in the selected group the five performances would be uncorrelated. We want to say that the five performances measure just one generic quality in common, and apart from this they are unique in what they measure. What can we say beyond this? Can we "name", or "label," x? Can we state what, conceptually, it seems to be? A cautious response to the challenge to name x would be to say that x is "general scholastic quality." This is hardly more than a restatement of the bare facts. Spearman (1904) chose to say (in the context of other evidence, it is only fair to add) that x is *general intelligence*. Both these statements are justified by simply thinking of x as "what the variables have in common." But we can use further information. The correlations of the measures with x are known, and they range down from .9 for classics, to .5 for music, becoming lower as we move from linguistic performances to nonlinguistic, so we could argue that x is a generic "linguistic ability."

It is hoped that so far we have established the following basic principles:

1. We can find a correlation matrix that exhibits an extremely regular law of formation, describable, say, by "proportionality of columns."

2. Such a matrix behaves "as if" all the correlations could be explained by the regressions of the variables on just one unobserved variable, with all residual correlations becoming zero.

3. The one unobserved variable is thought of as a pure, generic property in common to all the observed variables, measurable by any one of them. In addition, each observed variable has a residual part, consisting in what it measures uniquely (including its error of measurement).

4. We can at least begin to speculate, with a show of rationality, about the nature of the generic property that the variables measure in common from the knowledge that (a) it is *these* known and understood measurements that have that something in common and (b) some of them are more closely related to it than others.

After all the emphasis in the preceding sections on the importance of the distinction between sample and population, the reader should be wondering by now whether we have been considering a sample, a population, or both. Strictly speaking, nearly every remark in this section so far could only be made about a population, with supposedly known correlation matrix. If we have a population whose correlation matrix fits the "proportional-columns" law of formation, then almost certainly any sample drawn from it will not. The law becomes a statistical hypothesis, and we must test whether our sample correlation fits the hypothesis

TABLE 1.5.2

Classics	1.00	.83	.78	.70	.66	.63
French	.83	1.00	.67	.67	.65	.57
English	.78	.67	1.00	.64	.54	.51
Mathematics	.70	.67	.64	1.00	.45	.51
Discrimination	.66	.65	.54	.45	1.00	.40
Music	.63	.57	.51	.51	.40	1.00

well enough for it to be tenable or departs from it so far that we should reject it. (This fact was well recognized in the earliest phase of factor analysis, from 1904 to the 1930s but somehow tended to be ignored thereafter, until quite recently, with the result that much of the literature on factor analysis is in a confused state.) Table 1.5.2 gives the correlation matrix, published by Spearman (1904), on which was laid the foundations of the common factor model by recognition of the proportionality criterion and its implications by way of correlation theory. Clearly, the sample matrix does not closely obey the theoretical law of formation, but we can show by the methods of Chapter 2 that it is statistically con-
:nt with the law. That is, we cannot reject the hypothesis that just one common factor explains the correlations in the population from which the sample was drawn. In practice, then, we shall need a method for statistical estimation of the six correlations of the variables with the factor (the basic parameters in this hypothesis), and we shall need a criterion for retaining or rejecting the hypothesis of just one common factor on the basis of a sample.

Suppose now that we have a correlation matrix that clearly does not fit the hypothesis of just one common factor. That is, suppose it is evident that there cannot be just one unobserved variable that will explain the correlations, reducing them to zero when we partial it out. Could it be that, in theory, two or more than two variables might be partialled out, thereby reducing the partial correlations to zero? Expressions for partial correlations with two or more variables partialled out are unpleasantly complicated, especially for correlated independent variables. This is partly because of denominator terms that we can ignore for our purposes. In the case where the independent variables $x_1, \ldots, x_m$ are mutually uncorrelated, we can write the general expression as

$$r_{jk \cdot x_1 x_2 \ldots x_m} = \frac{r_{jk} - (r_{j1}r_{k1} + r_{j2}r_{k2} + \cdots + r_{jm}r_{km})}{\text{a denominator}}. \quad (1.5.2)$$

(The denominator is just a scaling term, which in effect puts the residuals into standard measure.) We do not have to write the expression for the denominator (which is also a function of the correlations $r_{j1}, \ldots, r_{jm}; r_{k1}, \ldots, r_{km}$), because we only want to ask what the condition is that the partial correlations are zero. Independent of the value of the denominator, we see that if

$$r_{jk \cdot x_1 x_2 \ldots x_m} = 0 \tag{1.5.3}$$

then

$$r_{jk} - (r_{j1}r_{k1} + r_{j2}r_{k2} + \cdots + r_{jm}r_{km}) = 0 \tag{1.5.4}$$

which can be arranged in the form

$$r_{jk} = r_{j1}r_{k1} + r_{j2}r_{k2} + \cdots + r_{jm}r_{km}. \tag{1.5.5}$$

The implication is that if m (uncorrelated) variables explain the $n(n-1)/2$ correlations between n dependent variables, then each such correlation can be written as a sum of m products of two numbers—the correlation of each dependent variable with each independent variable. For example, Table 1.5.3 gives the correlations of six dependent variables, bordered above and on the left by their correlations with two (uncorrelated) independent variables. The use of (1.5.4) shows that their partial correlations are all zero. We observe that the 15 correlations in Table 1.5.3 are all of the form

$$r_{jk} = r_{j1}r_{k2} + r_{j2}r_{k2}. \tag{1.5.6}$$

For example,

$$r_{12} = .9 \times .8 + .0 \times .0$$

$$r_{35} = .7 \times .1 + .1 \times .7.$$

The reader, if in doubt, should compute a few more.

In exactly the same way as in the case of one common factor, we convert this argument into an argument about *multiple* common factors, as theoretical ex-

TABLE 1.5.3

			Correlations					
	x_1	1.0	.0	.9	.8	.7	.2	.1	.0
	x_2	.0	1.0	.0	.0	.1	.6	.7	.8
French	y_1	.9	.0	1.00	.72	.63	.18	.09	.00
English	y_2	.8	.0	.72	1.00	.56	.16	.08	.00
Geography	y_3	.7	.1	.63	.56	1.00	.20	.14	.08
Chemistry	y_4	.2	.6	.18	.16	.20	1.00	.44	.48
Physics	y_5	.1	.7	.09	.08	.14	.44	1.00	.56
Mathematics	y_6	.0	.8	.00	.00	.08	.48	.56	1.00

plainers of observed correlations. It is a matter of empirical fact about a correlation matrix whether or not its $n(n - 1)/2$ correlations can be explained as sums of products of numbers from an $(n \times m)$ list of numbers like the (6×2) list bordering the matrix in Table 1.5.3. As a rough guide, provided that $n(n - 1)/2$ is larger than nm, we again have a law of formation governing the correlations in the matrix, which constitutes an interesting fact about it. It is a law of formation that does not reveal itself to simple inspection of the correlation matrix, but it is quite as lawful as the law of proportionality by columns.

Here again we are talking about a population. In practice we shall expect to set up the hypothesis that 2, or 3, or some specified number of common factors, small enough to be restrictive, explains the correlations in the population. We shall then want to estimate the correlations of the tests with these factors and to calculate a statistical criterion measuring the goodness of fit of the sample to the hypothesis. We shall expect to reject the hypothesis of just m factors (just 2, no more; just 3, no more; etc.) if the test criterion reaches our chosen level of significance. Otherwise, we shall regard the hypothesis as tenable.

Unfortunately, it turns out that when we try to allow more than one common factor as explainers of our correlations, if our hypothesis only specifies the number of factors to be fitted and makes no further specifications of what we expect, we are not supplying enough a priori conditions to determine the properties of the common factors that we wish to study. For example, Table 1.5.4 gives an alternative set of correlations of the observed variables from Table 1.5.3, with a pair of factors, that explains their correlations just as well as the set studied in Table 1.5.3 For example,

$$r_{35} = .566 \times .566 - .424 \times .424 = .14.$$

In effect, there are many (in fact, infinitely many) interchangeable sets of correlations between observed variables and common factors that will explain the

TABLE 1.5.4

	x_1	x_2
y_1	.636	.636
y_2	.566	.566
y_3	.566	.424
y_4	.566	-.283
y_5	.566	-.424
y_6	.566	-.566

observed correlations equally well. This creates a problem at the stage at which we wish to understand our results. As in the case of just one common factor, if we have reached the point where we have two (or *m*) common factors that explain our correlations and we know the correlations of the variables with the factors, we want now to go beyond the bare statistical facts. We want to think of the two (or *m*) common factors as pure measures of distinct properties that our variables "impurely" measure in common. We would hope to name these two (or *m*) hypothetical properties on the basis of the nature of the measures of which they are the common conceptual core, so to speak. We would expect to depend heavily on the magnitudes of the variable-factor correlations for this purpose. For example, in Table 1.5.3, we note that the first three variables have high correlations with the first factor and low correlations with the second, whereas for the last three the reverse is true. From the labels of the measures, we might be willing to call the first factor *linguistic* aptitude and the second *mathematical aptitude*. But the alternative set of variable-factor correlations given in Table 1.5.4 seems to require a quite different interpretation. Here all six variables are correlated about equally with the first factor; the first group of three have positive correlations, whereas the second group of three have negative correlations with the second factor. We might try to say that all six variables measure in much the same way a general scholastic aptitude, whereas the second factor is positively related to linguistic performances and negatively related to mathematical performances. We could actually call it a linguistic versus mathematical factor.

Basic intolerance of the ambiguity of multiple factor results of the type just illustrated has led psychometricians to adopt additional principles aimed at eliminating alternative sets of test-factor correlations that will explain given observations and narrowing these down to one "preferred" set of numbers. The almost universally adopted principle is to have some test-factor correlations either as small as possible or equal to zero. The first form of this principle is used when we fit a hypothesized number of common factors to a sample correlation matrix without worrying about which set of test-factor correlations we obtain and then perform manipulations on whatever test-factor correlations happen to come out in order to transform them into a set with as many small test-factor correlations as possible, arranged in a satisfactory pattern in their matrix. This is the usual procedure in what we call *exploratory factor analysis*, and it is treated in Chapter 2. The second form of the principle is used when we are prepared a priori to guess not only the number of common factors but also that specified variables will be quite unrelated to specified common factors. Either on the basis of a deep, considered, conceptual analysis of the nature of our measures or on the basis of prior exploratory or other past analyses of data, we can build very detailed hypotheses. For example, it might have been reasonable to postulate for the measures in Table 1.5.4 that the first three measures would be related to a linguistic factor only; the last two would be related to a mathematical factor only, whereas number 4, science, would relate to both. We would then express this hypothesis in a prescription of the "pattern" of zeros versus numbers to be estimated in fitting the detailed hypothesis. (It is necessary to mention, however, that we would usually then allow a further complication by letting the common factors themselves be correlated. See the following.)

Fitting and testing a detailed hypothesis in which we postulate both the number of common factors and also postulate that relations between prescribed variables and prescribed factors are zero is known as *confirmatory factor analysis* and is discussed in Chapter 3. At the time of writing, confirmatory factor analysis is not in very wide use; yet it can be claimed that exploratory factor analysis should only be used, if at all, to aid in developing hypotheses that are detailed enough to be unambiguous, and then these should be tested by confirmatory factor analysis. Further, we can do without exploratory factor analysis altogether in cases where we choose our measures, with great care, on the basis of a deep theoretical analysis of the subject matter under study. It is these views that lead to a rather strong emphasis in this book on confirmatory methods and to a positive removal of emphasis from some of the exploratory methods.

One further complication has to be mentioned to complete this outline of the basic foundations of common factor analysis. In order to simplify the expression for partial correlation in (1.5.2) and the discussion that followed that expression, it was quietly supposed that the independent variables happened to be uncorrelated. This supposition continued to operate when we substituted common factors for independent variables. Because common factors are hypothetical measures, we are always free to have uncorrelated common factors as part of the definition of our hypothesis. Certainly, if common factors were allowed to be very highly correlated, it might be hard to give them distinct names and to think of them as generic properties of our subjects that are of distinct kinds. Some investigators would argue that common factors are fundamental principles of classification, or fundamental dimensions of variation, and they should be uncorrelated by definition. Others would claim that as fundamental quantities they should be correlated by analogy with some observable "fundamental" quantities that are, in fact, correlated. Perhaps the most convincing argument for allowing common factors to be correlated, is that correlations are definitely influenced by the selection of subjects. Variables that are highly correlated in one population may have low or zero correlations in another. Regression weights, on the other hand, the rates of change of dependent variables as functions of independent variables, remain the same from one population to another under a wide and reasonable principle of selection. (See Chapter 6.) The emphasis in our discussion so far has been on correlations, essentially to keep things simple. We now find it desirable to shift the emphasis to regression weights, as these represent the more fundamental terms if we seek invariant relationships in multivariate data.

Assume now that all variables are in standard measure in the population. If we have uncorrelated independent variables, according to the theory of regression, the regression weights in the regression of each dependent variable on the m independent variables are the same as their correlation with the independent variables, and the condition that the partial correlations vanish is the one given by (1.5.5). If, on the other hand, the independent variables are correlated, the regression weights are not numerically the same as the correlations. They may then, in fact, range from minus infinity to plus infinity instead of being bounded by minus one and plus one. Generally, they do not become very large or small, but beginners should not be surprised when regression weights of variables on correlated factors stray outside the sacred bounds of plus and minus one. Again we leave to our factor-analytic computer programs the actual business of computing regression weights of variables on factors and suppose that we may receive them in the form of an ($n \times m$) matrix whenever we want them. We shall write f_{jp} for the element in the jth row and pth column of this matrix and understand it to be the regression weight of the jth variable on the pth common factor. Given this matrix of regression weights and the ($m \times m$) matrix of correlations between the independent variables, of which the (p, q)th correlation will be denoted by ρ_{pq}, then it turns out that in place of (1.5.5) we have a more complicated condition, namely,

$$r_{jk} = \sum_{p=1}^{m} \sum_{q=1}^{m} f_{jp} f_{kq} \rho_{pq} \tag{1.5.7}$$

That is, if all the partial correlations vanish, then each correlation is a sum of m^2 terms, one for each element in the ($m \times m$) matrix of correlations of the independent variables. Each term is a triple product of two weights and the relevant correlation (including the unit ''self''-correlations).

Thus we see that if the $n(n - 1)/2$ correlations among the members of a set of observed variables can be explained by m correlated common factors, then they can be written as the functions of nm numbers f_{jp} and $m(m - 1)/2$ numbers ρ_{pq} (together with unities for ρ_{pp} of course) given by (1.5.6). There is extra freedom to choose such numbers because of the choice of correlations between the factors. This results in extra freedom to make some regression weights small or zero. Note that we remove a deliberate ambiguity from the previous statement about variables being unrelated to factors. With correlated factors, we usually make the regression weights of the variables on the factors small, not their correlations. (This is on the grounds that regression weights are, as argued previously, fundamental quantities, invariant under usual forms of selection.)

We quote another useful result without proof. Given the regression weights f_{jp} of variables on factors (or on known independent variables) and the correlations ρ_{pq} of the factors (or of the known independent variables), we can compute the correlations, which, to avoid ambiguity, we shall denote by s_{jp}, of the variables and the factors by using the simple expression

$$s_{jp} = \sum_{q=1}^{m} f_{jp} \rho_{qp} \tag{1.5.8}$$

TABLE 1.5.5

(a)

Correlation Matrix

$$\begin{bmatrix} 1.000 & .720 & .630 & .315 & .360 & .405 \\ .720 & 1.000 & .560 & .280 & .320 & .360 \\ .630 & .560 & 1.000 & .245 & .280 & .315 \\ .315 & .280 & .245 & 1.000 & .560 & .630 \\ .360 & .320 & .280 & .560 & 1.000 & .720 \\ .405 & .360 & .315 & .630 & .720 & 1.000 \end{bmatrix}$$

(b)	(c)	(d)
Regression Weights of Variables on Factors	Correlation Matrix of Factors	Correlations of Variables with Factors

$$\begin{bmatrix} .9 & .0 \\ .8 & .0 \\ .7 & .0 \\ .0 & .7 \\ .0 & .8 \\ .0 & .9 \end{bmatrix} \qquad \begin{bmatrix} 1.0 & .5 \\ .5 & 1.0 \end{bmatrix} \qquad \begin{bmatrix} .90 & .45 \\ .80 & .40 \\ .70 & .35 \\ .35 & .70 \\ .40 & .80 \\ .45 & .90 \end{bmatrix}$$

In Table 1.5.5, these results are put to work. We are given the correlation matrix shown and told that the computer offers us (after performing work on the given correlations) the matrix of regression weights of variables on factors and the correlation matrix of factors that are also shown. We see, for example, that the correlation between the first and second variable is given by

$$r_{12} = .9 \times .8 \times 1.0 + .9 \times .0 \times .5$$
$$+ .0 \times .8 \times .5 + .0 \times .0 \times 1.0$$
$$= .72$$

and that

$$r_{34} = .7 \times .0 \times 1.0 + .7 \times .7 \times .5$$
$$+ .0 \times .0 \times .5 + .0 \times .7 \times 1.0$$
$$= .245$$

The entire matrix of correlations between variables and factors is given also in Table 1.5.5. We notice that the fact that a regression weight is zero does not imply that the corresponding correlation is zero. Similarly, a correlation of zero would not imply a corresponding regression weight of zero. This does, as we might expect, create problems in the interpretation of correlated factors, or rather it represents one symptom of the general difficulty (noted already in Section 1.3) of interpreting correlated sources of variation. We also notice that the example chosen has a very clear pattern of zeros and nonzeros in its regression weights. If we had prespecified the locations of these and not estimated them, our hypothesis here would be almost as parsimonious as a single-factor hypothesis. There is a long tradition of measuring the parsimony of our hypotheses in factor analysis just by the number of factors we fit. This is a habit of thought that we need to lose. Chapter 3 elaborates on the point, but it should be clear already that the simplest hypothesis will be the one with the fewest parameters estimated. This need not be determined by the number of factors, which could even be greater than the number of variables.

At this point, some readers should be feeling very frustrated about things that have not been said. Here is an entire section purporting to give the foundations of common factor analysis; yet with the sole exception of the term *common factor* none of the language of common factor theory, already met elsewhere and either readily understood or puzzled over, has been used. Where are the usual *factor loadings, factor pattern, factor structure, communalities, orthogonal factors, oblique factors, unique factors, specific factors, rotation, simple structure, principal axes* (or *components*), etc.? The view taken here is that none of these terms is necessary, either for a beginner's understanding of factor analysis or for a complete mathematical exposition of the subject. For a technical exposition of the subject, we would need other terms from statistics and algebra, of course. We need and have used correlations among factors, regression weights of variables on factors, and residuals. These are the primitive terms of our vocabulary. We could avoid some clumsiness by the use of abbreviations, say *v–v correlations, v–f correlations, f–f correlations,* and *v–f weights,* with immediately obvious meaning. In fact, these will be used later as reminders of the meaning of other terms. However, a specialized language has become traditional among factor theorists and users of factor analysis, and we must bow to existing usage and learn the traditional vocabulary. For many of the terms, a glossary can be given immediately. A few other words are introduced later.

General Note: All the material in this chapter is very well known. For further reading, at an intermediate level of difficulty, on the concepts of factor analysis, see Gorsuch (1974) or Rummel (1970). For a more technical account, see Mulaik (1972). Classical texts that still have a great deal to offer the interested student are Thomson (1950) and Thurstone (1947).

GLOSSARY

(Common) factor loading: Regression weight of a variable on a common factor (sometimes, *common factor coefficient*). The word *loading* is an engineering metaphor, due to Thurstone, replacing the metaphor ''weight'' from nineteenth-century physics.

(Common) factor pattern: The entire ($n \times m$) matrix of regression weights of the n variables on the m common factors.

(Common) factor correlation: The correlation of a variable with a common factor.

(Common) factor structure: The entire ($n \times m$) matrix of correlations of the n variables with the m factors.

(In these four terms the word *common* is commonly omitted.)

Communality: The squared multiple correlation of a variable with all the common factors—thought of as the proportion of the variance of the variable ''in common'' because explained by the common factors. Often used, ambiguously, to refer to crude approximations to communality. All references to communality should be regarded with suspicion unless the context makes the use of the term absolutely unambiguous.

Uniqueness: The residual variance of a variable about its regression on the common factors. (Also *unique variance.*)

Unique factor loading (rare): The standard deviation of the residual of a variable. Sometimes, perhaps regrettably, the residual part is thought of as rescaled to be in standard measure; then what was its standard deviation becomes a coefficient resembling a regression weight.

Orthogonal factors: Uncorrelated factors. (The term derives from a widely used geometrical picture of correlation.)

Oblique factors: Correlated factors. (Same remark as previous.)

Rotation: Performing arithmetic to obtain a new set of factor loadings (v–f regression weights) from a given set and perhaps to obtain also the correlation matrix of the obtained factors. (The term derives, correctly, from a geometrical picture of transformation from one set of uncorrelated factors to another but is also used, incorrectly, to describe any derivation of a set of correlated factors from another set of factors. The word *transformation* is to be preferred.)

Simple structure: This term has two radically different meanings that are often confused. Its primary meaning is exhibited when we say that a factor pattern (a matrix of v–f regression weights) has *simple structure* if (1) each row has at least one zero, (2) each column has at least as many zeros as there are common factors, (3) for every pair of columns there should be at least as many pairs of variables with a zero regression weight on one factor and a nonzero regression weight on the other, as there are common factors. The intention is to try to express in a recipe for action the notion that each variable should have its correlations with other variables explained by as few of the factors as possible.

Its secondary meaning is obtained by substituting the undefined word *small* for the definite word *zero* in the primary definition. This is a crucial change. In the first version it is a matter of fact whether a correlation matrix will yield simple structure or not, and the question can be tested by the methods of Chapter 3. In the second version, we can only ask how *well* the correlation matrix yields simple structure by rotation. Users of factor analysis then tend to treat as "simple structures" factor patterns that have virtually not attained any simplicity at all. *Rotation* methods, by their nature, can only yield simple structure in the second sense. Confirmatory factor analysis is necessary for the first. It is here strongly recommended that we speak of the first only as simple structure and the second as *approximate simple structure*.

Further additions to the glossary will be made when appropriate. We note that, rather strangely, there does not seem to be a specialized term for the correlations between the factors. This is the main place where a new term might be needed to distinguish quick;y between (v–f) factor correlations and (f–f) correlations between factors.

1.6   MATHEMATICAL NOTES ON CHAPTER 1[2]

(a) Multiple Regression and Partial Correlation

Suppose we have m independent variables $x_1, \ldots, x_m$ and a single dependent variable y in standard measure in the population. Let $\mathbf{R}_{xx} = \mathrm{E}\{\mathbf{xx}'\}$ be the ($m \times m$) correlation matrix of the independent variables and $\mathbf{r}_{xy} = \mathrm{E}\{\mathbf{xy}\}$ be the ($m \times 1$) vector of correlations between y and the m components of the vector $\mathbf{x}' = [x_1, \ldots, x_m]$. Writing

$$\hat{y} = \mathbf{b}'\mathbf{x} \qquad (1.6.1)$$

for the regression of y on $\mathbf{x}$, where $\mathbf{b}' = [b_1, \ldots, b_m]$ is an ($m \times 1$) vector of regression weights, we have by the results in A1.9 on expected values,

$$\sigma_{\hat{y}}^2 = \mathrm{E}\{\mathbf{b}'\mathbf{xx}'\mathbf{b}\} \qquad (1.6.2)$$

that is,

$$\sigma_{\hat{y}}^2 = \mathbf{b}'\mathbf{R}_{xx}\mathbf{b} \qquad (1.6.3)$$

[2]This section may be omitted, but the reader is encouraged to peruse it and decide whether it would help him or her to work with it seriously.

for the variance of $\hat{y}$, and

$$c_{y\hat{y}} = E\{\mathbf{b}'\mathbf{x}_y\} \tag{1.6.4}$$

that is,

$$c_{y\hat{y}} = \mathbf{b}'E\{\mathbf{x}y\} = \mathbf{b}'\mathbf{r}_{xy} \tag{1.6.5}$$

for the covariance of y and $\hat{y}$. Because by the chosen scaling the variance of y is unity, the squared correlation between y and $\hat{y}$ is given by

$$\rho_{y\hat{y}}^2 = \frac{(\mathbf{b}'\mathbf{r}_{xy})^2}{\mathbf{b}'R_{xx}\mathbf{b}}. \tag{1.6.6}$$

The usual line of argument at this point invokes the differential calculus to obtain the condition for a maximum of $\rho_{y\hat{y}}^2$ with respect to choices of $\mathbf{b}$. Instead, we shall use the property of the regression surface that the residual

$$e = y - \hat{y} \tag{1.6.7}$$

is uncorrelated with the independent variables $\mathbf{x}$; that is,

$$E\{\mathbf{x}e\} = \mathbf{0} \tag{1.6.8}$$

which is to say that

$$E\{\mathbf{x}(y - \mathbf{x}'\mathbf{b})\} = \mathbf{0} \tag{1.6.9}$$

that is,

$$E\{\mathbf{x}y\} - E\{\mathbf{x}\mathbf{x}'\}\mathbf{b} = \mathbf{0} \tag{1.6.10}$$

that is

$$\mathbf{r}_{xy} - R_{xx}\mathbf{b} = \mathbf{0} \tag{1.6.11}$$

whence we have

$$R_{xx}\mathbf{b} = \mathbf{r}_{xy} \tag{1.6.12}$$

and, finally,

$$\mathbf{b} = R_x^{-1}{}_x\mathbf{r}_{xy} \tag{1.6.13}$$

the required expression for the regression weights in terms of the given correlations. Substituting (1.6.13) in (1.6.6) gives

$$\rho_{y\hat{y}}^2 = \mathbf{r}_{xy}'R_x^{-1}{}_x\mathbf{r}_{xy}. \tag{1.6.14}$$

Alternatively, the squared multiple correlation is given by

$$\rho_{y\hat{y}}^2 = \mathbf{b}'R_{xx}\mathbf{b}. \tag{1.6.15}$$

For example, from Table 1.3.2a, we may write

$$R_{xx} = \begin{bmatrix} 1.000 & .707 \\ .707 & 1.000 \end{bmatrix} \quad \mathbf{r}_{xy} = \begin{bmatrix} .000 \\ .350 \end{bmatrix}.$$

It may be verified that

$$R_{xx}^{-1} = \begin{bmatrix} 2.000 & -1.414 \\ -1.414 & 2.000 \end{bmatrix}$$

hence

$$\mathbf{b} = \begin{bmatrix} 2.000 & -1.414 \\ -1.414 & 2.000 \end{bmatrix} \begin{bmatrix} .000 \\ .350 \end{bmatrix} = \begin{bmatrix} -.4949 \\ .7000 \end{bmatrix}.$$

Further,

$$\rho_{y\hat{y}}^2 = [.000 \quad .350] \begin{bmatrix} 2.000 & -1.414 \\ -1.414 & 2.000 \end{bmatrix} \begin{bmatrix} .000 \\ .350 \end{bmatrix}$$

$$= .245.$$

(Hence $\rho_{y\hat{y}} = .4949$ as in Table 1.3.2).

More generally, suppose we have m independent variables $x_1, \ldots, x_m$ and n dependent variables $y_1, \ldots, y_n$ in standard measure in a population. We arrange them in a partitioned vector $[\mathbf{x}':\mathbf{y}'] = [x_1, \ldots, x_m:y_1, \ldots, y_n]$, and correspondingly partition their $(n + m) \times (n + m)$ correlation matrix as

$$\begin{bmatrix} \mathbf{R}_{xx} & \vdots & \mathbf{R}_{xy} \\ \cdots & \vdots & \cdots \\ \mathbf{R}_{yx} & \vdots & \mathbf{R}_{yy} \end{bmatrix}$$

where $\mathbf{R}_{xx}$, of order $(m \times m)$, is the correlation matrix of the independent variables; $\mathbf{R}_{yy}$, of order $(n \times n)$, is the correlation matrix of the dependent variables; $\mathbf{R}_{xy}$, of order $(m \times n)$, is the matrix of cross-correlations; and $\mathbf{R}_{yx}$, $(n \times m)$, is the transpose of $\mathbf{R}_{xy}$. The n vectors of regression weights $\mathbf{b}_1, \ldots, \mathbf{b}_n$ that we would obtain for the regression of each dependent variable $y_1, \ldots, y_n$ on the m independent variables may be adjoined to form the $(m \times n)$ matrix $\mathbf{B} = [\mathbf{b}_1:\mathbf{b}_2: \ldots :\mathbf{b}_n]$. Then the matrix $\mathbf{B}$ of regression weights for the regression of $\mathbf{y}$ on $\mathbf{x}$ may be written as

$$\mathbf{B} = \mathbf{R}_{xx}^{-1}\mathbf{R}_{xy}. \tag{1.6.16}$$

This requires no new argument. It is just a matter of combining, in one expression, n results of the type (1.6.13); that is,   ·

$$\mathbf{b}_j = \mathbf{R}_{xx}^{-1}\mathbf{r}_{xyj} \quad j = 1, \ldots, n.$$

Then (1.6.16) is a single expression containing these n results.

The vector $\mathbf{e}' = [e_1, \ldots, e_n]$ of the residuals of the dependent variables about their regressions on $\mathbf{x}$ is given by

$$\mathbf{e} = \mathbf{y} - \hat{\mathbf{y}} \tag{1.6.17}$$

that is, by

$$\mathbf{e} = \mathbf{y} - \mathbf{B}'\mathbf{x} \tag{1.6.18}$$

which may be written as

$$\mathbf{e} = \mathbf{y} - \mathbf{R}_{yx}\mathbf{R}_{x\,x}^{-1}\mathbf{x}. \tag{1.6.19}$$

The covariance matrix of the residuals is then given by

$$
\begin{aligned}
E\{\mathbf{ee}'\} = {}& E\{\mathbf{yy}'\} \\
& + \mathbf{R}_{yx}\mathbf{R}_{x\,x}^{-1}E\{\mathbf{xx}'\}\mathbf{R}_{x\,x}^{-1}\mathbf{R}_{xy} \\
& - \mathbf{R}_{yx}\mathbf{R}_{x\,x}^{-1}E\{\mathbf{xy}'\} \\
& - E\{\mathbf{yx}'\}\mathbf{R}_{x\,x}^{-1}\mathbf{R}_{yx}
\end{aligned} \tag{1.6.20}
$$

that is, by

$$\mathbf{C}_{yy\cdot x} = \mathbf{R}_{yy} - \mathbf{R}_{yx}\mathbf{R}_{x\,x}^{-1}\mathbf{R}_{xy}. \tag{1.6.21}$$

This is the covariance matrix of $\mathbf{y}$ with $\mathbf{x}$ (partialled out.'' The partial *correlation* matrix cannot be written in a convenient form but would be obtained by first obtaining the standard deviations of the residuals from the square roots of the diagonal elements of (1.6.21) and then dividing each element of the residual covariance matrix by the product of the two relevant standard deviations. We may, alternatively, write $\mathbf{C}_{yy\cdot x}$ as

$$\mathbf{C}_{yy\cdot x} = \mathbf{R}_{yy} - \mathbf{B}'\mathbf{R}_{xx}\mathbf{B}. \tag{1.6.22}$$

The results (1.6.21) and (1.6.22) are used repeatedly throughout this book in one application or another. The reader may wish to interpret as an example of multiple regression and partial correlation methods the material, actually presented as a factor-analytic example, given in Table 1.5.5. Regard matrix (a) as $\mathbf{R}_{yy}$, matrix (c) as $\mathbf{R}_{xx}$, and matrix (d) as $\mathbf{R}_{yx}$. Note also that in this example

$$\mathbf{R}_{xx}^{-1} = \begin{bmatrix} 1.333 & -.667 \\ -.667 & 1.333 \end{bmatrix}.$$

Then it is easy to "verify" equations (1.6.16), (1.6.21), and (1.6.22) on this example, noting that the diagonal elements of the matrix $\mathbf{C}_{yy\cdot x}$ are the squared multiple correlations of the components of $\mathbf{y}$ with $\mathbf{x}$.

(b) The Hypotheses of Section 1.4

The hypothesis that all the variables in a set are mutually uncorrelated is the hypothesis that their $(n \times n)$ correlation matrix $\mathbf{R}$ is equal to the identity matrix, that is, that

$$\mathbf{R} = \mathbf{I}_n. \tag{1.6.22}$$

It may be shown that if $\mathbf{A}$ is the usual sample correlation matrix from a sample of N observations, then the quantity

$$\Theta = -2N \log |\mathbf{A}| \tag{1.6.23}$$

is distributed approximately like chi-square, with degrees of freedom given by

$$\mathrm{df} = \frac{n(n-1)}{2} \tag{1.6.24}$$

if N is sufficiently large.

The hypothesis that two groups of variables are uncorrelated is the hypothesis that their partitioned correlation matrix has null off-diagonal submatrices (i.e., is *diagonal block*). We denote this by writing

$$\mathbf{R} = \begin{bmatrix} \mathbf{R}_{xx} & \mathbf{R}_{xy} \\ \mathbf{R}_{yx} & \mathbf{R}_{yy} \end{bmatrix} = \begin{bmatrix} \mathbf{R}_{xx} & \mathbf{O} \\ \mathbf{O} & \mathbf{R}_{yy} \end{bmatrix} \tag{1.6.25}$$

for the $(m + n) \times (m + n)$ matrix $\mathbf{R}$, partitioned as before. If $\mathbf{A}$ is the usual sample correlation matrix partitioned in the same way, that is,

$$\mathbf{A} = \begin{bmatrix} \mathbf{A}_{11} & \mathbf{A}_{12} \\ \mathbf{A}_{21} & \mathbf{A}_{22} \end{bmatrix} \tag{1.6.26}$$

then the quantity

$$\theta = -2N \log \left\{ \frac{|\mathbf{A}|}{|\mathbf{A}_{11}| \, |\mathbf{A}_{22}|} \right\} \tag{1.6.27}$$

is distributed approximately like chi-square, with degrees of freedom given by

$$\mathrm{df} = mn \tag{1.6.28}$$

if N is sufficiently large.

(c) The Algebra of the Common Factor Model

Given n variables $y_1, \ldots, y_n$ in standard measure in the population, we write

$$\mathbf{R} = \mathrm{E}\{\mathbf{y}\mathbf{y}'\} \tag{1.6.29}$$

for the correlation matrix of $\mathbf{y}' = [y_1, \ldots, y_n]$. The assumption of the common factor model is that there exists a vector of m variables, $\mathbf{x}' = [x_1, \ldots, x_m]$, such that the residual covariance matrix

$$\mathbf{R}_{yy \cdot x} = \mathbf{R} - \mathbf{FPF}' \qquad (1.6.30)$$

is diagonal, where we are writing $\mathbf{F}$, an $(n \times m)$ matrix, for the matrix of regression weights of the n variables $y_1, \ldots, y_n$, on the m variables $x_1, \ldots, x_m$ and $\mathbf{P}$ is the $(m \times m)$ correlation matrix of $x_1, \ldots, x_m$. We write $\mathbf{U}^2$ in place of $R_{yy \cdot x}$ as a mnemonic to indicate that the diagonal elements u_{jj}^2 of $\mathbf{U}^2$ are (necessarily nonnegative) *unique variances* and rearrange (1.6.30) in the form

$$\mathbf{R} = \mathbf{FPF}' + \mathbf{U}^2. \qquad (1.6.31)$$

This form of the assumption can be taken to assert that if the common factor model holds, the $(n \times n)$ correlation matrix $\mathbf{R}$ can be expressed as the product of an $(n \times m)$ matrix $\mathbf{F}$, an $(m \times m)$ matrix $\mathbf{P}$, and the transpose of $\mathbf{F}$, plus a diagonal matrix. We refer to $\mathbf{F}$ as the *common factor pattern*, to $\mathbf{P}$ as the matrix of correlations between the factors, and to $\mathbf{U}^2$ as the *uniqueness* matrix. We may also occasionally wish to consider the matrix

$$\mathbf{S} = E\{\mathbf{yx}'\}$$

of correlations between the components of $\mathbf{y}$ and the components of $\mathbf{x}$. We refer to $\mathbf{S}$ as the *common factor structure*. Because, by (1.6.16),

$$\mathbf{F} = \mathbf{SP}^{-1}$$

it follows that

$$\mathbf{S} = \mathbf{FP}. \qquad (1.6.32)$$

If we take Table 1.5.5 to illustrate these results, we see for example that (1.6.31) yields

$$
\begin{bmatrix}
1.000 & .720 & .630 & .315 & .360 & .405 \\
.720 & 1.000 & .560 & .280 & .320 & .360 \\
.630 & .560 & 1.000 & .245 & .280 & .315 \\
.315 & .280 & .245 & 1.000 & .560 & .630 \\
.360 & .320 & .280 & .560 & 1.000 & .720 \\
.405 & .360 & .315 & .630 & .720 & 1.000
\end{bmatrix}
$$

$$
=
\begin{bmatrix}
.9 & .0 \\
.8 & .0 \\
.7 & .0 \\
.0 & .7 \\
.0 & .8 \\
.0 & .9
\end{bmatrix}
\begin{bmatrix}
1.0 & .5 \\
.5 & 1.0
\end{bmatrix}
\begin{bmatrix}
.9 & .8 & .7 & .0 & .0 & .0 \\
.0 & .0 & .0 & .7 & .8 & .9
\end{bmatrix}
$$

and (1.6.32) yields

$$
\begin{bmatrix}
.90 & .45 \\
.80 & .40 \\
.70 & .35 \\
.35 & .70 \\
.40 & .80 \\
.45 & .90
\end{bmatrix}
=
\begin{bmatrix}
.9 & .0 \\
.8 & .0 \\
.7 & .0 \\
.0 & .7 \\
.0 & .8 \\
.0 & .9
\end{bmatrix}
\begin{bmatrix}
1.0 & .5 \\
.5 & 1.0
\end{bmatrix}
$$

Unless we restrict the model further, if m is greater than unity, the parameters, $\mathbf{F}$ and $\mathbf{P}$, of the common factor model are not *identified*. That is, for a given $\mathbf{R}$ satisfying (1.6.31) with one set of numbers $\mathbf{F}$ and $\mathbf{P}$, there are infinitely many other sets of numbers also yielding the given $\mathbf{R}$ by (1.6.31). This is because we can introduce the identity matrix in the form of an arbitrary matrix multiplied by its inverse, into (1.6.31), that is, choose any

$$\mathbf{NN}^{-1} = \mathbf{I}_m \tag{1.6.33}$$

and write (1.6.31) as

$$\mathbf{R} = \mathbf{FNN}^{-1}\mathbf{PN}'^{-1}\mathbf{N}'\mathbf{F}' + \mathbf{U}^2 \tag{1.6.34}$$

and thence obtain

$$\mathbf{R} = \mathbf{F}^*\mathbf{P}^*\mathbf{F}^* + \mathbf{U}^2 \tag{1.6.35}$$

where

$$\mathbf{F}^* = \mathbf{FN} \tag{1.6.36}$$

and

$$\mathbf{P}^* = \mathbf{N}^{-1}\mathbf{PN}'^{-1}. \tag{1.6.37}$$

(Note that it is necessary to restrict the scaling so that $\mathbf{P}^*$ will be a correlation matrix, that is, will have diagonal elements equal to unity, but this is an unimportant complication on the present argument.)

If we restrict the model to be the *orthogonal common factor model* (i.e., make the correlation matrix of the factors $\mathbf{P} = \mathbf{I}_m$), we can still find infinitely many alternative sets of numbers $\mathbf{F}$ that equally, with $\mathbf{U}^2$, "explain" $\mathbf{R}$ by what then becomes

$$\mathbf{R} = \mathbf{FF}' + \mathbf{U}^2 \tag{1.6.38}$$

in place of (1.6.31). Section A1.5 describes how to generate *orthogonal* matrices, that is, how to generate $(m \times m)$ matrices $\mathbf{Q}$ such that

$$\mathbf{QQ}' = \mathbf{I}_m. \tag{1.6.39}$$

Given an arbitrary orthogonal matrix $\mathbf{Q}$, we can write (1.6.38) as

$$\mathbf{R} = \mathbf{F}(\mathbf{QQ'})\mathbf{F'}$$
$$= (\mathbf{FQ})\,(\mathbf{Q'F'})$$
$$= \mathbf{F*F*'} \qquad (1.6.40)$$

where

$$\mathbf{F*} = \mathbf{FQ}. \qquad (1.6.41)$$

For example, the matrix in Table 1.5.4 is obtained from the regression weight submatrix in Table 1.5.3 by multiplying it by a (2×2) orthogonal matrix.

One mathematically convenient way to restrict $\mathbf{F}$ in the orthogonal factor model so that it is free from indeterminacy is to require that it have $m(m - 1)/2$ fixed zero values in, say, the upper triangle of the first m rows of the matrix, as illustrated by

$$\mathbf{F} = \begin{bmatrix} f_{11} & 0 & 0 & 0 \\ f_{21} & f_{22} & 0 & 0 \\ f_{31} & f_{32} & f_{33} & 0 \\ f_{41} & f_{42} & f_{43} & f_{44} \\ f_{51} & f_{52} & f_{53} & f_{54} \end{bmatrix}.$$

It may be shown that this is always possible and that with this restriction the matrix is determined uniquely given $\mathbf{R}$ and $\mathbf{U}^2$ (for the appropriate order m). We notice that there are then $mn - \frac{1}{2}m(m - 1)$ nonzero elements in $\mathbf{F}$ to be determined, from $\frac{1}{2}n(n - 1)$ distinct elements in $\mathbf{R}$. On this ground, we generally believe that the model is restrictive if

$$\tfrac{1}{2}n(n - 1) > mn - \tfrac{1}{2}m(m - 1)$$

which may be written as

$$\tfrac{1}{2}\{(n - m)^2 - n - m\} > 0. \qquad (1.6.42)$$

This quantity is the same as the degrees of freedom in the chi-square test for the unrestricted model, described in Section 2.2.

The reader should be warned about a point that has been glossed over in the main text. At times it is convenient to speak as though the parameters of the model are the elements of $\mathbf{F}$ (and of $\mathbf{P}$ if we have correlated factors) and to proceed as though the n numbers in $\mathbf{U}^2$ are determined, given $\mathbf{R}$, $\mathbf{F}$, and $\mathbf{P}$, as the diagonal elements of $\mathbf{R} - \mathbf{FPF'}$. In some circumstances this would yield incorrect conclusions, in particular, in connection with estimation problems. In that connection, we find it necessary to consider that we are estimating the $mn - \frac{1}{2}m(m - 1)$ nonzero parameters in $\mathbf{F}$ [the $m(m- 1)/2$ distinct correlations in P, if working with correlated factors] and the n uniquenesses, but we are doing this on the basis of the $\frac{1}{2}n(n - 1)$ correlations between distinct variables in our sample *and* their n sample variances. The n additional pieces of information exactly balance the n additional parameters that we are in reality estimating. In order to simplify the text, this matter has been deliberately left somewhat ambiguous.

2 Exploratory Common Factor Analysis

2.1. THE PARAMETERS OF THE COMMON FACTOR MODEL

Let us first bring together the central notions of Section 1.5.

In Section 1.5 we saw that the basic assumptions of the common factor model can be expressed in two distinct but equivalent ways. We can say that there exists a number of unobserved variables (common factors) that explain our observed correlations, in the sense that when these are partialled out, the partial correlations of our observed variables all become zero. Alternatively, we can say that each of our observed variables can be expressed as the sum of a (common) part that is its regression on a number of unobserved variables (common factors) and a residual about that regression and that the residuals are uncorrelated.

For the simple case where we suppose that the common factors are uncorrelated, the first of these descriptions is expressed mathematically in the statement

$$r_{jk} = f_{j1}f_{k1} + f_{j2}f_{k2} + \cdots + f_{jm}f_{km} \quad \begin{aligned} & j \neq k \\ & j = 1, \ldots, n \\ & k = 1, \ldots, n \end{aligned} \quad (2.1.1)$$

where r_{jk} is the correlation (in the population) between the jth and kth variable, and f_{jp} is the regression weight of the jth variable on the pth factor (or its correlation with the pth factor, because these are the same when the factors are uncorrelated). The second of these descriptions is expressed in the statement that

$$y_j = f_{j1}x_1 + f_{j2}x_2 + \cdots + f_{jm}x_m + e_j \quad j = 1, \ldots, n \quad (2.1.2)$$

where y_j is the jth observed variable; x_p is the pth common factor, $p = 1, \ldots,$ m; e_j is the residual of y_j about its regression on the factors (the unique factor); and f_{jp} is, again, the regression weight of y_j on x_p (the common factor loading— or coefficient—of variable j on factor p), together with the statement that the residuals are uncorrelated.

The statement in (2.1.1) is the testable numerical implication of the common factor hypothesis, as shown in Section 1.5, and is sometimes described as the *fundamental theorem of factor analysis*. The statement in (2.1.2) is the statistical common factor model itself.

The parameters of the model that we would want to estimate from a given sample are the nm factor loadings (v–f weights) f_{jp} and the n residual variances (variances of the residuals e_j), which are otherwise known as *unique variances* and which will be denoted by u_j^2. If our hypothesis specifies only the number m of common factors, this hypothesis is not sufficiently definite to *identify* the numbers in the ($n \times m$) matrix of factor loadings (i.e., in the factor pattern). We say that these parameters are *not identified*. For example, in Tables 1.5.3 and 1.5.4, we had two sets of numbers, looking quite unlike each other so to speak, that give on computation by way of (2.1.1) exactly the same correlations. Given any one set of factor loadings that yield a set of correlations, the mathematician knows how to generate from these given numbers all the other sets of numbers that give the same correlations. These are *transformations* of the given numbers, and in factor analysis the process of transforming a given set of factor loadings into an alternative, equivalent set ("equivalent" in yielding the same correlations) is known as *rotation*. This nomenclature is correct for uncorrelated factors and incorrect for correlated factors. In what we call *exploratory factor analysis*, the user is unwilling (and just conceivably unable) to specify any more detail, so the mathematician arranges a two-step calculation for the user. In the first step, one set of fitted (estimated) factor loadings is calculated from the sample data supplied, perhaps a set that is mathematically convenient. This will give an *unrotated factor pattern* and is usually ignored by the user when it is supplied in the printed output. In the second step, the computer program performs arithmetic on the unrotated factor pattern, to obtain a "rotated" factor pattern in which the coefficients approximate simple structure (Section 2.4) while equally fitting the data.

In exploratory factor analysis, as we saw, the testable hypothesis is a hypothesis specifying the number of common factors. Using any rational best-fitting procedure for fitting the model to a sample, it seems obvious that the hypotheses that there are 1, 2, . . . , n common factors form a sequence in which more factors must give a better fit. (The hypothesis that there are zero factors is the same as the hypothesis, Section 1.4, that the variables are mutually uncorrelated.) For a sufficiently large number of factors, the fit to any sample must be perfect, and the model would not constrain the data, and so be falsifiable. In exploratory work, then, we follow Thurstone and regard the best number of common factors as the smallest number that will account for the correlations (i.e., the smallest number with which the data are consistent). The weaknesses of this approach are pointed out in Chapter 3.

We might expect that all the relevant information for the estimation of the parameters (the factor loadings and uniquenesses) of the common factor model from a sample of N subjects is contained in the sample correlation matrix and that the sample means and standard deviations are irrelevant (not to mention the scores of individual subjects). Broadly, this is true, though it is a very technical matter to prove it true. We shall describe two methods of obtaining "best" estimates: the method of maximum likelihood (ML) and the method of least squares (LS). The mathematician is able to show that ML estimates are, effectively, independent of the scale of the variables, so there is no important information in the sample standard deviations (or means). In the case of LS estimates, this is not actually true, but if we choose to use the sample correlations, we are minimizing the measure of fit (actually, of misfit), in the scale of (or, in technical language, *in the metric of*) the observed variables as standardized in the sample. This is rational behavior, so the reader is encouraged to remember from this paragraph the main point that it is technically all right to submit sample correlation matrices (rather than sample covariances) to an exploratory factor-analysis program.

2.2. ESTIMATION

Suppose now that we have drawn N subjects independently from a population, measured the n values of the variables under study on each subject, and computed the $(n \times n)$ matrix of sample correlations. It is necessary to distinguish three sets of numbers at this point and to adopt distinguishing notation for them. We shall write r_{jk} for the (unknown) correlation in the population and, correspondingly, f_{jp}, u_j^2 for the population factor loadings and unique variances. We shall write $\hat{r}_{jk}$, $\hat{f}_{jp}$, and $\hat{u}_j^2$ for our best estimates of these quantities obtained from our sample, and to avoid confusion we shall write a_{jk} for the sample correlation coefficient (i.e., the correlation between the measures of variable j and the measures of variable k obtained from our sample). (It would be nice to distinguish a fourth set of numbers—the *possible* values of the estimates out of which we are going to choose the best set—but we shall not do so.)

In least squares (LS) estimation we follow a widely used mathematical notion of "best" in fitting one set of quantities to another. We ask the mathematician to develop some computer arithmetic that will give us estimates $\hat{f}_{jp}$ and $\hat{u}_j^2$ that are better than any other numbers, in the sense that the quantity

$$Q = \sum_{j=1}^{n} \sum_{k=1}^{n} (a_{jk} - \hat{r}_{jk})^2 \qquad (2.2.1)$$

where

$$\hat{r}_{jk} = \hat{f}_{j1}\hat{f}_{k1} + \hat{f}_{j2}\hat{f}_{k2} + \cdots + \hat{f}_{jr}\hat{f}_{km} \qquad (2.2.2)$$

and

$$\hat{r}_{jj} = \hat{f}_{j1}^2 + \cdots + \hat{f}_{jm}^2 + \hat{u}_j^2$$

(and $\hat{r}_{jj} = 1$) is smaller than any other quantity we can get by choosing other values of f_{jp}. The expression (2.2.1) is a sum of squares and so must always be greater than or equal to zero. It could be zero only if every estimated correlation $\hat{r}_{jk}$ was exactly the same as the sample correlation a_{jk}. In that case the hypothesis would not be restrictive, and the fit would be perfect. With a small enough number of factors, we expect the fit to be imperfect in the sample, but we hope that the "residual correlations," the discrepancies between the sample a_{jk} and fitted $\hat{r}_{jk}$, will be small enough to allow the belief that the model is true of the population from which the sample was drawn. Table 2.2.1 gives a small example of estimates fitted by least squares.

The reader can try, with the aid of a calculator, varying the values of f_{jp} or u_j^2 slightly, in order to discover that any other values we choose will make the quantity Q larger and the fit worse. After the computer supplies us with a set of LS best-fitting numbers $\hat{f}_{jp}$, we can ask it to transform them (Section 2.4) to give a new set that will be equally well fitting (with the same value of Q and the same matrix of discrepancies $a_{jk} - \hat{r}_{jk}$) but will also approximate simple structure.

TABLE 2.2.1

```
          Correlation Matrix = A    Factor Loadings (F)
         ⎡1.000  0.700  0.600  0.500⎤    F₁ ⎡-0.842⎤
         ⎢0.700  1.000  0.600  0.500⎥    F₂ ⎢-0.842⎥
         ⎢0.600  0.600  1.000  0.400⎥    F₃ ⎢-0.707⎥
         ⎣0.500  0.500  0.400  1.000⎦    F₄ ⎣-0.587⎦

                     FF'              Residual Matrix - A - FF'
⎡0.709  0.709  0.595  0.494⎤    ⎡ 0.291  -0.009   0.005   0.006⎤
⎢0.709  0.709  0.595  0.494⎥    ⎢-0.009   0.291   0.005   0.006⎥
⎢0.595  0.595  0.499  0.415⎥    ⎢ 0.005   0.005   0.501  -0.015⎥
⎣0.494  0.494  0.415  0.345⎦    ⎣ 0.006   0.006  -0.015   0.655⎦

Unique Variances:    U₁ = 0.291085
                     U₂ = 0.291085
                     U₃ = 0.500221
                     U₄ = 0.654269

Q = 0.00083152   (Where Q = sum of squares of the off-
                  diagonal elements of the residual matrix)
```

The method of least squares has the advantage that we develop a sound and simple intuition for the way in which "fit" is measured and made optimal. (It is actually better to speak of Q as measuring "misfit," or badness-of-fit, which we aim to minimize.) The method of least squares has the disadvantage, however, that with or without the stringent assumption of normality of the distribution of the population, it does not give us a test of significance of the hypothesis.[1]

The method of maximum likelihood is a very widely used method of estimation. Under normality assumptions, in many kinds of problem it gives the same mathematical expressions for estimates as the method of least squares but not in the cases considered in this book. The basic idea of the method is extremely simple, but mathematically its application here is too complicated to describe, even to the point of offering an expression like (2.2.1), without introducing some concepts from matrix algebra that are preferably omitted from an elementary book. The basic principle, quite simply, is that we ask the mathematician to give us arithmetic procedures for getting values of the population parameters that would make the probability of occurrence of our sample from that population as large as possible. (Pedants would insist that this statement assumes distributions that are not mathematically continuous. They would be right, but it doesn't matter.) When we calculate the probability of our sample as a function of various possible values of the population parameters, we refer to it as the *likelihood*, and we choose values to maximize the *likelihood* of the sample.

In applying the method of maximum likelihood to models for multivariate data, assuming normality, the mathematician finds it convenient to define a function of the likelihood that is also an algebraic measure of fit of the parameters (or, rather, of "misfit"). That is, it is positive and increases with an increase of the discrepancies between a_{jk} and $\hat{r}_{jk}$ and is zero only if the fit is perfect in the sample. This quantity is the natural logarithm of the ratio of the

---

[1]Instead of minimizing the *ordinary* least-squares function (2.2.1), we can minimize a weighted or generalized least-squares function

$$Q^* = \sum_{j=1}^{n} \sum_{k=1}^{n} \sum_{l-1}^{n} \sum_{m=1}^{n} w_{jklm}(\alpha_{jk} - \hat{r}_{jk})(\alpha_{lm} - \hat{r}_{lm})$$

with weights w_{jklm} chosen to compensate for the variances and covariances of the residual covariances. A reasonable choice is

$$w_{jklm} = b_{jk}b_{lm}$$

where b_{jk} is the (j, k)th element of the inverse of the sample correlation matrix and approximates the expected value of the covariance of a_{jk} and a_{lm} in repeated sampling. Corresponding to (2.6.2), this generalized least-squares function can be written as

$$Q^* = \text{Tr} \{[A^{-1}(A - FF' - U^2)]^2\}$$

The advantage of the generalized least-squares function over the ordinary least-squares function is that it yields a chi-square test of fit in large samples, just as the likelihood function does.

likelihood of our data under the restrictive hypothesis to the likelihood of our data when we put no restrictions on the nature of the population from which it comes. It reaches a minimum when the likelihood is a maximum. Because of a very general result in the mathematical theory of statistics, we can choose to scale this measure of misfit so that its minimum is distributed as chi-square if the hypothesis of m factors is true, and if the sample size is large enough. We shall therefore assume that a computer program gives us a quantity that we shall denote by λ and just call the *likelihood ratio criterion* (LRC). (1) This quantity is a distribution-free measure of "misfit" of the estimated parameters to the sample correlations, which has been minimized by the computer program. Indeed, it is a direct measure of the departure of the correlation matrix of the residuals from an identity matrix and in this sense measures misfit of the model to the sample data. (2) It is the log-likelihood ratio for testing the hypothesis of m factors against the alternative "hypothesis" that the population is not constrained in any way. (3) It is distributed like chi-square, assuming normality, if the sample size is large enough, with degrees of freedom given by

$$\text{df} = \tfrac{1}{2}\{(n - m)^2 - (n + m)\}. \tag{2.2.3}$$

We can use ML estimates whether or not we assume normality. *If* we assume normality, we can also compare the LRC with tabulated chi-square for the given degrees of freedom. If the LRC does not exceed the chi-square value for, say, the 5% level, we have no reason to reject the postulated number of factors in favor of a larger number. If we reject the hypothesis, we can go on to test the fit with a larger number of factors.

Most social scientists have been nurtured in the classical Neyman–Pearson tradition for the testing of a statistical hypothesis. In this tradition we usually set up a restrictive hypothesis that we hope to reject in favor of an alternative, less restrictive hypothesis that is really our preferred outcome of the study. For example, we seek to reject a hypothesis that the means of a control group and an experimental group are equal in order to affirm that they are different and, the important outcome, that the treatment had a "significant" effect. In contrast, in factor analysis and in almost all models of any complexity for multivariate data, our interpretation of a notion of parsimony or, to put it more straightforwardly, the need to keep our account of the data as simple as possible gives us a desire to affirm the most restrictive hypothesis that is tenable. (It should preferably be substantively reasonable and interpretable as well as statistically tenable.) However, failure to reject a restrictive hypothesis usually means only that we do not have a large enough sample to reject it.

In exploratory factor analysis, the user may not have a hypothesis as to the number of factors. Indeed, to develop such a hypothesis genuinely and not just choose an arbitrary number, the user would need to classify the tests into sets (possibly overlapping) on substantive grounds and hypothesize a number of factors equal to the number of sets. That is, logically we cannot postulate how many factors we have without postulating what they are. In that case our hypothesis is detailed enough to permit the immediate application of the confirmatory methods described in Chapter 3 and thus avoid exploratory analysis altogether.

Suppose, nevertheless, that the user insists that nothing is known about the tests that are to be factor analyzed and that the data are to be used to determine "how many factors to extract." (The notion of *extracting* factors is analogous to extracting the roots of a polynomial and has nothing to do with dentistry.) If we start with an arbitrary small number and fit m, $m + 1$, $m + 2$, . . . common factors until the chi-square is not significant at our favorite conventional level (5% or 1% presumably), we shall not have much idea of the probability to be associated with the entire nested sequence of statistical decisions. It is, however, known that the probability that we would thereby decide to fit more than the true number of factors is less than our chosen significance level.

We can be very sure that as we increase our sample size, the number of factors needed to reach a nonsignificant chi-square will increase. One might claim that all common factor hypotheses are false, because all restrictive statistical hypotheses are false, and they will be proved false by the use of a sufficiently large sample size. It seems not unreasonable to recommend that we use the chi-square test one-sidedly. It would be a worse error to retain and interpret factors that are "not real," that is, factors that are random error masquerading as genuine structure in the data, than to omit some not-very-detectable factors that are "real." More precisely, we should not retain m factors if $m - 1$ factors do not yield a significant chi-square, for we shall be pretending that random error is genuine structure. On the other hand, it would be rational to ignore a significant chi-square that seems to be requiring at least $m + 1$ factors, if the $(m + 1)$st factor were to supply little to the fit, or to the meaning of the analysis. That is, the chi-square test, combined with the efficiency of maximum likelihood estimation, serves primarily as a protection against overfactoring in relatively small samples, a tendency to which traditional approximate methods of factor analysis are prone (see Section 2.3).

From one point of view, inspection of the entire residual covariance matrix gives us more useful information about the fit of the model to the data than we obtain from the chi-square test.

Clearly, if the residual covariances of distinct variables are all sufficiently small, then m factors have accounted sufficiently well for the correlations of the variables. Accounting for correlations is the purpose of the model, and the smallness of the residual covariances is by definition the measure of its success in doing so. It should be noted, by the way, that some computer programs still in use for exploratory factor analysis do not print out any information about the residual covariances. Such programs cannot be recommended, as it is impossible to tell from them whether the analysis fits the data well, badly, or not at all. The trouble with direct inspection of residual covariances as a basis for determining whether or not the model fits the data well enough is of course lack of the

comforting sense of objectivity that comes from choosing a statistical significance level and consistently applying it. Acknowledging, with a deliberately
mixed metaphor, that rules of thumb should be taken with a grain of salt, we
might get a rough guide by combining the fact that a common factor seems to
need at least three tests with loadings above .3 to define it adequately (see
Section 2.3) with the elementary arithmetic result that $.3 \times .3 = .09$, to find a
rule that if all residual covariances are less than .1, we are unlikely to be able to
fit a further common factor that would be well defined and possibly interpretable.
It is also possible to examine the largest residual covariances for evidence that
they cluster, indicating the constitution of the additional factor that might be
fitted if the chi-square is significant and some residual covariances are too large.

Technically, the mathematics and the computer arithmetic involved in minimizing either the function Q for LS estimates or the LRC for ML estimates is
quite complex, and different procedures of varying efficiency have been recommended and programmed. The important fact remains, however, that programs
do exist yielding LS and ML estimates, and in the latter case we also have a chi-
square test of the hypothesis. The LS and ML solutions will usually be slightly
different as they are based on different measures of fit. They can disagree widely
in some cases, as when one gives a Heywood case while the other does not (see
Section 2.3). But we seldom find a difference that matters.

Table 2.2.2 gives a sample correlation matrix obtained by selection from a
study by Thurstone, with sample size $N = 213$. We know from previous work
that the variables would be classified into three measures of verbal ability, V1,
V2, and V3, say; three measures of word fluency, W1, W2, and W3; and three
measures of reasoning ability, R1, R2, and R3, say. But we perform an exploratory factor analysis to see what it will tell us. The ML estimation procedure under
the hypothesis of three common factors gives us an estimated factor pattern as
shown in Table 2.2.3, "unrotated," meaning, not yet transformed to meet the

TABLE 2.2.2

Correlation Matrix

1.000	.828	.776	.439	.432	.447	.447	.541	.380
.828	1.000	.779	.493	.464	.489	.432	.537	.358
.776	.779	1.000	.460	.425	.443	.401	.534	.359
.439	.493	.460	1.000	.674	.590	.381	.350	.424
.432	.464	.425	.674	1.000	.541	.402	.367	.446
.447	.489	.443	.590	.541	1.000	.288	.320	.325
.447	.432	.401	.381	.402	.288	1.000	.555	.598
.541	.537	.534	.350	.367	.320	.555	1.000	.452
.380	.358	.359	.424	.446	.325	.598	.452	1.000

CODE: 1 = sentences   2 = vocabulary
       3 = sentence completion   4 = first letters
       5 = four-letter words   6 = suffices
       7 = letter series   8 = pedigrees
       9 = letter grouping

TABLE 2.2.3

Unrotated Factor Pattern (ML)			Communality	Uniqueness
.867	-.269	.021	.825	.175
.881	-.237	-.057	.835	.165
.826	-.222	-.031	.732	.268
.657	.445	-.320	.732	.268
.630	.429	-.219	.628	.372
.597	.237	-.290	.496	.504
.603	.320	.502	.718	.282
.646	.053	.291	.504	.496
.540	.381	.301	.527	.473

requirement of approximating to simple structure. The coefficients in this matrix (the factor loadings) are both the regression weights of the variables on the factors and their correlations with the factors. The value of the LRC is 2.916 on

$$df = \tfrac{1}{2}\{(9 - 3)^2 - (9 + 3)\} = 12$$

which from the table of chi-square has a probability of being exceeded that is equal to .995, so we do not reject the hypothesis of three factors. The matrix in Table 2.2.4 contains the residual covariance matrix, commonly abbreviated to *residual matrix*. As mentioned already, it should be printed out by a good factor-analysis program, for we can use it to see if the discrepancies between the model

TABLE 2.2.4
Residual Matrix

.175	.001	.001	-.005	.006	-.001	-.000	-.011	.007
.001	.165	.003	.001	-.002	.003	.006	-.003	-.010
.001	-.003	.268	.006	-.006	-.006	-.010	.022	.007
-.005	.001	.006	.268	-.001	.000	.004	-.004	-.004
.006	-.002	-.006	-.001	.372	.000	-.005	.002	.008
-.001	.003	-.006	-.000	.000	.504	-.002	.007	-.000
-.000	.006	-.010	.004	-.005	-.002	.282	.003	-.000
-.011	-.003	.022	-.004	.002	.007	.003	.496	-.004
.007	-.010	.007	-.004	.008	-.000	-.000	-.004	.437

and the data are small and evenly distributed or if there is an arrangement of the worst discrepancies that suggests an additional factor that we have otherwise failed to detect. For example, Table 2.2.5 shows a reanalysis of this sample with two factors hypothesized, and apart from the fact that the chi-square is significant, we can also see a definite bunching of the worst discrepancies in the residual matrix of Table 2.2.5(b) in the last block of variables. On the other hand, the residuals from three factors in Table 2.2.4 show, apart from the nonsignificant chi-square, that a fourth factor would certainly be ill-defined and unnecessary, because none is larger than .022. It is traditional in common factor analysis to present also the estimates of the *communalities* of the variables, the row sums of squares of the loadings, which are best thought of as the squared multiple correlation of each variable with all the common factors. These are also given in Table 2.2.3. In a modern analysis we tend to emphasize instead the unique variance (residual variance) of each variable. It is the proportion of the variance of each variable that is not explained by the factors. This is a piece of information that is complementary, equivalent information to the squared multiple correlations, and it lacks the ambiguities that the term *communality* has picked up over 40 years or so. For completeness, we also present the *rotated* factor pattern, using an algorithm called VARIMAX (see Section 2.4) in Table 2.2.6. The important point to note about this now is that the fit after "rotation" to a new set of factor loadings is just as good (or poor) as before "rotation." Table 2.2.7(a) gives the (unrotated) LS estimate of the common factor pattern, Table 2.2.7(b) gives the (varimax) rotated pattern and Table 2.2.7(c) gives the resulting residual matrix.

Because of the simplicity of the example chosen, the interpretive phase of our work is very simple. We declare, on the basis of the factor pattern in Table 2.2.6(a), that the first three variables have high correlations with (and are "heavily" weighted with) the first factor, the second three with the second factor, and the last three with the third factor. We then take this to mean that the factors are

TABLE 2.2.5

(a) Two-Factor
Pattern (ML)

.883	.236
.891	.174
.838	.174
.640	-.515
.620	-.519
.594	-.329
.543	-.152
.622	.007
.497	-.270

(b) Two-Factor Residual

.166	.001	-.005	-.005	.007	.000	.003	-.010	.005
.001	.177	.002	.012	.002	.017	-.026	-.018	-.038
-.005	.002	.267	.013	-.004	.003	-.028	.011	-.011
-.005	.012	.013	.325	.010	.041	-.045	-.045	-.034
.007	.002	-.004	.010	.346	.002	-.014	-.015	-.003
.000	.017	.003	.041	.002	.539	-.085	-.047	-.059
.003	-.026	-.028	-.045	-.014	-.085	.682	.218	.287
-.010	-.018	.011	-.045	-.015	-.047	.218	.613	.144
.005	-.038	-.011	-.034	-.003	-.059	.287	.144	.679

Table 2.2.6
Varimax Factor Patterns

(a) Three-Factor (ML)			(b) Two-Factor (ML)	
.833	.243	.268	.868	.283
.827	.317	.226	.841	.339
.774	.283	.230	.798	.311
.228	.792	.230	.257	.780
.213	.706	.290	.237	.773
.315	.616	.135	.319	.599
.229	.180	.796	.373	.423
.444	.166	.528	.526	.333
.151	.312	.638	.270	.498

the three generic properties that, respectively, these groups of measures indicate in common, and presumably we name these generic properties *verbal ability, word fluency,* and *reasoning ability.* It is desirable to remark that in worthwhile research with factor analysis, one would hope to make a detailed examination of the measures used and to use relevant substantive theory to arrive at a deeper understanding of what might be operations, processes, or theoretical concepts requiring imagination to postulate, of which the measures are joint indicators. The example, we hope, is unrepresentatively mechanical.

It should be remarked that even in this rather dull example we have genuinely gained information. It was perfectly possible, a priori, that just one common factor would account for the correlations, or that two, say word fluency and reasoning, would do so with verbal ability a complex "resultant" of those two. It is sometimes suggested that "we only get out of a factor analysis what we put into it." This statement is never put quite precisely enough for one to come to grips with it, but at least we can say that it does not mean that the results of the analysis are entirely foreordained and uninformative. We can certainly get out things that we did not think that we had put in and, occasionally, not get things out that we felt confident we had put in.

The trouble with exploratory factor analysis, however, is that we often know far more than we are pretending to know and we fail to use this knowledge. A better analysis of the present example is given in Chapter 3, where we specify in our hypothesis not only the number of factors but which variables have zero regression weights on which factors. Thereby we create an unambiguous and satisfying hypothesis and test the hypothesis precisely as it stands.

TABLE 2.2.7

(a)

.821	-.379	-.025
.838	-.350	-.104
.789	-.334	-.66
.705	.372	-.307
.679	.358	-.205
.618	.175	-.288
.650	.197	.511
.654	-.061	.272
.593	.279	.308

Three-Factor (LS)
Pattern
Unrotated

(b)

.828	.249	.264
.828	.320	.217
.779	.281	.229
.233	.796	.207
.213	.715	.273
.317	.616	.120
.255	.199	.796
.447	.179	.523
.152	.330	.627

Three-Factor (LS)
Pattern
Rotated
(varimax)

(c)

.182	.005	.001	-.007	.005	-.001	.001	-.012	.007
.005	.165	-.006	.001	-.001	.003	.009	-.004	-.009
.001	-.006	.262	.008	-.005	-.005	-.012	.016	.005
-.007	.001	.008	.270	-.001	.001	.006	-.005	-.004
.005	-.001	-.005	-.001	.369	-.000	-.006	.001	.006
-.001	.003	-.005	.001	-.000	.505	-.001	.005	-.002
.001	.009	-.012	.006	-.006	-.001	.277	.003	-.000
-.012	-.004	.016	-.005	.001	.005	.003	.495	-.003
.007	-.009	.005	-.004	.006	-.002	-.000	-.003	.475

Residual Matrix

2.3. COMPONENT THEORY, IMAGE THEORY, APPROXIMATE METHODS, AND HEYWOOD CASES

There are two "theories" of multivariate data, quite logically distinct from common factor analysis, which tend to give enough numerical and conceptual similarities to it to make them be seen as competitive alternatives to it or sometimes to cause them to be confused with it and which certainly make them useful approximations to it. Some readers, on the basis of other knowledge, will in fact object to the treatment here of these two topics in one brief section, subordinated to exploratory factor analysis. Let it be emphasized that this is because it suits the overall plan of this book to do so. Principal component theory, sometimes under the guise of *optimal scaling* or *optimal weighting,* has a considerable body of literature in its own right. It is preferred by some investigators to common factor analysis. *Factor analysis* as a generic term is generally taken to include component theory and image theory. We shall continue, therefore, to use the word *common* before *factor analysis* in its narrow sense and accept, but not deliberately follow, the general usage of factor analysis as a broader, looser term.

(a) Principal Component Theory

Conceptually, the best way to understand principal components is rather different from the way favored by the mathematician. Suppose we have a set of n observed variables $y_1, \ldots, y_n$, and we make a weighted sum of them, say,

$$s = w_1 y_1 + w_2 y_2 + \cdots + w_n y_n \tag{2.3.1}$$

just as we might in regression theory, where we want to choose the weights in some "best" way. But unlike the regression case we do not have an external criterion with which to correlate the weighted "mixture." Instead, we want to consider just internal relationships. We want a simple combination of all the measures that "resembles" each individual measure as much as possible. Now one way to make this rather vague notion mathematically definite is to say that if we calculated the square of the correlation of s with each of the variables, y_1, $\ldots, y_n$, then s would on the whole resemble all of them most when we choose weights so that the sum of the squares of the n correlations of s with y_1, s with y_2, $\ldots, s$ with y_n is as large as possible. Given the $(n \times n)$ matrix of correlations of $y_1, \ldots, y_n$, there is a definite mathematical answer to this question, though its arithmetic is rather unpleasant and requires a computer program. For example, Table 2.3.1 gives the correlation matrix of a set of variables and shows the weights to give them that will yield a weighted sum whose total of squared correlations is the largest possible. No other choice of weights will increase the value beyond that shown. (The effects of making small arbitrary changes in the weights are demonstrated in the table.) We note that we could, of course, multiply all the weights by a common constant without changing the sum of

TABLE 2.3.1
From Hotelling (1933)

					Weights	Correl-ations
y_1 = Reading Speed	1.000	.701	.266	.084	.602	.618
y_2 = Reading Power	.701	1.000	-.059	.092	.512	.695
y_3 = Arithmetic Speed	.266	-.059	1.000	.596	.448	.608
y_4 = Arithmetic Power	.084	.092	.596	1.000	.425	.578

Sum of squares of correlations = 1.846

Full set of weights

.602	-.362	-.404	.587
.512	-.512	.399	-.560
.448	.557	-.521	-.472
.425	.545	.636	.350

If we take weights all equal to .5, we get a sum of squares of correlations = 1.840.

---

squared correlations. What matters is the proportions in the mixture, as in the regression of a dependent variable on independent variables. Now suppose that we record, but set aside, the "best" combination that we have found and look for a "second-best" combination. To avoid confusion, we label the best combination s_1 and write

$$s_1 = w_{11}y_1 + w_{12}y_2 + \cdots + w_{1n}y_n \qquad (2.3.2)$$

adding a subscript unity to the first set of weights we found. Now we look for a "second-best" combination

$$s_2 = w_{21}y_1 + w_{22}y_2 + \cdots + w_{2n}y_n \qquad (2.3.2)$$

To avoid just finding s_1 again, we ask that s_2 be uncorrelated with s_1 and that subject to this condition, it should have a maximum sum of squares of its n correlations with $y_1, \ldots, y_n$. Again we obtain a set of weights $w_{21}, \ldots, w_{2n}$ that provide the weighted sum we require. We can now ask for a third-best weighted sum, with maximum squared correlations with $y_1, \ldots, y_n$ and uncorrelated with s_1 and with s_2. This process is continued. We can find n weighted sums, $s_1, \ldots, s_n$, each of which is uncorrelated with all the other sums, and each in turn has the largest sum of squares of correlations with the n variables that it can have. We shall call these sums *principal component* scores.

Now let p_{jl} be the correlation between the jth variable and the lth sum, s_l. We find that there is a converse relationship between the variables and the principal component scores. We already have each principal component score as a weighted sum of variables

$$s_1 = w_{11}y_1 + w_{12}y_2 + \cdots + w_{1n}y_n$$
$$s_2 = w_{21}y_1 + w_{22}y_2 + \cdots + w_{2n}y_n \qquad\qquad (2.3.4)$$
$$\dots\dots\dots\dots\dots\dots$$
$$s_n = w_{n1}y_1 + w_{n2}y_2 + \cdots + w_{nn}y_n \;.$$

For example, from Table 2.3.1,

$$s_1 = .602y_1 + .512y_2 + 448y_3 + .425y_4$$
$$s_2 = .362y_1 - .512y_2 + .557y_3 + .545y_4$$
$$s_3 = -.404y_1 + .399y_2 - .521y_3 + .636y_4$$
$$s_4 = .587y_1 - .560y_2 - .472y_3 + .350y_4$$

It turns out that we can interchange roles and write the variables as weighted sums of the n components, with the correlations p_{jl} as the weights; that is, we have

$$y_1 = p_{11}s_1 + p_{12}s_2 + \cdots + p_{1n}s_n$$
$$y_2 = p_{21}s_1 + p_{22}s_2 + \cdots + p_{2n}s_n \qquad\qquad (2.3.5)$$
$$\dots\dots\dots\dots\dots\dots$$
$$y_n = p_{n1}s_1 + p_{n2}s_2 + \cdots + p_{nn}s_n \;.$$

For example, from Table 2.3.1,

$$y_1 = .818s_1 - .438s_2 - .292s_3 + .240s_4$$
$$y_2 = .695s_1 - .620s_2 + .288s_3 - .229s_4$$
$$y_3 = .608s_1 + .674s_2 - .376s_3 - .193s_4$$
$$y_4 = .578s_1 + .660s_2 + .459s_3 + .143s_4$$

We began with a regression of a sum of variables on each of those variables, and we have thence obtained a regression of each of the observed variables on those sums. Further, because the component scores are uncorrelated, the expression of each observed variable as a sum of components gives an analysis of its variance into n additive parts, one due to each component. That is, if y_j is in standard measure, then its unit variance is given by

$$\sigma_j^2 = 1 = p_{j1}^2 + p_{j2}^2 + \dots p_{jn}^2 \qquad\qquad (2.3.6)$$

for example

$$\sigma_1^2 = .818^2 + (-.438)^2 + (-.292)^2 + .240^2 = 1.00$$

As we saw initially, each component in turn explains the maximum possible proportion of the variance of all n of the variables; for example, the first component explains

$$.818^2 + .695^2 + .608^2 + .578^2 \text{ units of variance.}$$

If we wanted to substitute just one combined measurement for our n measurements $y_1, \ldots, y_n$, we could not do better than to use the first principal component score, s_1, which is maximally correlated with all of them and explains more of their variance than any other composite measurement could. If we wanted to keep some m measures, less than all n of them, we could not do better than to keep the first, second, . . . , mth principal component scores, ordered in terms of the magnitude of the sum of variance explained. We might call principal components "best approximate descriptions" of multivariate data.

As in the common factor model, we find that the correlation between any two variables can be written as the sum of the products of the correlations of the two variables with all n of the components. That is,

$$r_{jk} = p_{j1}p_{k1} + p_{j2}p_{k2} + \cdots + p_{jn}p_{kn} \tag{2.3.7}$$

For example,

$$r_{12} = .818 \times .695 + .438 \times .620 - \\ .292 \times .288 - .240 \times .229 = .701$$

Except in the special case where there are redundant variables in the set (i.e., where some variables in the set can be perfectly predicted from the rest, usually because we have included sums of part scores along with their parts in the set), we require all n of the components to explain the correlations by (2.3.7). This is in contrast to the common factor model, where we usually have m factors, where m is much less than n, explaining the correlations (but not the variances) of the variables.

It is reasonable to hope that "a few" of the principal components will explain a large part of the variance of the given variables. However, the point deserves emphasis that we cannot in general find correlation matrices of n variables that can be entirely explained by less than n components, either in respect to the variance of the variables or in respect of their correlations only. Hence, principal component theory does not yield a falsifiable hypothesis. Typically, in social science work, the output of a principal component analysis is presented as a matrix of the correlations p_{jl} between the variables and the components, usually omitting the columns of correlations that are supposed by the investigator to be "negligible" in some sense. We shall refer to these correlations as *principal component coefficients.* (Sometimes they are known as principal component loadings, following usage in common factor analysis.) The sum of squares of the elements in each column of this matrix is the variance of all the variables that is explained by that principal component, in terms of the analysis of the variance of the variables into uncorrelated parts.

Occasionally we may feel that we can interpret the component score as a weighted sum of the given variables on the basis of the relative magnitudes and signs of the parts of the "mixture." Tables 2.3.1 and 2.3.2 give an example from Hotelling (1933). His interpretation, which is plausible enough, is that

> the chief component seems to measure general ability; the second, a difference between arithmetic and verbal ability. These two account for eightythree percent of the variance (of the four variables). An additional thirteen percent seems to be largely a matter of speed vs. deliberation. The remaining variance is trivial.

It should be clear from this example that principal component theory resembles common factor theory but with important differences. Its output gives us correlations between observed variables and components. We interpret those components, if we can, in terms of what is measured by the variables that are correlated with each component. However, the principal components are themselves known weighted sums of the given variables, chosen to explain variance in terms of multiple correlation principles; whereas common factors are unknown variables, chosen to explain correlations in terms of partial correlation principles.

To take another example, from Thomson (1934), the constructed correlation matrix in Table 2.3.3 is precisely fitted by the common factor model with one common factor. Its five principal components have the coefficients indicated and successively explain 2.683, 0.890, 0.652, 0.448, 0.328 units of variance (these sum to five as they must). The one common factor explains the correlations perfectly, although not even four of the five components explain the correlations' perfectly. On the other hand, the first principal component alone explains more variance than the one common factor.

TABLE 2.3.2
Hotelling (1933)
Principal Component Coefficients

	1st Comp.	2nd Comp.	3rd Comp.	4th Comp.
Reading Speed	.818	-.438	-.292	.240
Reading Power	.695	-.620	.288	-.229
Arithmetic Speed	.608	.674	-.376	-.193
Arithmetic Power	.578	.660	.459	.143
Sum of Squared Correlations	1.846	1.465	.521	.167

TABLE 2.3.3
Thomson (1934)

(a) The Correlation Matrix

$$\begin{bmatrix} 1.000 & .669 & .592 & .458 & .251 \\ .669 & 1.000 & .566 & .438 & .240 \\ .592 & .566 & 1.000 & .387 & .212 \\ .458 & .438 & .387 & 1.000 & .164 \\ .251 & .240 & .212 & .164 & 1.000 \end{bmatrix}$$

This matrix is explained perfectly
by one factor with loadings

$$[.837 \quad .800 \quad .707 \quad .548 \quad .303]$$

(b) Principal Component Coefficients

$$\begin{bmatrix} .856 & -.092 & -.152 & -.217 & -.436 \\ .840 & -.098 & -.173 & -.346 & .365 \\ .790 & -.116 & -.294 & .523 & .060 \\ .673 & -.182 & .713 & .083 & .020 \\ .413 & .908 & .069 & .022 & .009 \end{bmatrix}$$

(c) Residuals from First Principal Component

$$\begin{bmatrix} .267 & -.050 & -.084 & -.118 & -.103 \\ -.050 & .294 & -.098 & -.127 & -.107 \\ -.084 & .098 & .376 & -.147 & -.114 \\ -.118 & -.127 & -.147 & .547 & -.114 \\ -.103 & -.107 & -.114 & -.114 & .829 \end{bmatrix}$$

A word is necessary about the relation between the account of principal component theory just given and the one that the reader is most likely to encounter elsewhere. Hotelling (1933) introduced principal component theory in his first paper, both as above and in a different fashion. The idea of finding a weighted sum that resembles *all* our variables most, by having maximum (squared) correlations with all of them, is conceptually a good way to think about principal components, but it leads to rather difficult mathematics. The most commonly preferred way to introduce principal components is to say that we are looking for a set of weights to give a score with maximum variance, subject to the condition that the sum of the squares of the weights be held constant, thus varying the proportions in the "mixture" but not the amount. Newcomers to multivariate analysis sometimes follow the mathematics of this notion, which are much easier, and yet do not understand the notion itself (i.e., *why* we want such sums). We shall simply accept the fact that the two problems have the same mathematical answers (when the variables are standardized). Further, the mathematical answers happen to be the same as certain considerably older problems in astronomy and geometry. The geometrical problem is that of finding the principal axes of ellipsoids; hence we sometimes find *principal axes* (perhaps loosely) used as a synonym for principal components. Also, because of prior usage in writings on the fundamental problem of finding equivalents of our maximized sum of squared correlations, which is also the total variance' explained by each component when the variables are in standard measure, these quantities are sometimes published as the *eigenvalues, latent roots,* or *characteristic roots* of the correlation matrix, and the corresponding sets of principal component coefficients are sometimes labeled *eigenvectors, latent vectors,* or *characteristic vectors.*

It is quite usual to find matrices of principal component coefficients presented in the literature as substitutes for common factor coefficients. It is also usual to find, under titles like "principal axes factor analysis" or "principal components, iterated once," modified principal component analyses that have made one or two arithmetic steps of unstated nature toward obtaining least squares estimates in the common factor model. These are legacies of the era from the 1930s to the 1950s when problems of estimation were not well understood. Such results in the literature are hard to evaluate. More will be said about them later.

It will be noticed that no distinction has been made so far in this section between principal components in a population and principal components in a sample. In fact, the ambiguity, which was deliberate, leaves us free to read all these remarks in terms of either, especially as there are no restrictive hypotheses to test.

(b) Image Theory

The mathematics of image theory is a simple application of regression theory. It is interesting, partly, because of a particular conception about the way in which we choose, or we should choose, which measurements to make. Generally, we know or think we know well enough how to define a population of subjects that is of interest to us and to choose subjects from it. Besides choosing our subjects, we also decide how many things and just what things to measure on them. Suppose we pretend that this decision is, like the matter of choosing subjects, one of selection from a population. In imagination, we suppose that given time we could have listed all the distinct measurable properties, or behaviors in various situations, of our subjects that can be conceived. We regard the things we choose to measure as a subset of all the distinct choosable measurements, imagined or as yet unimagined, that could ever be made on our subjects. It is not obvious for a given class of subjects whether or not this list is infinitely long. Now suppose that instead of such an *entire* list, we are imagining a list of attributes of a given, more or less definable, kind (e.g., cognitive attributes, emotional attributes, attitudes; or at a more detailed level of description, arithmetic performances or vocabulary knowledge). To the extent that we have a definite denotation of the "kind" so that we can recognize if a measurement is that kind of measurement or not, we can imagine using all distinct measures of the kind in question. Such an entire set of conceivable measures has been discussed at times under the name of a *behavior domain* or of a *universe of content*. It might be claimed that the object of factor-analytic methods is to discover what measures belong to what behavior domains. On the other hand, it can be claimed that the investigator has a duty at the beginning of a study to be as clear as possible about the definition of the behavior domain that he is about to investigate. In practice we are likely to have notions about the behavior domain whose degree of precision varies from vague to precise, depending on how little or how much we know already. It seems easy to mark off all the items requiring a subject to add numbers together and give the sum from all the items that require something else or something more. We could say, therefore, that numerical addition is a well-defined behavior domain. On the other hand we might not be able to get all psychologists and all psychiatrists to pick out just the same items as measures of "anxiety." (Do you have bad dreams? Do you perspire a lot? Do you think the world is fundamentally an evil place?) Presumably a sensitive interplay of clinical theory, measurement, and multivariate analysis should lead us from a vague conception of the behavior domain of "anxiety" to an increasingly precise denotation of it. But generally, although we can try to be precise in our conception of the behavior we wish to study, we have to be willing to work with conceptions ranging all the way from vague intuitions to precise denotations that serve as instructions for inventing all the possible measures that belong to the domain.

It is important to note that the behavior domain (the "kind" of property) we investigate need not be thought of as conceptually simple but may in fact be subdivisible, or cross-classifiable, into a number of more elementary attributes. For example, addition items form a behavior domain, but they can be further classified in terms of (a) the number of terms in the sum, (b) the number of digits in the terms, and so on. The attempt to define complex behavior domains as logical combinations of elementary attributes has been described under the title *facet theory*. In some areas of inquiry, we can indeed use logic, or substantive knowledge, to describe a behavior domain as a combination of distinct attributes or *facets*. It is then a matter of fact whether the logical analysis we produce of the kind of thing we measure will serve to predict the statistics of the measures in some population. The basic expectation of psychometricians seems to be that the more two measures resemble each other in the nature of the properties measured, the higher should be the correlation between them in any or all or most populations. This is not a logical necessity, of course. It is a postulated empirical law that is based on the "common-elements" explanation of the "why" of correlation. Why are two variables correlated? Because they (in part) measure the same thing. As we change the properties of a given item to derive less and less similar items, we usually expect their correlations with the given item to decrease. Out of a strong a priori conceptual analysis of measures, we should be able to group them into kinds or perhaps arrange them in an ordered sequence in respect of one or more attributes. For example, we could group all the one-digit addition items together, all the two-digit addition items together, etc. Alternatively, we could *order* the items in terms of number of digits. We would then hope to find, in the correlational behavior of the measures, confirmation of our conceptual analysis.

The notion that behavior domains "exist" and that we should try to make our measures "represent" them is an interesting way to describe the notion that we should come to know what properties we are measuring and to know which alternative measures will serve as indicators of those properties.

The basic mathematical idea of image theory is independent of the conception of behavior domains. Given any set of n variables, $y_1, \ldots, y_n$, in standard measure, we can obtain the regression estimate of each variable in turn on the remaining $n - 1$ variables. We write

$$\hat{y}_j = b_1 y_1 + b_2 y_2 + \cdots + b_{j-1} y_{j-1} + b_{j+1} y_{j+1} + \cdots + b_n y_n.$$ (2.3.8)

(Note the way in which we indicate the omission of y_j itself from the expression on the right.) The regression weights and the multiple correlations can be calculated by the standard arithmetic procedures that were taken for granted in Chapter 1. No new arithmetic is needed. Tables 2.3.4 and 2.3.5 give the regression weights and squared multiple correlations for the Spearman case of Table 1.5.1, and the case previously factor analyzed in Tables 2.2.2 to 2.2.7.

We now think of each variable as the sum of two parts, its regression upon the remainder, $\hat{y}_j$, and its residual about that regression, e_j, say. Guttman calls the regression part $\hat{y}_j$ the *partial image* of y_j and the residual e_j the *partial antiimage* of y_j. Now suppose that there are infinitely many measures in the same behavior domain as our given measures $y_1, \ldots, y_n$ (i.e., infinitely many distinct measurable properties of the same kind). Then we define the *total image* of each y_j as its regression on all the remaining measures in the same behavior domain and its *total antiimage* as the residual about that regression.

TABLE 2.3.4
Image Analysis of
Spearman Matrix (Table 1.5.1)
Regression of Each Variable on Remainder

Variable	Squared Multiple Correlation	w_1	w_2	w_3	w_4	w_5
1	.653	.0	.431	.266	.182	.129
2	.550	.532	.0	.154	.105	.075
3	.428	.418	.196	.0	.083	.059
4	.317	.341	.160	.099	.0	.048
5	.221	.276	.130	.080	.055	.0

TABLE 2.3.5
Image Analysis of
Thurstone Matrix (Table 2.2.2)
Regression of Each Variable on Remainder

Variable	Squared Multiple Correlation	Regression Weights								
		w_1	w_2	w_3	w_4	w_5	w_6	w_7	w_8	w_9
1	.738	.0	.529	.304	−.038	.016	.027	.051	.052	.027
2	.750	.506	.0	.286	.067	.028	.069	.028	.059	−.043
3	.675	.378	.372	.0	.065	−.003	.024	−.030	.110	.017
4	.553	−.065	.120	.089	.0	.421	.261	.039	−.027	.090
5	.520	.030	.054	−.004	.452	.0	.172	.059	.022	.124
6	.426	.058	.157	.042	.335	.206	.0	−.052	.006	.026
7	.477	.102	.058	−.048	.046	.064	−.048	.0	.293	.390
8	.450	.110	.130	.185	−.034	.025	.006	.308	.0	.114
9	.429	.059	−.009	.029	.115	.148	.026	.426	.118	.0

Unlike the residuals in common factor analysis, the partial antiimages are not mutually uncorrelated, so the partial images of the variables do not explain their correlations (in the partial-correlation sense of "explain"). Hence the partial images cannot serve as "common parts" in the factor-analytic sense. Yet there is an obvious sense in which we might feel that image theory should, like common factor theory, be about "what variables have in common," because it is, by definition, about "what each variable has in common with the remaining $n - 1$ variables." It is possible to show that the partial image variance of each variable (the squared multiple correlation of each variable with the remaining $n - 1$) is always less than its communality (squared multiple correlation with the common factors). This also means that its partial antiimage variance (residual variance about its regression on the remaining $n - 1$ variables) is always greater than its uniqueness (residual variance about its regression on the common factors). However, if the common factor model with its limited number of factors correctly describes the entire behavior domain and if the behavior domain contains infinitely many distinct measures, then the total image of each variable is the same as its common part, the two residual parts are the same, the total image variance is equal to the communality, the total antiimage variance is equal to the uniqueness, and generally the two theories coincide completely.

It is important to note the requirement, rather loosely stated, that the common factor model must correctly describe the entire (infinite) behavior domain. If, as we add more variables to our list, we add more factors, so that by the time we "have an infinity" of variables, we "have an infinity" of common factors, then we do not find total images and common parts coinciding in the limit. More precisely, the ratio of the number of factors to the number of variables should go to zero in the limit. We can and should contemplate the possibility that the common factor model is a quite inappropriate model for a given set of measures. Evidence for this is obtained if we fit, successively, m, $m + 1$, . . . factors to a sample correlation matrix and the fit successively improves but not nearly fast enough, and we have many factors of not very pleasing appearance before we can feel satisfied with the fit. Experience and representative mathematical calculation suggest that infinity, in practice in this area, is not as far away as we might think. That is, the behavior of as few as a dozen or, conservatively, 20 measures can give a very good idea of the behavior of the entire set from which we are pretending they were drawn. It may be shown that the partial image weights should all tend to zero if the common factor model "holds" in the limit and should all be "small" in observed correlation matrices of reasonable size (a dozen or more variables). Table 2.3.6 gives a correlation matrix for which the common factor model is entirely inappropriate, and gives an image analysis of it. The weights for this case may be contrasted with the weights in Tables 2.3.4 and 2.3.5.

The main contribution of image theory to common factor analysis so far has been the provision of approximate methods for exploratory analysis, recom-

TABLE 2.3.6
Image Analysis of Chain Model Data
[See section 4.2 (c)]

Correlation Matrix

1.000	.500	.333	.250	.200	.167
.500	1.000	.666	.500	.400	.333
.333	.666	1.000	.750	.600	.500
.250	.500	.750	1.000	.800	.667
.200	.400	.600	.800	1.000	.833
.167	.333	.500	.667	.833	1.000

Regression of Each Variable on Remainder

Variable	Squared Multiple Correlation	Regression Weights				
1	.250	.0	.500	.000	.000	.000	.000
2	.531	.313	.0	.561	.000	.000	.000
3	.675	.000	.388	.0	.556	.000	.000
4	.754	.000	.000	.421	.0	.545	.000
5	.801	.000	.000	.000	.440	.0	.539
6	.694	.000	.000	.000	.000	.831	.0

mended by Jöreskog and Kaiser, to be discussed shortly. Perhaps the more important contribution it has to offer is the way it supports the view that factor-analytic investigations should be directed at clearly conceived and defined behavior domains, using clearly representative measures. Such investigations will usually be confirmatory rather than exploratory.

(c) Approximate Methods

Factor analysis has been developed in the course of 70 years of work, of which only the last 20 have been aided by electronic computers. Especially in the work from the 1930s to the 1950s, tremendous emphasis had to be placed on methods for turning the mathematics of factor analysis into feasible arithmetic for desk calculation. Unfortunately, this has led to much confusion in the literature, some of it built into the traditional language of factor analysis; confusion between sample and population, between measures of fit and methods of fitting, and between central concepts of the theory and arithmetic devices including crude approximation devices for saving work.

The modern view is that the common factor model is a statistical hypothesis that may be "true" of a population and that at least prescribes the number of common factors. Given at least this prescription, we can use any one of a number of arithmetic algorithms to get (least squares or maximum likelihood) "best" estimates of the population factor loadings and of the population uniquenesses and use the likelihood ratio criterion or inspection of residual covariances to reject or retain the hypothesis, as described in Section 2.2.

Partly because of the pressure of arithmetic problems in multiple factor analysis and partly from an actual failure to be as precise about concepts as we, the inheritors of decades of creative work on the subject can be, the earlier workers have handed down to us a number of confused modes of thought that are still to be recognized in the vocabulary of factor analysis. The reader will find, elsewhere, the persisting notion that in factor analysis we first "guess" the communalities of the variables and then "extract" common factors one by one until the residuals are small enough to suit our taste. This process yields "obtained" communalities that are different from the "guessed" communalities. These treatments (1) tend to confuse basic conceptual aspects of the model with crude, simplified arithmetic procedures for fitting it; (2) cannot by their nature produce best fit. We can obtain best fit only when, under a hypothesis as to the number of common factors, we produce $nm + n$ estimated quantities (the factor loadings and the uniquenesses), each of which is best in the context of the others. Any method that computes the first column of factor loadings and never changes it when the others are computed cannot be choosing best numbers. Such treatments should be thought of as approximate methods, replacing "best" estimation procedures.

There would seem to be at least four valid reasons for using approximate methods. The first is, quite simply, to save computing costs. The cost of ML estimation in common factor analysis can be a considerable percentage of the cost of the entire research project. A saving here could certainly be justified if an approximate analysis or a series of analyses were used to guide decisions governing a final, "best" analysis of the data, by the methods of Section 2.2 or of Chapter 3. The second is that a study may involve so many variables that its dimensions will not fit the limitations of the available ML computer program. We could, as a matter of fact, question whether a really large-scale study should ever be carried out. That is, will an investigator ever be able to collect together, on good, rational grounds, a really large number of measures that are likely to yield a clear, interpretable analysis? But one cannot legislate against such studies. The third use for approximate methods is one that the ordinary user does not even have to know about as it is hidden away inside a computer program for an exact method. That is, it saves money to have an approximate analysis that provides a starting point, not far away from the solution, for the numerical methods that yield ML or LS estimates. The fourth reason for using approximate methods is extremely questionable. The frequency of occurrence of Heywood cases (see following) in ML estimates leads some workers to recommend approximate analyses because these do not yield Heywood results. (For the moment, think of these as "impossible" estimates.) On the other hand, when a Heywood case occurs, the data may be trying to tell us something, namely, that the study has not been well designed in the sense that not enough variables have been included to define each factor adequately. In any case, if we are otherwise convinced that the model is appropriate, we can use the Bayesian estimation procedure described in the following.

Approximate methods that have been strongly advocated and/or are in common use include: (1) the use of principal components of the sample correlation matrix, instead of common factors; that is, we compute correlations between the variables and the m main principal component scores and regard these as factor loadings; (2) the use of "squared multiple correlations (SMCs) as communalities"; that is, we use the residual variance of each variable about its regression on the remaining $n - 1$ (its partial antiimage variance) as an approximation to the estimate of its unique variance; (3) the use of principal components of the partial images of the variables as common factors; (4) the use of "reduced" partial antiimage variances as unique variances; that is, we find a constant, less than one, by which to multiply these variances, to allow for the fact that they are strictly greater than the unique variances.[2]

Table 2.3.7 gives the results when these four methods are applied to a simple one-factor case. Table 2.3.8 lists the values of the LS fit function Q (equation 2.2.1) for representative published correlation matrices. From these cases it is fairly clear that method (4) is best, followed closely by (2), and then (3) and (1) virtually tied.

At this point we should note also that a traditional problem of exploratory factor analysis has concerned nonstatistical criteria for deciding what the number of common factors, m, might be. A criterion that can indeed be a useful guide for a first analysis has been recommended for a number of different reasons. It is often mentioned briefly in accounts of applications as "eigenvalues (or latent roots) greater than one." Interpreted, this means that the number of principal components of the observed variables that explain more than one unit of variance (whose sum of squares of correlations with the n variables is greater than unity) indicates the smallest number, or the actual number, of common factors that should account for the correlations. A discussion of the logical basis of this criterion is a highly technical matter, and the reader is invited to accept that it is sometimes a good practical guide (and occasionally very very bad). We therefore expect to find that an ML estimation program for exploratory factor analysis will allow us to prescribe the number of common factors, if we are prepared to do so, or will let us tell the computer to choose a first hypothesis on the basis of the number of eigenvalues of the correlation matrix greater than one or greater than a number that we supply (and we are expected to supply the number one). We can

---

[2]Of these four methods, it is difficult to attribute the first or the second to an individual investigator. The third is due to Kaiser (1970), and the fourth to Jöreskog (1962). All the last three methods are based on Guttman's classical results on image theory (see Mulaik, 1972).

TABLE 2.3.7

	Correlation Matrix (Repeated)					Correct Solution

$$
\begin{bmatrix}
1.00 & .72 & .63 & .54 & .45 & .36 \\
.72 & 1.00 & .56 & .48 & .40 & .32 \\
.63 & .56 & 1.00 & .42 & .35 & .28 \\
.54 & .48 & .42 & 1.00 & .30 & .24 \\
.45 & .40 & .35 & .30 & 1.00 & .20 \\
.36 & .32 & .28 & .24 & .20 & 1.00
\end{bmatrix}
\qquad
\begin{bmatrix}
.9 \\ .8 \\ .7 \\ .6 \\ .5 \\ .4
\end{bmatrix}
$$

(1)   Principal
       Component
"Factor Pattern"   Residual Matrix

$$
\begin{bmatrix}
.8832 \\
.8326 \\
.7697 \\
.6937 \\
.6044 \\
.5023
\end{bmatrix}
\qquad
\begin{bmatrix}
.220 & -.015 & -.050 & -.073 & -.083 & -.084 \\
-.015 & .307 & -.081 & -.089 & -.103 & -.098 \\
-.050 & -.081 & .4-7 & -.114 & -.115 & -.107 \\
-.073 & -.098 & -.114 & .519 & -.119 & -.108 \\
-.083 & -.103 & -.115 & -.119 & .635 & -.104 \\
-.084 & -.098 & -.107 & -.108 & -.104 & .748
\end{bmatrix}
$$

$$Q = .0088523$$

(2)   SMCs
       Factor Pattern   Residual Matrix

$$
\begin{bmatrix}
.8467 \\
.7898 \\
.7025 \\
.6071 \\
.5083 \\
.4078
\end{bmatrix}
\qquad
\begin{bmatrix}
.283 & .051 & .035 & .026 & .020 & .014 \\
.051 & .376 & .005 & .000 & -.001 & -.002 \\
.035 & .005 & .506 & -.006 & -.007 & -.006 \\
.026 & .000 & -.006 & .631 & -.009 & -.008 \\
.020 & -.001 & -.007 & -.009 & .742 & -.007 \\
.015 & -.002 & -.006 & -.008 & -.007 & .834
\end{bmatrix}
$$

$$Q = .0003664$$

(3) Partial Image
    Factor Pattern   Residual Matrix

$$
\begin{bmatrix}
.7769 \\
.7248 \\
.6447 \\
.5571 \\
.4664 \\
.3742
\end{bmatrix}
\qquad
\begin{bmatrix}
.396 & .157 & .129 & .107 & .088 & .069 \\
.157 & .475 & .093 & .076 & .062 & .049 \\
.129 & .093 & .584 & .061 & .049 & .039 \\
.107 & .076 & .061 & .690 & .040 & .031 \\
.088 & .062 & .049 & .042 & .782 & .025 \\
.069 & .049 & .039 & .031 & .025 & .860
\end{bmatrix}
$$

$$Q = .0064568$$

(4) "Reduced" Partial
Antiimage Uniquenesses   Residual Matrix

$$
\begin{bmatrix}
.8566 \\
.7991 \\
.7108 \\
.6142 \\
.5143 \\
.4126
\end{bmatrix}
\qquad
\begin{bmatrix}
.266 & .035 & .021 & .014 & .009 & .006 \\
.035 & .361 & -.008 & -.011 & -.011 & -.010 \\
.021 & -.088 & .495 & -.017 & -.015 & -.013 \\
.014 & -.011 & -.017 & .623 & -.016 & -.013 \\
.010 & -.011 & -.015 & -.016 & .735 & -.012 \\
.006 & -.010 & -.013 & -.013 & -.012 & .830
\end{bmatrix}
$$

$$Q = .002464$$

TABLE 2.3.8

	Harman: 8 Physical Variables	Harman: 24 Psychological Tests	Matrix in Table 2.2.2
(1)	.002765	.003356	.003662
(2)	.000570	.001711	.000432
(3)	.002651	.002461	.004630
(4)	.000532	.001710	.000113

also expect to find that many published factor analyses, especially the approximate ones, will say that the number of factors was determined as "the number of eigenvalues greater than one." As mentioned briefly at the end of the discussion of principal components, the reader should be wary of ambiguities in published applications of factor analysis. Many applications, right up to the current decade, use an approximate method. It is sometimes difficult to tell what approximation has been used, and usually it is impossible to evaluate the goodness of fit of the model and hence to decide how seriously the results can be taken. It is hard to give advice about this situation. If the investigator has published the correlation matrix, or it is accessible, we can always reanalyze it properly if sufficiently concerned. But often editors do not permit the correlation matrix to be published, and the description of the analysis is so scant that we would not even know how to repeat it to compare our results with details of the original. It must, then, be admitted that many published factor analyses do not meet the usual criteria for respectable research reporting of presenting sufficient detail to enable independent testing.

Broadly, if enough information is given to let us believe that the sample correlation matrix is a reasonably stable estimate of the population matrix, an approximate exploratory analysis will often as a matter of fact resemble a "best-fitted" analysis enough to yield the same conclusions. But if we are given only, say, the rotated factor matrix, it is perhaps better to regard the study as never having been carried out at all.

A high percentage of published studies present something like the following information: "The correlations were factored using principal components with eigenvalues greater than one, and rotated to simple structure using varimax, yielding the rotated factor loadings shown in Table 2.3.9." Sometimes also "loadings below .3 are omitted," as though leaving out these numbers helps the reader to comprehend the results. The statement is ambiguous, for we do not know, and indeed the investigator may not know, if the program borrowed from the computer center obtained only principal components, as in approximation (1), or crudely fashioned a closer approximation to LS estimates out of these.

TABLE 2.3.9
Varimax Factor Pattern

	I	II	III	IV	V	h^2
1	0.143	.522	.197	.478	-.084	.568
2	.224	.197	.608	.225	.166	.537
3	-.049	.134	.002	-.186	.790	.678
4	.737	.303	.177	-.131	-.118	.697
5	.024	.270	.065	-.800	.148	.741
6	.746	-.267	-.161	.099	.070	.669
7	.012	-.526	.002	.004	-.329	.386
8	.261	-.271	.050	.489	.488	.621
9	.155	.081	-.819	.197	.102	.752
10	.059	.672	-.347	.081	-.151	.605

"The data were factor analyzed using principal
components with eigenvalues greater than one,
followed by varimax rotation."

- How to lie with factor analysis.

Documentation of package programs for "factor analysis" does not always make this clear.

If we are presented with just the result in Table 2.3.9, we are at a loss to evaluate it. In fact, it is an analysis of the correlation matrix in Table 1.4.4. The correct number of common factors is zero, not five; hence the "eigenvalues greater than one" guide fails us completely. It is disconcerting to find that the process of transformation toward approximate simple structure can yield enough large and small values of the factor loadings to give what some factor analysts quaintly refer to as a "compelling" simple structure (i.e., presumably, one that "compels" our faith in it.) It is comforting to know that a reanalysis of the correlation matrix, if this were available to us, would have given us "the truth," namely that it is drawn from a population of uncorrelated variables with no common factors (i.e., no generic properties in common).

(d) Heywood Cases (Improper Solutions)

With the increasing use of good methods of estimation, investigators are increasingly encountering cases where the best-fitted estimates are *improper*, because one or more estimates of uniqueness (residual variance) are negative. This of course is unacceptable, as variances are essentially positive quantities (means of squares). Even a zero residual variance is unacceptable, as it implies exact dependence of an observed variable on the common factors. This could only be true if the variable has no measurement error. That negative uniquenesses might arise was first pointed out by Heywood (1931); hence it is commonly referred to as a *Heywood case*. Alternatively, it is known as an *improper solution*. We can summarize the situation in just six points and draw some tentative conclusions.

(i) Some investigators tend to regard the fact that Heywood cases can occur as an indication that something is wrong with the basic principles of the common factor model and that we should use some other technique of multivariate data analysis instead—perhaps principal components or image analysis.

(ii) A Heywood correlation matrix is a perfectly possible correlation matrix for a population.

(iii) On the other hand, a "non-Heywood" population can give samples, by chance, in which the *estimators* of some positive population residual variances are negative; hence a Heywood case in a sample does not *prove* that the population is a Heywood case. A second sample might yield a different conclusion.

(iv) Sometimes a Heywood case can be cured by fitting fewer factors, but often this gives unacceptably poor fit.

(v) Most modern programs for ML or LS estimation are arranged to stop the search for a minimum of the function with respect to any uniqueness before it becomes negative. Such a procedure is at best a makeshift, as we know that we have not found the required minimum, and a zero uniqueness is still really unacceptable.

(vi) A very common cause of Heywood cases seems to be a failure on the part of the investigator to represent each factor by a sufficient number of tests with large loadings on it. Consider the two simple general-factor correlation matrices in Table 2.3.10. In case (a), by simple inspection, as in the earlier discussion in Chapter 1, we deduce that the single-factor model fits the correlations with loadings .6, .5, and .4. These loadings are determined precisely by the data, as are the corresponding unique variances, .64, .75, and .84. In case (b), we find that the loadings and unique variances are not uniquely determined by the data. We can choose loadings of .6, .5, and zero or 1.2, .25, and zero or .2, 1.5, and zero or, indeed, any two numbers whose product is .30 for the first two loadings with zero for the third. And we note immediately that if we can easily find pairs of numbers for the loadings in which one or the other number is greater than unity and the corresponding unique variance is negative, so can the computer, of course. This fact seems to have been well-known to Thurstone in the 1930s as an indeterminacy of the parameters of *doublet factors*—factors with only two non-zero loadings—but its implications for the occurrence of Heywood cases have not been widely recognized. More generally, if one or more of m common factors have only two tests with nonzero loadings, then those loadings and the

TABLE 2.3.10

(a)

$$\begin{bmatrix} 1.00 & .30 & .24 \\ .30 & 1.00 & .20 \\ .24 & .20 & 1.00 \end{bmatrix}$$

(b)

$$\begin{bmatrix} 1.00 & .30 & .00 \\ .30 & 1.00 & .00 \\ .00 & .00 & 1.00 \end{bmatrix}$$

(c)

$$\begin{bmatrix} 1.00 & .30 & .024 \\ .30 & 1.00 & .02 \\ .024 & .02 & 1.00 \end{bmatrix}$$

corresponding unique variances are not *identified* (uniquely determined by the correlations), and Heywood cases are likely to occur. Notice that the negative unique variance is not specifically associated with one of the variables, and the phenomenon need not be eliminated by deleting the variable with negative residual variance from the analysis.) More generally still, if one or more factors have only one or two tests with large loadings and the rest of the loadings are small (*singlet* or *doublet* factors, in Thurstone's terminology), the factor loadings on this factor may be very poorly estimated from even a large sample. Consider case (c) in Table 2.3.10. The correlations are consistent with only one set of loadings, .6, .5, and .04, but because the last loading is close to zero, it is easy to imagine that in finite samples it would behave like case (b), yielding estimates of loadings greater than unity, and estimates of residual variances that are negative. (It is not yet common practice to compute standard errors of estimate of factor loadings and uniquenesses, to put confidence bounds on them and determine how well they have, individually, been estimated. It is technically possible and desirable to do so.) Generally, experience suggests that we can hope to avoid Heywood cases and, indeed, poorly estimated common factor loadings and unique variances, if we make sure that every common factor is defined by at least three and preferably four or more variables having large loadings on it. This is reasonable in terms of the substantive aims of factor analysis, because we can hardly expect a common abstract attribute to be well defined by just two measured of it.

Negative estimates of essentially positive quantities occur in statistical problems other than those of factor analysis. One approach to these problems involves the adoption of the Bayesian philosophy of statistical estimation. Briefly, in this way of thinking, we attribute a probability distribution to the population parameters we wish to estimate in which we may incorporate and give fairly exact expression to our beliefs about the population studied. Here, for example, we might turn our belief into the assertion that the probability of finding a negative or zero residual variance is zero, whereas the probability of finding nonzero values is greater than zero. It is possible to turn this thinking into a plausible probability distribution of uniquenesses, which leads to a simple modification of a ML estimation program that prevents it from obtaining negative or zero uniquenesses.[3] This approach to the problem is possibly better than the common device mentioned before of stopping the analysis at the point where a residual variance reduces to zero; but before either of these devices is adopted, the investigator should check whether the data yield one or more singlet or doublet factors, in which case there is a more serious problem in the form of ill-defined factors and underidentified (nonuniquely determined) parameters with the study.

2.4. DEVICES FOR APPROXIMATING SIMPLE STRUCTURE

The simple hypothesis of exploratory common factor analysis that prescribes only the number of common factors is not specific enough to determine unique estimates of the common factor loadings if the number is more than one. We say that these parameters are not "identified." When we obtain a set of estimates, we have to recognize that infinitely many alternative sets would fit the data equally well. The mathematician can tell us how to compute from a given set of factor loadings all the possible alternative values, which are *transformations* of the values we first happen to obtain.

A widely accepted goal, in transforming a given factor pattern into another, is contained in the notion of *simple structure*. Given an explanation of the intercorrelations of our n variables in terms of a minimum number, m, of common factors, the basic notion of simple structure is, further, that we explain the correlation of each variable with the others by a minimum number of those common factors. That is, broadly, a factor pattern has simple structure when each variable has nonzero loadings (regression weights) on as few of the factors as possible. Partly on the basis of experience, five rules have been given for simple structure that are supposed to legislate an unambiguous choice among alternative solutions that might be equally acceptable in terms of the fundamental definition. These are: (1) Each row of the factor pattern should have at least one zero element. (2) Each column should have at least m zero elements. (3) For every pair of columns there should be at least m variables with a zero coefficient in one column and a nonzero in the other. (4) In the case where m is greater than

---

[3]See Martin and McDonald (1975).

three, for every pair of columns there should be a large proportion of variables with zeros in both columns. (5) For every pair of columns, there should be a small proportion of variables with nonzeros in both columns. Notice that only the first three of these rules are objective. It is customary to illustrate simple structure by using zeros and crosses as in Table 2.4.1 to indicate the positions of zero and of nonzero elements. Table 2.4.1(a) shows a simple structure that fits all the criteria. Table 2.4.1(b) shows a more specialized structure that is certainly a simple structure and actually fits the stronger principle that every variable has a nonzero loading on only one factor. This structure is known as *independent clusters*.

Thurstone originally advocated the simple structure principle as reflecting a truth about the psychology of cognition where the concept originated (viz., that we do not seem to use all our "mental faculties" in any one cognitive task). (Thurstone, at the time of the introduction of simple structure, explicitly regarded factors as a scientific revival of an old discredited unscientific notion of mind as made up of "faculties.") The concept also carried with it a second principle of parsimony to supplement the first, by which we first explain all the correlations with as few factors as possible and then explain each correlation with as few of those few as possible.

The unquestioning acceptance of simple structure in factor patterns is possibly a reflection of human conceptual preferences rather than of anything in the subject matters we study. Essentially, a practice of factor interpretation has evolved, again without formal and explicit argument, in which we describe a factor as that which is in common to those variables that have large positive

TABLE 2.4.1

(a)			(b)		
Simple Structure Factor Pattern			Independent Clusters Factor Pattern		
X	0	*X*	*X*	0	0
X	*X*	0	*X*	0	0
X	0	0	*X*	0	0
0	*X*	*X*	0	*X*	0
X	*X*	0	0	*X*	0
0	*X*	0	0	*X*	0
0	0	*X*	0	0	*X*
0	*X*	*X*	0	0	*X*
X	0	*X*	0	0	*X*

regression weights on it. The factor is "most like" the variables that increase most rapidly as the factor score increases. It is unlike the variables with zero loadings, as these do not vary as the factor varies, and *least* like those variables that have large negative regression weights on it (i.e., the variables that decrease most rapidly as the factor score increases). But for large classes of data the methods of scoring employed combined with the simple structure criterion tend to eliminate negative loadings and leave a contrast between large positive loadings and zero loadings. The interpreter can then ask what the high-loading group of variables has in common in order to identify the factor. He or she does not have to ask what the zero-loading variables have in common, of course. If there are any large negative loadings, one can usually think of those variables as, in effect, scored in reverse (extraversion scored as lack of introversion or anxiety scored as lack of calmness). The task of interpretation seems easier when we just ask what a given group of variables have in common than when we have to contrast them with another group of variables. In fact, unfortunately, investigators sometimes miss the elementary precaution of making sure that variables with zero loadings on a factor do not *also* have the generic property that the high-loading variables seem to have. This would make nonsense of the proposed interpretation of the factor. It might seem, then, that zeros in the factor pattern are desired because the zero–nonzero contrast is easy to think about.

It follows from the definition of simple structure that if we have a population whose correlation matrix can be explained by a factor pattern with a definite simple structure, it is quite impossible (i.e., there is a zero probability) that a sample drawn from that population could be made to yield simple structure by transforming a given set of estimates in which no factor loadings have been set equal to zero. At best we could hope to invent devices that yield an approximation to simple structure that is "good" in some sense. We might also hope to find a way to decide when the approximation is "good" enough to enable us to believe that the variables possibly have simple structure in the population. Unfortunately, in the literature, no distinction is made between "simple structure" and "approximate simple structure" or between simple structure in the population and simple structure in the sample. A habit has grown up, with no formal or explicit basis, of regarding sample loadings less than .3 as "near-zero" in a loose definition of simple structure. Simple structure in this loose definition seems rather too easy to obtain, and investigators often interpret their results *as though* they had simple structure when they might be said not to have it at all.

Many devices have been invented for "rotation to simple structure" (i.e., for transforming a given estimated factor pattern so that it approximates the definition of simple structure as closely as it is able to, perhaps not at all closely). Just about any of these devices are adequate to indicate to us, in combination with rational thought about the objects of the study, where to postulate zero loadings in a detailed hypothesis that can be tested by the methods of Chapter 3. It seems illogical to be content with an approximate simple structure in which some of the coefficients in the factor pattern are "small" and others are "large." We either believe the small coefficients are zero in the population, or we do not. If we do, we should not get nonzero estimates of the zero coefficients. If we do not, we should not pretend to be using simple structure.

Essentially, there are four main approaches to the problem of obtaining a transformation to approximate simple structure. These are (1) graphical methods, (2) counting methods, (3) simplicity function methods, and (4) target methods.[4]

1. The oldest method involves the drawing of graphs, pairwise plots of the columns of factor loadings against each other, by human operators and the selection by eye of new axes for the graphs. This is an extremely complicated art. Most investigators consider it satisfactorily replaced by methods that can run themselves off on a computer, thus saving human effort. It does seem, though, that the results of graphical transformations tend to be considered the standard by which the results of other methods are judged.

2. The intention behind counting methods is that we count the number of variables that have a loading less than a given size (say .3) on each factor and look for a solution that maximizes this number. Because of the geometry of the problem, originating in the graphical treatments, this count of small values is known as the *hyperplane count* (the number of points close enough to a plane in multidimensional space). However, as carried out in practice, instead of a simple count of the number of small-enough values, a weight is given to each element counted that makes the total count a function of the size of the large coefficients rather than just an integer representing the number of small-enough coefficients. This seems to constitute a departure from the original principle, according to which simple structure is a matter of the number of small factor loadings and surely should be quite independent of the size of the large ones.

3. In the *simplicity function* methods, the basic problem put to the mathematicians is to define a quantity that is computed as a function of all nm elements of the common factor pattern and will vary as we transform the numbers in the factor pattern, becoming a minimum (or, for some functions, a maximum) at a set of values of the factor loadings that we would regard as a reasonable approximation to simple structure. Such a function is called a *simplicity function*.

On the face of it, it looks impossible to define a usable simplicity function. In the first place, there are a number of distinct ingredients to the original recipe for simple structure. It would seem impossible to capture them all in a single mathematical function. In the second place, it would seem incorrect to have a function that depends on the values of the "large" elements in the transformed pattern, because the simple structure concept has no implication at all for the sizes of elements that are thought to be nonzero. Nevertheless, a number of simplicity functions have been defined that appear to work well in practice. No attempt will

---

[4]For general comments, see Hakstian (1971) and Hakstian and Abel (1974).

be made here to distinguish the different variations that have been invented. We just examine the general idea.

Broadly, a solution to the problem of defining a simplicity function can be based on the commonsense reflection that a factor pattern matrix that exhibits simple structure has an extreme distribution of the absolute sizes of its elements, in which there are many large (positive or negative) values and many small values with few of intermediate size. Such a spread of the values to the extremes could be measured by one of the usual measures of variability in descriptive statistics. A convenient choice would be to square the *nm* elements of the factor pattern, because we want the contrast to be between absolute values—very large versus very small—rather than signed values—large positive versus large negative. We would then try to find a transformation that maximizes the variance of the *nm squared* numbers.

Competing variants on this idea have been developed, and claims made about the general relative qualities of the results obtained. It seems impossible to find a simplicity function that is "better than" other simplicity functions in the sense that it always gives results nearer to (a) the known simple structure of artificial test data or (b) graphical solutions. Because simplicity functions depend on the irrelevant "large" values of the factor loadings, the solution given by one simplicity function will differ from the solution given by another simplicity function *and* from the "best" solution as otherwise judged, by reason of irrelevant values of factor loadings that differ from one example to another. It is doubtful, therefore, if there could be a way to show that one simplicity function is "generally best." If we use an approximate simple structure only as a guide for setting up detailed hypotheses, as in Chapter 3, this does not matter.

4. In target methods, (also rather unfortunately described as *Procrustean* methods), we suppose we know where the zeros would be in an exact version of the simple structure, and we choose a transformation to make the loadings corresponding to the "target" zeros as small as possible. (Usually we minimize the sum of squares of those numbers.) The main advantage is that the result is independent of the large loadings. The main disadvantage is that we must first choose a target. In practice, we can use a target method to improve a result obtained by one of the other methods, which also yields an automatic decision as to the location of the exact zeros.

The user of computer programs for "rotation to simple structure" could obtain some guidance from Table 2.4.2. The main choice is between "orthogonal rotation," yielding a new solution that is also in terms of uncorrelated (orthogonal) factors, with a common factor pattern in which the factor loadings are *v–f* regression weights and also *v–f* correlations, and "oblique rotation", yielding a common factor pattern (*v–f* regression weights), a common factor structure (*v–f* correlations), and the correlation matrix of the factors (*f–f* correlations). The main argument for orthogonal transformation is that factors

TABLE 2.4.2

(a) Orthogonal Transformations

(i) QUARTIMAX: Simplicity Function $s_q = \sum_{j=1}^{n} \sum_{p=1}^{m} f_{jp}^4$

the sum of the fourth power of loadings. (Maximized)
Tends to "simplify" the rows but not the columns of
the factor pattern--may leave a "general factor"
with no near-zero loadings. (Due to Carroll, 1953.)

(ii) VARIMAX: Simplicity Function

$$s_v = \sum_{p=1}^{m} \left[\frac{n\sum_{j=1}^{n} (f_{jp}^2)^2 - (\sum_{j=1}^{n} f_{jp}^2)^2}{n^2} \right]$$

the sum across columns of the "variances" of the
squared loadings in the m columns. Usually the
method is applied with the loadings "normalized"--
divided by the square root of the communality--to
make each row sum of squares equal unity.(Maximized)
Tends to avoid a "general" factor. (Due to Kaiser,
1958.)

(iii) TRANSVARIMAX: A weighted sum of s_q and s_v is used as
simplicity function. (Due to Saunders, 1962.)
General Comment: VARIMAX is most widely available,
and most popular. In exploratory work, it seems to
suffice.

(b) Oblique Transformations

(i) (DIRECT) OBLIMIN Simplicity Function

$$s_{do} = \sum_{p \ne q}^{m} \sum_{}^{m} \left[\sum_{j=1}^{n} f_{jp}^2 f_{jq}^2 - \frac{1}{n} (\Sigma_j f_{jp}^2) (\Sigma_j f_{jp}^2) \right]$$

(Minimized) We minimize the "covariance" of squared
loadings in distinct columns. Recommended by Hakstian
(1974). (Due to Jennrich and Sampson, 1966.)

continued

continued

(ii)   OBLIMAX Simplicity Function

$$s_o = \frac{\sum\limits_{j=1}^{n} f_{ip}^{*4}}{(\sum\limits_{j=1}^{n} f_{ip}^{*2})^2} \qquad p = 1, \ldots, m$$

For each factor in turn, the function is maximized, then the process is repeated. The quantities f_{jp}^{*} are not the common factor loadings but are related to them by a scale transformation. (They are known as <u>reference-structure</u> loadings.) Not recommended by Hakstian, 1974. (Due to Saunders, 1961.)

(iii)   BIQUARTIMIN. Simplicity function resenbles s_{do}. Not recommended by Hakstian. (Due to Carroll, 1957.)

(iv)   MAXPLANE. Originally intended to maximize the number of loadings whose absolute value is greater than a given number--a <u>counting method</u> (i.e., to maximize the <u>hyperplane count</u>). In practice, weights are used as discussed in the text. Not strongly recommended. (Due to Cattell and Muerle, 1960.)

(v)   PROMAX A target method. Using, say, VARIMAX, we obtain an approximate simple structure. The loadings are raised to an even power to exaggerate the difference between the large and small loadings. Then an oblique transformation is chosen that uses the "powered" loading matrix as a target. Recommended. (Due to Hendrickson and White, 1964.)

(vi)   Harris-Kaiser oblique transformations: Essentially a method for restricting the kind of transformation chosen. Cannot be described here. Certain methods suggested are recommended by Hakstian. (Due to Harris and Kaiser, 1964.)

---

are principles of classification that should be as independent as possible (i.e., uncorrelated). The main argument for oblique transformation is that factors that are uncorrelated in one population may well be correlated in another, and correlated factors will tend to give invariant v–f regression weights (suitably scaled— see Chapter 6) from one population to another. We would have the best of all worlds if a set of variables gave us uncorrelated factors, simply as a matter of fact, in all the populations we happen to care about, but this cannot be expected.

2.5. RELATED METHODS

In this section we briefly consider three techniques that bear some relationship to exploratory factor analysis, namely inverse factor analysis, optimal scaling, and multidimensional scaling. At least the last two of these topics are major fields of psychometric theory, and each requires no less than a book-length account to do it justice. As in the discussion of principal component theory and image theory, the treatment of these topics here is partial in both senses of the word, being both incomplete and biased toward a perspective that is essentially that of common factor analysis.

(a) Inverse Factor Analysis

An extremely confused issue in factor theory concerns the notion of "factoring persons instead of tests" in the usual context of persons taking tests as the source of our data. If we think of factor analysis as something we "do to" an $(n \times n)$ matrix of correlations between n tests measured on N persons, and if we think of sample correlations as mean products of standardized deviations of persons from their means on two tests, then it is easy to invent "inverse" or "obverse" or "converse" factor analysis as something we would "do to" an $(N \times N)$ matrix of "correlations" between N persons measured on n tests. We would immediately perceive difficulties with such an "inverse" factor analysis. If n tests are measured in n different sets of units, with n different origins and scales, we would wonder what the correlation between Smith's and Brown's sets of n scores would mean, and we would notice that the correlation would be sensitive to changes of unit. For example, measuring weight in tons versus milligrams, height in feet versus millimicrons, and length of big toe in inches versus miles would change the correlations dramatically. In spite of these difficulties, a large literature has developed on the subject of "factoring persons." Much of it has been devoted to the question whether the factor loadings obtained from correlations between persons should be in correspondence to their usual factor loadings. Much too was concerned with the effects on such correspondence of "taking out" or "leaving in" means or of rescaling the variables to comparable units before computing correlations between persons.

If we do not accept the view that factor analysis is something we do to correlation matrices and if, specifically, we regard the common factor model as a special case of latent trait theory, based on the principle of local independence (see Chapter 7), we may find it difficult to see why the notion of "factoring persons" ever arose in the first place. That is, it is fairly easy to understand a common factor as a latent trait such that in a subpopulation of persons for whom that trait is a fixed number the correlation between two tests is zero. It is hard to understand a factor, whose loadings are obtained by analyzing correlations between persons, as a latent trait such that, in a subpopulation of tests for which that trait is a fixed number, the correlation between two persons is zero. Thus, the main difficulty with the notion of applying the common factor model to a matrix of "correlations between persons" would be the logical difficulty of interpreting the residual covariances as partial covariances, the uniqueness of a person as the residual variance about the regression of the person on the factors, and so on. The position taken here is that the common factor model is a statistical model and not a device that is applicable "inversely" to "correlations" between persons. Nor, it seems, has any cogent need to apply the model in this way ever been demonstrated.

The case is somewhat different with component theory. If we have scores y_{ji} of N subjects on n measures, which for the moment we suppose to be in raw score form, we may approximate the scores by sums of products of principal component weights and principal component scores. The detailed mathematics of the problem can be presented so as to give the impression that we choose between first obtaining and operating on sums of products of the scores of pairs of variables, or sums of products of the scores of pairs of subjects. These resemble "correlations between variables" and "correlations between persons." We might very loosely describe these procedures as "factoring tests" and "factoring persons," but either is just a device to solve the entire minimization problem with convenient arithmetic. It is not to be expected that if we first transform the scores to deviation measure or to standard measure in the sample the best-fitting weights and scores will be related to the weights and scores before rescaling in any simple way. This fact, however, does not seem to be a problem of any depth or consequence for psychometric theory. Any wish to obtain a best-fitting representation of a given set of scores will presumably be in turn motivated by rational research considerations. These in turn, in most cases, should dictate whether we wish to approximate the scores or their deviations from the mean or their deviations in standard measure by principal components; hence the discussions of the effects on the relationship between "factoring tests" and "factoring persons" of "taking out means" or "standardizing" do not yet seem adequately motivated.

The cavalier attitude expressed so far in this section toward problems that have been taken very seriously by very competent investigators should not deter the reader from inquiring more deeply into these matters if the nature of his or her research data would seem to make it necessary. On the other hand, it certainly seems desirable not to become involved with such problems if it is possible to avoid them.

The use of measures in a score matrix in which each row consists of deviations of the subject's scores from his or her own mean over n tests is sometimes solemnly discussed as *ipsative* scoring, with the obvious Latin derivation. The process of converting a score matrix to this form is known as *ipsatization*. Usually, to give such a scoring scheme the semblance of rationality, the scores would first have to be put in standard measure in the sample. The effects of ipsatization are not well understood, and it would seem very difficult to develop proper statistical theory to cover estimation problems for sample data so treated. There is need for further work, perhaps directed at the question whether we could ever have any good reason to ipsatize.

Problems of a rather different kind arise with other $n \times N$ data matrices that we might consider factor analyzing. If, for example, just one test is administered n times to N subjects, we are free to calculate the correlations between the n repeated measures and fit the common factor model to the data. If the n administrations of the test are all carried out under the same conditions, yielding N time series, one for each subject, the use of the common factor model would seem conceptually inappropriate, and we presumably would prefer to use a conventional time-series analysis. If we insist on using common factor analysis, it is unlikely that we shall be able to interpret the results in terms of common properties of times of testing, such as early versus late or middle versus early and late. If, on the other hand, the n repeated measures correspond to n distinct situations in which the test was administered, it may prove possible to interpret the analysis in terms of common properties of situations. See Chapter 6 for the analysis of data consisting of subjects by tests by occasions or situations.

(b) Optimal Scaling

Optimal scaling is one of several names (dual scaling, correspondence analysis) that have been given to certain applications of principal component analysis to multicategory data. If N subjects respond to n multicategory items, the responses can be coded in a data matrix of N rows and p columns, where p is the total number of categories in the n items. We record a unity in the column corresponding to the category of each item that each subject checks and zeros in all other columns. If the respondent is forced to choose a category in each item, each row of the data matrix must contain just n unities, one for each item. As a result, there is redundancy of information in the matrix. If we know the entries in all but one category of each item, then we know the entry in the remaining category. The object of optimal scaling is to choose weights for the item categories and scores for the subjects that are *optimal* in a mathematically well-defined sense of the word. A number of criteria have been proposed, all of which yield the same mathematical answer, which closely resembles principal component analysis. We write y_{jl} for the entry corresponding to the lth category of the jth item. If the respondent checks this category, then $y_{jl} = 1$. Consequently $y_{jk} = 0$ for every other category, k, of the item. We define a total score s, weights for each item category w_{jl}, and item scores s_j, by writing

$$s = \sum_j \sum_l w_{jl} y_{jl} \qquad (2.5.1)$$

and

$$s_j = \sum_l w_{jl} y_{jl} \qquad j = 1, \ldots, n \qquad (2.5.2)$$

(In fact, s_j is always the same as the weight assigned to the category checked, and s is the sum of the weights of all the categories checked.) We choose the weights to maximize the sum of the squares of correlations between the item scores s_j and the total score s. This is analogous to Hotelling's original treatment of principal components. Such alternatives as choosing the weights to maximize the ratio of the variance of the total score to the sum of the n variances of the item scores yield the same answer. These and certain other equivalent criteria are essentially designed to maximize the relationship between the total score and the item scores in some recognizable sense.

The optimal weights in (2.5.1) are regression weights of the (dependent) optimal score s on the p (independent) item categories. They are indeterminate because the independent variables contain redundant information. This means that further arbitrary restrictions need to be placed on the weights to determine them uniquely. Once they are determined, under any set of restrictions, we can, as in principal component analysis, compute a converse regression of the item categories on the optimal scores. These are invariant under arbitrary choices of the optimal weights and can be interpreted very much as in common factor analysis. In the practice of optimal scaling, the usual procedure is to obtain and interpret some set of optimal weights. From the factor-analytic point of view it seems preferable to obtain the regressions of the item categories on the optimal scores rather than the regressions of the optimal scores on the item categories.[5]

(c) Multidimensional Scaling

Multidimensional scaling is the generic term for a family of methods for representing *dissimilarities* between stimuli by distances in a multidimensional space. Because it is possible to think of a correlation coefficient as measuring the similarity of two tests, it may seem reasonable to take some function of the correlation coefficients chosen to increase as the correlation decreases to measure the dissimilarities of a set of n tests and to use multidimensional scaling as an alternative to common factor analysis to provide an account of the relations between them.

Just as the position of a point in two dimensions can be represented by its coordinates, x_1, x_2, measured on two axes at right angles, so an imagined point in m dimensions can be represented by its coordinates, $x_1, \ldots, x_m$, measured on m axes at right angles. By an extension of Pythagoras' theorem, given the coordinates of any two points in an m-dimensional space, we can calculate the square of the distance between the points as the sum of the squares of the m

---

[5]See Nishisato (1980) for a general account of optimal scaling. For a technical account of these remarks, see McDonald (1983).

differences between their coordinates. The converse problem is more difficult, but it can be solved.

In multidimensional scaling, given the squared distances between members of a set of n points in m-dimensional space, we can find a set of m coordinate values for each of the n points that is consistent with those squared distances. The obtained coordinates are subject to indeterminacies corresponding to both a rotation of the coordinate axes and a movement in space of the origin of the system of axes.

In metric multidimensional scaling we assume that a set of given dissimilarities measures the distances between the objects (tests, stimuli) to be mapped into a multidimensional space. The obvious difficulty with this assumption is that it can easily contradict itself. Suppose one investigator uses the quantity $\frac{1}{2}(1 - r)$ where r is the correlation coefficient between tests as a measure of their dissimilarity, ranging from zero to unity, whereas another uses $- \log \{\frac{1}{2}(1 + r)\}$, ranging from zero to infinity. The two measures of dissimilarity cannot be taken as measures of the same distance.

Nonmetric multidimensional scaling was introduced to avoid the self-contradictory assumption that distances are measured by dissimilarities. It is possible to avoid doing any arithmetic on the numbers representing dissimilarities by regressing the distances in the model on the observed dissimilarities, using a *monotone regression function*. This is a nondecreasing function of the independent variable that gives a least-squares best fit to a scatter diagram. It takes the form of a set of joined-up straight-line segments (parts of a polygon) that are either horizontal or sloping upward from left to right in the graph of the data. Arithmetic algorithms have been developed for the two steps of nonmetric multidimensional scaling, namely: (1) given a set of guessed coordinates of the objects, yielding a corresponding set of guessed distances, to regress the distances on the data using a monotone regression function; and (2) to move to a new set of coordinates chosen to reduce the residuals of the distances about their regressions on the dissimilarities. At the completion of a series of repetitions of these steps, we should have a set of coordinates for the objects that minimize the residuals of the distances about their regressions on the data. It is an unusual and interesting feature of these methods that the hypothetical quantities in the model are treated as dependent variables and regressed on the data as independent variables in order to avoid doing arithmetic on the observations.[6]

For our purposes, the important question concerns the relation between common factor analysis and nonmetric multidimensional scaling applied to quantities derived from correlations between tests. There is no direct mathematical relationship. In applications, users of nonmetric multidimensional scaling usually obtain an account of data in terms of fewer dimensions than do factor analysts.

---

[6]For a general account of multidimensional scaling, see Kruskal & Wish (1978).

This seems partly due to choices open to the investigator. A user wishing to avoid severe rotation problems in multidimensional space may deliberately choose a coordinate space of at most two dimensions to contain the data. It also seems partly due to the fact that multidimensional scaling allows a translation of origin that can commonly be used to eliminate one of the dimensions needed by the common factor model. Some reduction in the dimensionality of the data may also be due to the nonmetric properties of the former method. Allowing for these differences, it is possible to find a degree of consistency between these alternative analyses of the same data.[7]

Instead of using correlation coefficients with their built-in linear measurement of the relations between tests, it is possible to develop a nonmetric counterpart of principal component analysis, in which the monotone regression function is used to regress a weighted sum of components on the data.[8] Such a method recovers known parameters provided that the data contain only a small amount of unique variance. A nonmetric analog of the common factor model would presumably be able to cope with large amounts of unique variance, but it does not seem possible to develop a common factor model without doing arithmetic on the data, so such a model appears to be quite a challenge for research!

2.6.   MATHEMATICAL NOTES ON CHAPTER 2[9]

(a) Notes on Section 2.2

We write $\mathbf{A}$, of order $(n \times n)$, for the usual sample correlation matrix, computed from a sample of size N. (It is actually better to think of this and the matrix fitted to it as covariance matrices.) In the unrestricted common factor model, we wish to estimate $\mathbf{F}$ and $\mathbf{U}$ under the hypothesis that

$$\mathbf{R} = \mathbf{FF}' + \mathbf{U}^2$$

for $\mathbf{F}$ of order $(n \times m)$, with no further specification on the elements of $\mathbf{F}$.

---

[7]An unpublished study by McDonald and Chan reveals close similarities in configurations of common factor loadings and configurations of points in a nonmetric multidimensional scaling analysis of functions of the correlations, except for the loss of a dimension due to movement of the origin in multidimensional scaling. See, for example, Schlesinger and Guttman (1969) for an alternative view of these matters.

[8]Kruskal and Shepard (1974).

[9]This section may be omitted, but it may help, so try it.

General Note: Again all of the material in this chapter is very well known, and again Gorsuch (1974), Rummel (1970), and Mulaik (1972) are recommended for further reading. The analyses were done on computer programs written by the author.

In the method of least squares we choose $\mathbf{F}$ and $\mathbf{U}^2$ to minimize the quantity

$$Q = \text{Tr}\,\{(\mathbf{A} - \mathbf{R})^2\} \tag{2.6.1}$$

that is, the quantity

$$Q = \text{Tr}\,\{(\mathbf{A} - \mathbf{FF}' - \mathbf{U}^2)\,(\mathbf{A} - \mathbf{FF}' - \mathbf{U}^2)\}. \tag{2.6.2}$$

By differential calculus, omitted, we find that conditions for Q to be a minimum are

$$(\mathbf{A} - \mathbf{FF}' - \mathbf{U}^2)\mathbf{F} = \mathbf{0} \tag{2.6.3}$$

and

$$\text{Diag}\,(\mathbf{A} - \mathbf{FF}' - \mathbf{U}^2) = \mathbf{0} \tag{2.6.4}$$

This is a system of simultaneous nonlinear equations, for which a solution cannot be obtained in closed form. That is, we cannot obtain expressions for $\mathbf{F}$ and $\mathbf{U}^2$ in terms of elements of $\mathbf{A}$. However, for any given value of $\mathbf{U}^2$, we can solve (2.6.3) for $\mathbf{F}$ using the mathematics of principal component theory, rewriting it as

$$(\mathbf{A} - \mathbf{U}^2)\mathbf{F} = \mathbf{FF}'\mathbf{F} \tag{2.6.5}$$

and choosing to impose a condition that $\mathbf{F}'\mathbf{F}$ be a diagonal matrix. Conversely, for any given value of $\mathbf{F}$, we can solve (2.6.4) for $\mathbf{U}^2$, giving the "obvious" result

$$\mathbf{U}^2 = \text{Diag}\,\{\mathbf{A} - \mathbf{FF}'\} \tag{2.6.6}$$

In practice, therefore, there have been two main approaches to the numerical solution of the least-squares estimation problem. In one, we use a numerical algorithm to find values of $\mathbf{U}^2$ that successively approach nearer and nearer to the minimizing values, and for each of these we solve (2.6.5) by the methods of principal component theory. Methods for finding successively improved values of $\mathbf{U}^2$ range from ad hoc algorithms (such as one due to Thomson 1934) that "seem to work" to applications of modern Newton or quasi-Newton methods. In the other method, we use a numerical algorithm to find values of $\mathbf{F}$ that successively approach the minimizing values, and for each of these we obtain $\mathbf{U}^2$ by (2.6.6). The best known version of this method is Harman's MINRES.[10] We can also minimize Q directly with respect to both $\mathbf{F}$ and $\mathbf{U}^2$.

We turn now to maximum likelihood estimation. Not enough information has been given in Appendix A1 to enable us to derive this method from basic principles, and no attempt will be made to do so.

We shall accept as given a result obtained by Lawley (1940) that under the normal distribution assumption the quantity

---

[10]See Harman and Fukuda (1966).

$$\lambda = N[\text{Tr } \{AR^{-1}\} - \log |AR^{-1}| - n] \tag{2.6.7}$$

has its minimum at the point where the likelihood of our sample has a maximum, and λ is distributed asymptotically as N increases like chi-square with df = $\frac{1}{2}\{(n - m)^2 - (n + m)\}$. Whether the normal distribution assumption is true or not, the quantity λ is necessarily nonnegative. It is "large" when the fit of R to A is poor and "small" when the fit is good. It is zero only if we are able to obtain $R = FF' + U^2$ that exactly equals our sample A, for then $AR^{-1} = I_n$ and it is easily seen that Tr $\{I_n\} = n$ and $|I| = 1$, so log $|I| = 0$. (The reader may recognize that the quantity λ is of the form $x - \log x - 1$. It can be shown that such a quantity is essentially positive, becoming zero at $x = 1$.)

The conditions for a minimum of λ with respect to F and U^2 may be written as

$$R^{-1}(R - A)R^{-1}F = 0 \tag{2.6.8}$$

and

$$\text{Diag } \{R^{-1}(R - A)R^{-1}\} = 0. \tag{2.6.9}$$

Like the corresponding equations (2.6.3) and (2.6.4), these are simultaneous nonlinear equations that require a numerical algorithm for their solution. Again we can find numerical methods that yield a sequence of improved values of U^2, for each of which we obtain a solution to (2.6.8) in terms of the principal components of a certain matrix (usually, of $U^{-1}(A - U^2)U^{-1}$, but this has certain disadvantages). We cannot, in this case, solve (2.6.9) in closed form for U^2, given F. Nevertheless, methods that assume (2.6.6) to be true for F other than the required minimizing value do work quite well.

Very interestingly, it can be shown that the LRC l, given in (2.6.7), can also be expressed as

$$\lambda = -N \log|R_e| \tag{2.6.10}$$

where R_e is the *correlation* matrix (not the covariance) of the residuals. In trying to maximize the likelihood, assuming normality, we are trying to maximize the determinant of the residual correlation matrix.

3

The Analysis of Covariance Structures: Confirmatory Factor Analysis and Pattern Hypotheses

3.1. INTRODUCTION

In this and the next chapter we look at aspects of a more general class of models, of which common factor analysis is a special case. These provide hypotheses that constrain the $n(n + 1)/2$ elements of a covariance matrix by expressing them as functions of some smaller number k of parameters.

Some readers will require a remark at this point about the switch just indicated from correlations to covariances. As pointed out in Section 1.2, all the information about a normal distribution is summarized in the means and standard deviations of the variables and their correlations. Usually the student of social science is trained early to work with correlation coefficients as a convenient dimensionless index of the extent of covariation of two variables. For example, we understand a correlation between height and weight of .7 as a number independent of the units of measurement (inches or centimetres, pounds or kilograms). To the mathematical statistician the *covariance* of two variables, the mean product of the deviations of the variables from their means, is the more fundamental quantity. If we are given the standard deviations, σ_x and σ_y, of two variables x and y and their correlation, r_{xy}, then their covariance c_{xy} is given by

$$c_{xy} = \sigma_x \sigma_y r_{xy}. \tag{3.1.1}$$

For example, if the standard deviation of height is 10 in. (or 4 cm) and of weight is 22 lb (or 10 kg), then their covariance ($r = .7$) is 154 in.-lb (or 28 cm-kg). Changing the scale of the measures changes this number, so we typically cannot make comparisons of covariance (height and weight, length of nose and length of big toe) for the purpose of understanding the general structure of psychometric data. On the other hand, as indicated already, the decision to work in standard measure is one way to fix scale, and this decision makes covariances the same as correlations, because the standard deviations are then unity by definition. The widest applicability of the material in this chapter can be obtained if we think of the input information that we are aiming to explain as a matrix of covariances with variances in the diagonal. We would like to ask, at various times, (1) whether two pairs of variables have the same covariance, *usually* basing this on the belief that they have the same standard deviations and the same correlations; (2) whether two pairs of variables have the same correlation but possibly different standard deviations; (3) whether two variables have the same standard deviation. The relation between a correlation matrix and a covariance matrix is indicated in Table 3.1.1, and the possibilities just mentioned are also illustrated.

For the purposes of this chapter we would prefer to think about correlations rather than covariances. When we are free to do so, we shall speak of "correlations (covariances)". When it is better to think of covariances but possible to speak of correlations, we shall write "covariances (correlations)." If the word *correlations* is omitted, the reader should be warned that we are concerned about hypotheses (of equality, usually) that *must* be tested on covariances. Even if we can work with correlation matrices, it is convenient to pretend that these have $n(n + 1)/2$ distinct elements to explain, namely the $n(n - 1)/2$ correlations and the n diagonal unities, which are their unit variances.

We symbolize the covariances (correlations) between n variables in a population by $c_{jk}, j = 1, \ldots, n; k = 1, \ldots, n$, and we suppose we have a hypothesis that declares each covariance (correlation) to be computable as a function of t parameters, $\theta_1, \ldots, \theta_t$. If the hypothesis constrains the coefficients in the matrix in some way, so that not just *any* covariance (correlation) matrix would fit the hypothesis, we have a testable law of formation and can expect to estimate the numbers $\theta_1, \ldots, \theta_t$, given a sample from the population, and to retain or reject the hypothesis on the basis of a general test statistic. The exploratory common factor hypothesis of Chapter 2 is a special application of this idea, and we now consider others. For any such hypotheses we can invent, it is possible in theory to define the same log-likelihood ratio criterion introduced in Section 2.2 as a distribution-free measure of fit of the hypothesis to the sample, which also, under the assumption of a normal distribution, gives a chi-square test of the hypothesis, with degrees of freedom given by

$$\mathrm{df} = \tfrac{1}{2}n(n + 1) - t \qquad (3.1.2)$$

This general system for analyzing covariance (correlation) matrices is known as the *analysis of covariance structures,* and it includes just about all the theory of common factor analysis and other applications that are not usually thought of as common factor analysis. We might claim that the analysis of covariance structures is to correlational statistics as the analysis of variance is to "experi-

TABLE 3.1.1

Correlation Matrix

$$
\begin{bmatrix}
1 & r_{12} & r_{13} & r_{14} \\
r_{21} & 1 & r_{23} & r_{24} \\
r_{31} & r_{32} & 1 & r_{34} \\
r_{41} & r_{42} & r_{43} & 1
\end{bmatrix}
=
\begin{bmatrix}
1.00 & .60 & .45 & .30 \\
.60 & 1.00 & .40 & .20 \\
.45 & .40 & 1.00 & .60 \\
.30 & .20 & .60 & 1.00
\end{bmatrix}
$$

Standard Deviations

$$s_1 = 10$$
$$s_2 = 10$$
$$s_3 = 20$$
$$s_4 = 20$$

Covariance Matrix

$$
\begin{bmatrix}
c_{11} & c_{12} & c_{13} & c_{14} \\
c_{21} & c_{22} & c_{23} & c_{24} \\
c_{31} & c_{32} & c_{33} & c_{34} \\
c_{41} & c_{42} & c_{43} & c_{44}
\end{bmatrix}
=
\begin{bmatrix}
s_1^2 & s_1 r_{12} s_2 & s_1 r_{13} s_3 & s_1 r_{14} s_4 \\
s_2 r_{21} s_1 & s_2^2 & s_2 r_{23} s_3 & s_2 r_{24} s_4 \\
s_3 r_{31} s_1 & s_3 r_{32} s_2 & s_3^2 & s_3 r_{34} s_4 \\
s_4 r_{41} s_1 & s_4 r_{42} s_2 & s_4 r_{43} s_3 & s_4^2
\end{bmatrix}
$$

$$
=
\begin{bmatrix}
100 & 60 & 90 & 60 \\
60 & 100 & 80 & 40 \\
90 & 80 & 400 & 240 \\
60 & 40 & 240 & 400
\end{bmatrix}
$$

(Note that

$$r_{12} = r_{34} \text{ but } c_{12} \neq c_{34}$$
$$c_{12} = c_{14} \text{ but } r_{12} \neq r_{14})$$

mental'' statistics.[1] It allows the user to set up and test very detailed hypotheses about the relations of his measures. It requires detailed specification of the design of the study and conversion of that design by mathematical analysis into a specific hypothesis for the computer to fit and test. We consider some of the structural hypotheses for covariance (correlation) matrices that are known to be

---

[1]It is a straightforward matter to combine hypotheses about means with hypotheses about covariances in a single model for what is then called the *analysis of moment structures*. See, for example, McDonald (1980).

of interest, with illustrations, to give some indication of the general nature of this rapidly developing field. Presumably, those in the remainder of this chapter, the hypotheses of *confirmatory factor analysis,* will be of primary concern to the reader of this book, but the hypotheses treated in Chapter 4 represent the more interesting recent developments and further serve to correct a general bias toward the rather limited approach dictated by traditional exploratory factor analysis.

3.2. CONFIRMATORY FACTOR ANALYSIS

In this section we consider the hypotheses that naturally spring to the mind of an investigator who is steeped in the traditional modes of thought about common factor analysis. Essentially, these are variants on the ideas (1) of having fewer common factors than observed variables, (2) of prescribing (exact) simple structure, (3) with or without a *general* factor.

(a) Prescribed Simple Structure

From an inspection of the nature of our variables, we may be prepared to classify them on substantive grounds into separate groups each of which appears to "measure something in common." Possibly we shall obtain a mutually exclusive and exhaustive classification, in which each group seems to measure only one thing in common. Possibly some variables will appear to be *factorially simple* (i.e., measuring only one thing, in the context of the others), whereas some are *factorially complex* (i.e., measuring something that puts them in one group, and something else that puts them in another). However this works out in detail, our substantive hypothesis can be translated into a structural hypothesis constraining the correlation (covariance) matrix via the usual assumption that variables classified into the same group have a nonzero regression weight on a factor, this factor being the generic property of which the variables grouped together are multiple indicators. Our hypothesis is then expressed mathematically by the process of prescribing (i) the number, m, of common factors, which is the number of bases of classification we have listed on substantive grounds; and (ii) the elements in the $(n \times m)$ matrix of factor loadings that we would expect to be zero. That is, we state the number of factors, and we state which measures involve which factors. A convenient way to do this is to write zeros and numbers 1, 2, . . . to be thought of as subscripts of the parameters θ_1, θ_2, . . . in a matrix that represents the *design* of the factor pattern to be estimated. We shall call this hypothesis the hypothesis of *prescribed simple structure,* though the user may not necessarily place zeros in the matrix in a way that satisfies all five of the traditional criteria (Section 2.4).

We distinguish two forms of this hypothesis. In the first, we require the common factors to be uncorrelated. Following conventional usage we call this *prescribed orthogonal simple structure* (though it is the factors and not the *structure* to which the adjective *orthogonal,* meaning *uncorrelated,* applies). In the second, we allow the factors to be correlated. We call that case *prescribed oblique simple structure* (as the factors are "oblique," i.e., correlated).

The example of Table 2.2.2 is fitted in Table 3.2.1 with a prescribed orthogonal simple structure (actually, the special case of independent clusters— see Section 2.4). The fit is not very good, and the result is not very surprising, as the attempt is being made to explain correlations between cognitive tests, using uncorrelated primary mental abilities. This runs counter to the oldest finding of factor-analytic research, dating in a sense back to 1904, that tests of human cognitive performance all tend to be (positively) correlated and have a general factor—which we might call *general intelligence*—common to all of them without exception.

TABLE 3.2.1

Hypothesized Factor Pattern			ML Estimate			Unique Variance
1	0	0	.908			.176
2	0	0	.912			.169
3	0	0	.854			.270
0	4	0		.857		.265
0	5	0		.786		.382
0	6	0		.688		.527
0	0	7			.857	.265
0	0	8			.648	.581
0	0	9			.698	.513

Residual Matrix

.176						fill		
.000	.169					by		
.000	.000	.270				symmetry		
.439	.493	.460	.265					
.432	.464	.425	.000	.382				
.447	.489	.443	.000	.000	.527			
.447	.432	.401	.381	.402	.288	.265		
.541	.537	.534	.350	.367	.320	.000	.581	
.380	.358	.359	.424	.446	.325	.000	.000	.531

$$N = 213$$
$$\chi^2 = 216.4212$$
$$df = 27$$
$$p < .0005$$

The example under consideration rather obviously suggests that we could obtain good fit of the hypothesis of simple structure if we allow the factors to be correlated. Reasons are given in Chapter 6 for allowing factors to be correlated. Essentially, it comes down to the fact that regressions rather than correlations tend to be fundamental invariants of measures from one population to another. The prescribed oblique simple structure is fitted to the last example in Table 3.2.2. The parameters of the model are the nine free elements of the (9×3) factor pattern and the three correlations between the factors shown. The degrees of freedom are 24, compared with 12 for the exploratory analysis, and 27 for the orthogonal three-factor analysis that failed. The fit is borderline in terms of usual procedures for decision making, because we would reject the hypothesis at the 5% level, but it does seem reasonable to regard it as satisfactory, taking account of the sizes of the residual covariances. The difficulty with correlated independent variables is that we cannot with certainty untangle the contributions of the factors to the variance of each variable. Contrast the v–f regression weights (factor pattern) for this case, as given in Table 3.2.2(a), with the v–f correlations (factor structure) given in Table 3.2.2(d). We see that a variable with zero regression on a factor is nevertheless correlated with that factor. As remarked earlier, provided that the correlations between the factors are not too high and, consequently, the correlations of variables with "wrong" factors as in Table 3.2.2(d) are not too high, it seems reasonable enough in practice to treat the factors much as we would if they were uncorrelated.

TABLE 3.2.2

(a) ML Estimated
Factor Pattern

$$
\begin{bmatrix}
.905 & & \\
.914 & & \\
.856 & & \\
 & .836 & \\
 & .797 & \\
 & .703 & \\
 & & .781 \\
 & & .720 \\
 & & .703 \\
\end{bmatrix}
$$

(b) Correlations
of Factors

$$
\begin{bmatrix}
1.000 & .543 & .670 \\
.643 & 1.000 & .637 \\
.670 & .637 & 1.000 \\
\end{bmatrix}
$$

$$\chi^2 = 38,1963$$
$$df = 23$$
$$p = .033$$

(c) Residual Matrix

$$
\begin{bmatrix}
.181 & & & & & & & & \\
.001 & .165 & & & & & & & \\
.001 & -.003 & .267 & & & & & & \\
.047 & .002 & .000 & .301 & & & & & \\
.032 & -.004 & -.014 & .008 & .365 & & & & \\
.038 & .076 & .056 & .003 & -.019 & .507 & & & \\
-.026 & -.046 & -.047 & -.035 & .005 & -.062 & .391 & & \\
.104 & .096 & .121 & -.034 & .001 & -.022 & -.007 & .482 & \\
-.046 & -.073 & -.045 & .049 & .089 & .010 & .049 & -.055 & .506 \\
\end{bmatrix}
$$

fill
by
symmetry

$$
\begin{bmatrix}
.905 & .582 & .606 \\
.914 & .588 & .612 \\
.856 & .550 & .574 \\
.538 & .836 & .533 \\
.512 & .797 & .508 \\
.452 & .703 & .448 \\
.523 & .497 & .781 \\
.482 & .459 & .720 \\
.471 & .448 & .703 \\
\end{bmatrix}
$$

Contrast the example as treated in Table 3.2.2 with the typical exploratory treatment of it given in Tables 2.2.3 to 2.2.7 in which estimation, with no restrictions on individual factor loadings, has been followed by an attempt to transform the numbers in the estimated pattern to yield orthogonal simple structure. In the exploratory treatment, the model fits satisfactorily, with 12 degrees of freedom. If we follow recommendations in the informal "folklore" of factor-analytic practice, we would regard the numbers in the rotated factor pattern as a reasonable simple structure. In the confirmatory analysis, the model has 24 degrees of freedom, and it is almost as parsimonious as a model with just one factor (which would have 27). Further, it is unambiguously determined; that is, the nonzero factor loadings are identified and can be estimated uniquely. In this treatment, we take the concept of simple structure seriously and try to fit the model with zeros where the exploratory technique merely achieves "low" values. It is important to note also that the procedure was not guided by the exploratory analysis. It was based directly on an understanding of the nature of the variables.

In the exploratory approach, it might be claimed, we do not behave consistently. We first fit the model with many parameters and no constraint due to simple structure. We then transform the result to an equally fitting approximation to simple structure that may be very poor and speak as though we now have fewer parameters. But either the low numbers in the simple structure are consistent with exact zeros in the population or they are not. If they are, we should estimate only the nonzeros. If they are not, we do not in fact have simple structure at all.

Further, in the exploratory approach, the notion of parsimony is applied twice to the two steps involved in fitting the model. In the old tradition, we first "extract" factors in the hope of achieving a minimum number that will account for the correlations. We then transform the factor loadings with the hope that as many of these factors as possible will have a "negligible" influence on as many of the variables as possible. These two steps, based on particular notions of parsimony, can conflict with each other. In the confirmatory treatment, we decide the number of factors and the location of *exact* zeros on rational, substantive grounds. The notion of parsimony need not be invoked at all. Nevertheless, the results of our decisions will commonly be more parsimonious than the traditional results when we measure parsimony on the basis of the number of fitted parameters.

It should be clear, then, that we can break away from the tradition of exploratory analysis followed by transformation to approximate simple structure, at least in the final stage of a piece of research. Even in cases where we do not feel that we understand our measures well enough to prescribe the structure, it should be possible to use the exploratory methods in preliminary processing data only as ways to develop a detailed hypothesis that should be substantively convincing and not merely a patterning of numbers with little or no sense to it. Here we should have an interplay of research sense and the numerical information. Instead of accepting the approximate simple structure as it stands, we would modify it, choosing zeros versus nonzeros that tend to agree both with the exploratory output and our sense of what is reasonable. In fact, when a worker puts together measures to yield multivariate data, he or she usually has reasons for measuring just those things. Inability to formulate a detailed structural hypothesis with the aid of a technical adviser perhaps could be a sign that research aims were lacking in the first place. The attitude expressed in ''we appear to have these data—let's factor them and see what comes out'' is surely not one that should be encouraged. (Nor should we encourage the repeated analysis of a data set with variant confirmatory models until a good fit is found. This is hardly better than the mechanical application of exploratory methods.)

A further advantage of prescribed oblique structure over transformation to approximate it rests on the fact that we can also be prescriptive about the correlations between the factors. In Table 3.2.3, our example is refitted under the hypothesis that factor 2 and factor 3 are uncorrelated, whereas the other two correlations may be nonzero. This example is taken because it is convenient to introduce and not because it is suitable, but we can readily imagine situations where we might prescribe zero correlations between certain factors and nonzero correlations between others. Basically, the idea would be to ask whether the factors themselves (the generic properties indicated by groups of tests) have more general generic properties in common. Thus, just as verbal tests are correlated ''because they are indicators of verbal ability,'' we might say that *verbal ability* and *reasoning ability* are correlated because, at a higher level, they are indicators of *intelligence*. This remark leads us on naturally to the next type of case.

TABLE 3.2.3

Estimated Factor Pattern			Correlations of Factors		
0.7881	0.0	0.0	1.0000	0.4770	0.5742
0.7771	0.0	0.0	0.4770	1.0000	0.0
0.7174	0.0	0.0	0.5742	0.0	1.000
0.0	0.5838	0.0			
0.0	0.4943	0.0			
0.0	0.5383	0.0	x^2 = 68.9956		
0.0	0.0	0.5120	df = 25		
0.0	0.0	0.6043	p = 0.000		
0.0	0.0	0.3163			

(b) Higher-Order Factors

When we fit the oblique (correlated factors) model and have a matrix of correlations between the common factors, it seems natural to consider using the common factor model again to explain these correlations. From the first introduction of oblique simple structure, the possibility was recognized that we might fit *higher-order* factors (common generic properties *of* two or more given distinct generic properties) to the correlations between the factors. In principle, there can be more than one level to this process. If we call the correlated factors that explain the correlations of the observed variables, the first-order, or *primary* factors, we can explain the correlations between the primary factors by second-order factors, with oblique simple structure, whose correlations can be explained by third-order factors—and so on. Such a process could, in theory, go on until either the correlations between the highest-order factors reached are all zero; that is, we can have *orthogonal* simple structure, or until the number of higher-order factors is two or less so their correlations cannot be nontrivially explained by common factors.

Higher-order factoring has not been widely employed. Those who have used it have generally done an exploratory factor analysis by one of the traditional approximate methods, followed by transformation to approximate oblique simple structure, then a repeat of this analysis operating on the correlation matrix of the first-order factors. The properties of such crude estimates from sample correlation matrices are not known. We no longer need such multistage procedures, except perhaps for preliminary exploration to guide the development of a rational and numerically possible hypothesis, (i.e., one that both makes sense and is more or less indicated by the exploratory analysis).

Table 3.2.4 gives a reanalysis of the example we have been using throughout this section into three first-order factors (yes, verbal ability, word fluency, and reasoning) and one second-order factor, which we might be tempted to call intelligence.

Historically, in the 1930s there was a fierce controversy between advocates of oblique simple structure and advocates of the notion of a general factor (i.e., one on which all the variables have nonzero regressions) in the field of cognition. To Spearman and his followers, the advocates of *general intelligence,* it seemed as though oblique simple structure had been introduced perversely and deliberately to avoid just such a factor. To some, a grand reconciliation of views could be found in the reemergence of general intelligence, explaining the correlations among the first-order factors of cognition, the *primary mental abilities,* offered in Thurstone's work. McNemar[2] reviews a great deal of follow-up test development from primary mental ability work on the one hand and general intelligence work on the other and finds reasons to regard the general factor of intelligence as

---

[2]See McNemar (1964).

TABLE 3.2.4

First-Order Factor Pattern			Second-Order Factor Pattern
0.7105	0.0	0.0	1.0465
0.7176	0.0	0.0	0.9234
0.6723	0.0	0.0	0.9532
0.0	0.7066	0.0	
0.0	0.6749	0.0	
0.0	0.5948	0.0	
0.0	0.0	0.6677	$\chi^2 = 17.476$
0.0	0.0	0.6157	df = 21
0.0	0.0	0.6016	p = 0.682

Residual Matrix

0.0001								
0.0014	0.0001							
0.0016	-0.0032	0.0000						
-0.0468	0.0023	0.0003	0.0000					
-0.0313	-0.0040	-0.0134	0.0078	0.0002				
0.0387	0.0766	0.0566	0.0029	-0.0189	0.0001			
-0.0261	-0.0459	-0.0467	-0.0348	0.0054	-0.0615	0.0001		
0.1074	0.0963	0.1211	-0.0355	0.0012	-0.0023	-0.0071	0.0002	
-0.0463	-0.0726	-0.0444	0.0493	0.0887	0.0101	0.0488	-0.0545	0.0002

a more effective measure than the primary mental abilities. Broadly, we can expect problems in matching up the work of different investigators (see Chapter 6). One source of disagreement that can be turned into agreement by higher-order factoring is just this kind of case where one investigator uses tests at one level of generic similarity; whereas another uses tests at a more general or more specific level of generic similarity so that one worker's variables approximate the other researcher's factors, at some order, or one set of primary factors approximates another set of higher-order factors.

(c) Hierarchical Solutions

One way to treat the situation just discussed, where we choose to have or to avoid a general factor, is illustrated in Table 3.2.5. Here we have deliberately chosen to expect four uncorrelated factors, of which the first is allowed to be general and the other three are group factors (explaining correlations of groups of variables but not the entire set) in independent clusters. We can think of this as the representation by factors at just one order, of general and more specific bases of classification. Table 3.2.6(a) represents a more complex hypothesis of the kind in which a general factor is supplemented by two group factors, each of which is supplemented by further group factors in independent clusters. Each variable can be characterized by the general factor (i.e., the generic property of which they are all indicators) plus a choice of two group factors (i.e., one of two further mutually exclusive generic properties of which each variable is an indicator) plus a further group factor chosen out of a set *within* the preceding group, and so on.

TABLE 3.2.5

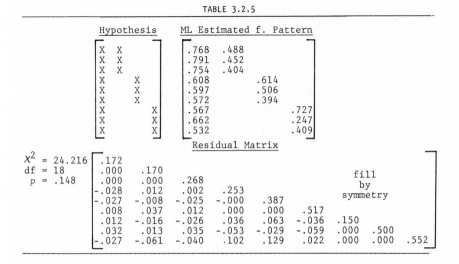

	Hypothesis			ML Estimated f. Pattern		
	X	X		.768	.488	
	X	X		.791	.452	
	X	X		.754	.404	
	X		X	.608		.614
	X		X	.597		.506
	X		X	.572		.394
	X		X	.567			.727
	X		X	.662			.247
	X		X	.532			.409

Residual Matrix

x^2 = 24.216
df = 18
p = .148

.172								
.000	.170							
.000	.000	.268						
-.028	.012	.002	.253					
-.027	-.008	-.025	-.000	.387				
.008	.037	.012	.000	.000	.517			
.012	-.016	-.026	.036	.063	-.036	.150		
.032	.013	.035	-.053	-.029	-.059	.000	.500	
-.027	-.061	-.040	.102	.129	.022	.000	.000	.552

fill
by
symmetry

TABLE 3.2.6

(a) Factor Pattern

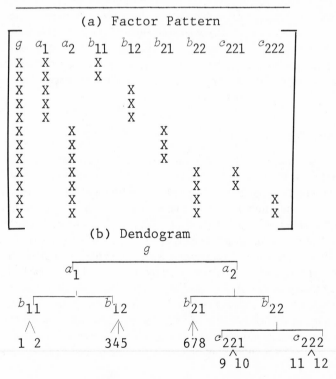

g	a_1	a_2	b_{11}	b_{12}	b_{21}	b_{22}	c_{221}	c_{222}
X	X		X					
X	X		X					
X	X			X				
X	X			X				
X	X			X				
X		X			X			
X		X			X			
X		X			X			
X		X				X	X	
X		X				X	X	
X		X				X		X
X		X				X		X

(b) Dendogram

This represents a hierarchical classification, which can alternatively be represented in an obvious way by the tree diagram—dendrogram—as used by taxonomists in Table 3.2.6(b). Both representations indicate the same thing, essentially that each variable can be classified as measuring several generic properties of different orders of generality. Variable 12 measures four properties (viz., g, a_2, b_{22}, and c_{222}, i.e., the general property and the second property of each level of classification). (There could be more than two properties at any level of classification, of course.) Variable 1 measures three properties (viz., g, a_1, and b_{11}, i.e., the general property and the first property at two of the other levels of classification). We note that the model, in traditional terms, aims to explain the correlations of twelve variables by nine factors. If we were proceeding in the traditional exploratory mode, we would never "discover" this description. In terms of exploratory analysis, there would be far too many factors, the degrees of freedom by (2.2.3) would be negative, and the fit in general would be perfect but useless because the hypothesis does not constrain the data. But the specification of the model in Table 3.2.6(a) includes many zeros, and the degrees of freedom for the detailed hypothesis are 38 yielding testability. Thus we notice by example that many interesting and testable hypotheses about correlation (covariance) matrices could never emerge and present themselves to our attention a posteriori if we use blind exploratory analysis with blind transformation to a possibly poor approximation to simple structure. The likely source of such hypotheses would be a facet analysis (i.e., a substantive content analysis) of our variables that suggests a tree such as that of Table 3.2.6(b) rather than a simple classification of the type that we call *simple structure*. Factor analysts have been criticized justly for their adherence to the assumptions inherent in the exploratory approach. These criticisms do not apply to the modern confirmatory treatment.

3.3. PATTERN HYPOTHESES AND PARALLEL TESTS

Among the hypotheses of this section, we could properly reconsider those already dealt with in Section 1.4. The hypotheses that all correlations are zero in a population or that all correlations between distinct sets of variables are zero are obvious special cases of structural hypotheses that constrain the elements of the correlation matrix.

A *hypothesis of pattern* for a correlation or covariance matrix consists in the assertion that one or more correlations or covariances are zero, or groups of two or more covariances or variances are equal. This includes the hypotheses that all the correlations are zero or that correlations between distinct groups of variables are zero, but we could also be postulating complicated hypotheses like that illustrated in Table 3.3.1. In Table 3.3.2, we set up and test a hypothesis of pattern, for our much analyzed correlation matrix from Table 2.2.2. In effect, we are postulating that the three verbal tests, the three word fluency tests, and the

TABLE 3.3.1
A Complex Pattern Hypothesis

Hypothesis:

$$R = \begin{bmatrix} 1 & \theta_1 & \theta_1 & 0 & 0 \\ \theta_1 & 1 & \theta_1 & \theta_2 & 0 \\ \theta_1 & \theta_1 & 1 & \theta_2 & \theta_2 \\ 0 & \theta_2 & \theta_2 & 1 & \theta_2 \\ 0 & 0 & \theta_2 & 0 & 1 \end{bmatrix}$$

three reasoning tests are interchangeable in all their relationships with each other. It is as though we declare that each measure of each ability measures the ability equally well and is equally related to the other abilities.[3]

A set of measures that have equal variances, equal covariances with each other, and equal covariances with all the other measures we might relate them to are known as *parallel measures*. In the context of true-score theory for mental tests where the concept originates, they are known as *parallel tests*. (This is not actually the definition, but it suits the purpose here to pretend that it is. It is a consequence of the definition and could reasonably be used as an alternative definition.) Clearly, we can never show that a set of measures are parallel, because to do this we would have to correlate them with every other measure in what we might call the *universal behavior domain* (the domain of all measurables). But evidence such as that in Table 3.3.2, if applied to the covariance matrix, would allow us to reject the hypothesis that we have three groups of parallel tests or to regard it as tenable in the context of the actual groups of measurements used. Interestingly, the hypothesis gives an acceptable fit to our data.

A necessary but not sufficient condition for parallel measures is the requirement that all the correlations within the set of measures be equal to a common value. The false impression can be gained that this condition is also sufficient and that we can regard a set of measures as equivalent and interchangeable if all their within-set correlations are the same.

The relationship between common factor theory and true-score theory is an interesting one. In Spearman's very earliest treatment of common factor theory,

---

[3]It is not strictly correct to apply this analysis to the sample correlation matrix. The covariance matrix should be used, for a valid test of significance.

TABLE 3.3.2

(a) Hypothesis for Matrix from Table 2.2.2

$$\begin{bmatrix} \theta_1 & \theta_2 & \theta_2 & \theta_7 & \theta_7 & \theta_7 & \theta_8 & \theta_8 & \theta_8 \\ \theta_2 & \theta_1 & \theta_2 & \theta_7 & \theta_7 & \theta_7 & \theta_8 & \theta_8 & \theta_8 \\ \theta_2 & \theta_2 & \theta_1 & \theta_7 & \theta_7 & \theta_7 & \theta_8 & \theta_8 & \theta_8 \\ \theta_7 & \theta_7 & \theta_7 & \theta_3 & \theta_4 & \theta_4 & \theta_9 & \theta_9 & \theta_9 \\ \theta_7 & \theta_7 & \theta_7 & \theta_4 & \theta_3 & \theta_4 & \theta_9 & \theta_9 & \theta_9 \\ \theta_7 & \theta_7 & \theta_7 & \theta_4 & \theta_4 & \theta_3 & \theta_9 & \theta_9 & \theta_9 \\ \theta_8 & \theta_8 & \theta_8 & \theta_9 & \theta_9 & \theta_9 & \theta_5 & \theta_6 & \theta_6 \\ \theta_8 & \theta_8 & \theta_8 & \theta_9 & \theta_9 & \theta_9 & \theta_6 & \theta_5 & \theta_6 \\ \theta_8 & \theta_8 & \theta_8 & \theta_9 & \theta_9 & \theta_9 & \theta_6 & \theta_6 & \theta_5 \end{bmatrix}$$

(b) Fitted ML Estimate

$$\begin{bmatrix} 1.000 & .794 & .794 & .455 & .455 & .455 & .443 & .443 & .443 \\ .794 & 1.000 & .794 & .455 & .455 & .455 & .443 & .443 & .443 \\ .794 & .794 & 1.000 & .455 & .455 & .455 & .443 & .443 & .443 \\ .455 & .455 & .455 & 1.000 & .602 & .602 & .367 & .367 & .367 \\ .445 & .445 & .445 & .602 & 1.000 & .602 & .367 & .367 & .367 \\ .445 & .445 & .445 & .602 & .602 & 1.000 & .367 & .367 & .367 \\ .443 & .443 & .443 & .367 & .367 & .367 & 1.000 & .535 & .535 \\ .443 & .443 & .443 & .367 & .367 & .367 & .535 & 1.000 & .535 \\ .443 & .443. & .443 & .367 & .367 & .367 & .535 & .535 & 1.000 \end{bmatrix}$$

$$\chi^2 = 54.238$$
$$df = 36$$
$$.1 > p > .05$$

the one general factor of the theory was regarded as a true score, and the residuals were regarded as errors of measurement. That is, alternative measures were thought of as having in common a true score and differing only by chance errors. He soon abandoned this view, and a careful distinction has been made ever since between factors specific to each measure that are part of its residual and mere errors of measurement that constitute the remainder of the residual. Yet the distinction between specific, nonerror variation and error variation is not always easy to make.

If we have a set of n measures, and we assume that they all measure a "true score" in common and differ by uncorrelated errors of measurement, it can be shown algebraically that their covariances must be all equal. Such a set of covariances can be explained "alternatively" by the assumption that they all indicate one common factor and differ by uncorrelated specific properties that they measure and that they have equal regression weights on the common factor. It is thus clear that the true-score-and-error explanation of such a matrix cannot be distinguished from the common-factor-and-specific-part explanation of it, at least on purely numerical grounds. Presumably we can ask, at least sometimes, if the measures are substantively equivalent as well as seeming so numerically. For example, if we found a vocabulary test, an arithmetic test, a music test, and so on, for which we could not reject the hypothesis that they had equal pairwise covariances, presumably we would reject the notion that they differ only by an error of measurement on substantive grounds. When we do indeed have a set of measures that appear to be equivalent so far as the evidence goes, it may yet be possible that any measure in the set can be embedded in another set of measures distinct from our first set that also behave like a set of equivalent measures but with a common value of their intercorrelation that might be higher or might be lower. The fact that we are able to find $n - 1$ "parallels" for a given test does not guarantee that we have succeeded in partitioning it into a true part and an error of measurement.

In many applications of factor analysis and of the structural hypotheses considered here, we would probably like to raise the question of a distinction between a generic/specific analysis of our measures and a true/error analysis of them. It is generally known that in most social science studies we cannot repeat measurements on subjects enough times to be able to assess errors of measurement in the fashion of physicists, say, because the process of measurement itself has all sorts of effects on the property measured. A cautious approach to the assessment of error in the context of parallel measures and other applications of structural hypotheses yielding residual variances about common factors is to regard these residual variances as giving upper limits to error variation. See Section 7.3 for further discussion.

3.4. MATHEMATICAL NOTES ON CHAPTER 3[3]

(a) Notes on Section 3.1

The general conception of the analysis of covariance structures is that each element c_{jk} of a covariance matrix $\mathbf{C}$ of order $(n \times n)$ can be written as a function

---

[3]To be omitted, unless it proves helpful.

General Note: Analyses such as those carried out in this chapter are usually performed by general-purpose programs for the analysis of covariance structures. Of these, the most widely distributed would be Jöreskog's LISREL series. A reference to this would rapidly become out of date, but most computer centers would recognize this identifier. The analyses in this book (this chapter and Chapter 6) were carried out on program COSAN, written by Colin Fraser to embody a general model by McDonald, discussed in Chapter 4. For further reading on confirmatory factor analysis, see Mulaik (1972).

$\phi_{jk}(\theta_1, \ldots, \theta_k)$ in k parameters that we may represent by the vector $\boldsymbol{\theta}' = [\theta_1, \ldots, \theta_k]$. The hypothesis is that

$$\mathbf{C} = \boldsymbol{\Phi}(\boldsymbol{\theta}) \tag{3.4.1}$$

where the $(n \times n)$ matrix

$$\boldsymbol{\Phi}(\boldsymbol{\theta}) = [\phi_{jk}(\theta_1, \ldots, \theta_k)]. \tag{3.4.2}$$

The expression given by Lawley for the special case of the unrestricted factor model, (2.6.7), can be rewritten here as

$$\lambda = N[\text{Tr} \{\mathbf{A}\mathbf{C}^{-1}\} - \log |\mathbf{A}\mathbf{C}^{-1}| - n] \tag{3.4.3}$$

the only difference being that we do not assume the variables to be in standard measure in the population. As in the special case, this quantity has its minimum at the point ($\boldsymbol{\theta} = \hat{\boldsymbol{\theta}}$, say) where the likelihood of our sample, under the given hypothesis, is a maximum and λ is distributed asymptotically like chi-square with, it may be supposed,

$$df = \tfrac{1}{2}n(n + 1) - k \tag{3.4.4}$$

(There are conditions under which this may not be true. Precise methods for determining degrees of freedom are known but not always convenient to implement.) Again, whether the observations have a normal distribution or not, the quantity λ is an essentially positive measure of "badness of fit."

(b) Notes on Section 3.2

We might take it that the model being employed in this section is the second-order factor model with zeros in prescribed locations in the matrices of the model. We could define this model by the equation

$$\mathbf{C} = \mathbf{F}_1(\mathbf{F}_2\mathbf{P}_2\mathbf{F}_2' + \mathbf{U}_2^2)\,\mathbf{F}_1' + \mathbf{U}_1^2 \tag{3.4.5}$$

where, in effect, we are decomposing the matrix of factor correlations, $\mathbf{P}$ in our usual notation, of order $(m \times m)$ into a second-order common factor specification

$$\mathbf{P} = \mathbf{F}_2\mathbf{P}_2\mathbf{F}_2' + \mathbf{U}_2^2 \tag{3.4.6}$$

where $\mathbf{F}_2$ is $(m \times m_2)$, say, $\mathbf{P}_2$, $(m_2 \times m_2)$, is the correlation matrix of second-order factors, and $\mathbf{U}_2^2$ is the $(m \times m)$ diagonal matrix of uniquenesses of the first-order factors. We expect to prescribe a number of the elements of $\mathbf{F}_1$ and $\mathbf{F}_2$ at least to be zero, and we may prescribe zeros for some correlations in $\mathbf{P}_2$. It is sufficient to describe such hypotheses by the traditional device illustrated in Table 3.2.5 of writing crosses where a parameter is to be estimated and blanks where we fix the quantity in question at zero. Care is needed on the part of the user to prescribe enough zeros, distributed through the matrices in such a manner that the parameters remaining to be estimated are identified, so that the estimates will be unique. Conditions at least as strong as Thurstone's criteria for simple structure would usually ensure this.

4 Models for Linear Structural Relations

4.1. CAUSAL RELATIONS AND CAUSAL MODELING

A major motive for the analysis of *linear structural relations* (linear relations between variables) is the desire to confirm hypotheses about *causal relations,* relations between causes and their effects. In the context of linear structural relations, discussion of causal modeling can tend to cut loose from its foundations in concepts of causal relations. It seems desirable to make at least a cursory examination of the problematic notion of a causal relation before we proceed to consider structural models for the causal analysis of multivariate data.

The notion of a causal relation is commonly employed in everyday life and in the social and biological sciences at least. It seems to be true that the notion has tended to be abandoned and is possibly not needed in certain parts of physics, and the notion is consciously avoided or used in a disguised form by those social scientists who have been persuaded that it is not a satisfactory scientific concept. For it must be admitted that the concept of a causal relation has been and remains a matter of controversy in the philosophy of science. We can take warning from Milton's fallen angels in Paradise Lost, who "reason'd high" on causality "and found no end, in wandring mazes lost."

Let us agree first that we do make statements of the type (a) (i) cigarette-smoking causes lung cancer (in humans), or (ii) (Mr. B.) contracted lung cancer because he smoked heavily; (b) (i) an increase in oil price at source causes an increase in gasoline price, and a decrease in consumption (in an oil-importing country), or (ii) the increase in gas price (in country A) at time T and decrease in consumption was caused by an increase in oil price by exporter W; (c) (i) drinking alcohol causes (drivers to have) road accidents, or (ii) the accident occurred because A was drunk; (d) (i) rain causes the use of protective coverings (by people), or (ii) rain caused Mr. A. to put up his umbrella; (e) (i) electroshock (applied to a human subject) causes a galvanic skin response, or (ii) electroshock (applied to A's hand) caused a galvanic skin response; (f) increasing the external pressure (on a bounded mass of gas) causes (its) volume to decrease.

Sceptical (positivist) philosophers of science have claimed that because all we ever observe empirically is regularity of succession of events, regularity of succession is all we can ever assert about them. We might take this argument as showing that a causal statement is not a statement of "observable fact," but it does not seem to prohibit us from postulating a causal relation in theory, if indeed we can clearly distinguish statements of fact from statements of theory. At least sometimes we hypothesize a process, a mechanism, a mode of action, whereby a cause is said to act upon a system to produce its effect, though perhaps the account is never as detailed or complete as we might wish and perhaps the intermediating process is no more than a set of further regularly occurring events. For example, we have at least a partial understanding of the carcinogenic action of cigarette smoke on lung tissue. In contrast, there have been remarkable achievements of folk medicine that surely rest on no more than fairly systematic observation. Consider for example the discovery that chewing cinchona bark (with its active ingredient quinine) prevents malaria. Presumably the original discoverers had little notion of a mechanism for the effect.

The notion introduced by the logical positivists that meaning is verification (i.e., that the meaning of any statement consists of the method or methods we would use to confirm it) has dominated methodology in the social sciences for the last several decades. However, the notion has been thoroughly discredited among professional philosophers for quite some time now, and we are not forced to take it seriously here.

We shall take the examples (a) through (f) to illustrate some general properties of causal statements.

First, it is indeed the case that we commonly make statements of the form C *(applied to S) causes E.* Because we make them, it is a reasonable presumption that we believe we understand them as being different from other statements about the relation between C and E. This belief could, of course, be universally mistaken. Yet at least we can hold the commonsense view that causal statements are reasonably offered and understood and that failure on the part of philosophers of science to give a universally acceptable analysis of causal statements is not in itself proof that they should not be made.

Second, causal statements commonly take either a general form, which constitutes an alleged law, as in version (i) of the examples, or a particular form, which constitutes an instance of the law, as in version (ii). We commonly "explain" the occurrence of a particular event by stating its cause, as when we say that A's accident was caused by his intake of alcohol. It is, however, a question requiring deep analysis whether explanation of a particular event by a particular cause is always founded on a more general causal law, making it of the same type as "*X* is *Y* because all *X*'s are *Y*'s," as in "Socrates is mortal because all men are mortal (and Socrates is a man)." For example, if we say that Napoleon's defeat at Waterloo was caused by such and such a strategic error, it may be hard to show that we imagine a more general causal law of which this is a supposed instance. At least we seem to require the particular instance to be justified by a general theory, as when we claim a general understanding (at least after the events) of the strategies by which battles have been, and will be, lost or won.

Third, in the specific instances the terms in the relation *C causes E* are particular *events,* occurrences, or happenings, in specifiable places and time intervals, and in the general laws they are classes of events (occurrences, happenings). Perhaps we avoid the circularity of dictionary definitions if we say that an event is a change of state of a part of the universe. It may be described qualitatively ("rain began," "electroshock was applied") or quantitatively ("the price of oil increased by five dollars per barrel on June 26, 1972").

Fourth, implicitly or explicitly a causal statement contains a reference to the entity upon which the causal event acts to produce its effect. In the examples, the entities (human beings, countries, drivers) have been put in parentheses both to identify them and to indicate that it is sometimes possible to rewrite these statements in their general form with the parenthetical references omitted. Yet typically the reference to a class of entities will be understood if the causal statement is clear. There seems to be no better word than *entity* for *that to which* the causal event is applied, but current fashions would probably dictate the word *system,* so we might agree to say that a causal statement is essentially of the form "event *C* acting on system *S* causes event *E*." Event *E* is a (short-term or long-term) change in a property or properties of a system or, a further consequence of changes in its properties, a response emitted by the system. This last distinction may not be of great importance, but if, for example, an experimental psychologist records lever presses in a Skinner box, he is observing changes in properties of the system if the system is a Skinner box with a rat in it and responses emitted by the system if the system is the rat itself. A distinction of a possibly more serious nature concerns the assignment of causal order to changes in distinct properties of a system—an economic community, a human subject, a country— possibly conceived of as a concatenation of interconnected subsystems.

Fifth, and the most problematic feature of a causal relation, it is asymmetric in the sense that "*C* causes *E* in *S*" does not imply and is not implied by "*E* causes *C* in *S*." It is certainly unlike a correlation, because "*X* is correlated with *Y*" implies and is implied by "*Y* is correlated with *X*." Rain causes Mr. *A* to put up his umbrella but Mr. *A*'s use of his umbrella does not cause rain. The attempt to characterize this easily recognized asymmetry, however, runs us into all sorts of philosophical difficulties. Here we can do no more than glance at them.

Attempts have been made to treat the causal relation as a relation of quasi-logical implication, to read "*C* causes *E*" as "*C* implies *E*." In the form "*E* occurred because *C* occurred" the ambiguous word *because* can seem to have the logical sense it has in "*p* is true because *q* is true." The trouble with this notion is that it leads immediately to the unwanted conclusion that "not-*E* causes not-*C*," because in logic "*p* implies *q*" is equivalent to "not-*q* implies not-*p*." Thus, we would have to say that Mr. A's not using his umbrella causes it not to rain.

Perhaps to avoid embarrassment in the face of arguments from sceptical philosophers of science against explicit causal statements, some writers have attempted to describe a causal relation as a functional relation between a dependent variable (replacing effect) and an independent variable (replacing cause). Because the function commonly can be inverted, that is, if we can write $y = f(x)$, then we can also write $x = g(y)$, this notion does not serve to distinguish a directed relationship from an undirected association of the values of two variables. It is true that many social scientists have learned to disguise intended causal statements in language of the type "*x* was chosen as the independent variable," "*x* was a factor in the determination of *y*," and the like. Example (f), the classical case of Boyle's law (pressure × volume = constant) offers a number of interpretations. In context, it asserts that the internal pressure and the volume of a given bounded mass of gas covary according to the law. This statement contains no causal assertion. Yet it implies that if the external pressure on the mass of gas is increased, the volume will decrease. This statement contains a causal direction, and its converse—if the volume is decreased, the external pressure increases—makes little sense. It also implies that if the external pressure is increased, the internal pressure of the mass of gas will increase to reach equilibrium with the external pressure and the volume will decrease. Here we have a cause with correlated effects. This last version begins to resemble example (b), in which an increase in external oil prices produces an increase in internal gas prices and a decrease in consumption in an economic system.

Attempts have also been made to base the notion of causal order on the notion of temporal order. This notion is built into the synonyms *antecedent* for cause and *consequent* for effect. The old Latin phrase, *post ergo propter* (after, therefore because), is badly stated. At most we can say "not-after, therefore not-because." That is, certainly we accept that a causal event cannot occur at a later time than its effect. In Lewis Carroll's *Through the Looking Glass,* time is imagined running in reverse, and the Red Queen cries out in pain because she is about to prick her finger with her needle. The absurdity of this imagined world seems to derive from the fact that between the onset of the pain and the pricking of the finger there is time to intervene and prevent the alleged causal event from occurring. Temporal order seems to be a secondary consequence of causal order, not a defining property. Further, merely establishing that *C* and *E* are correlated events and that *C* precedes *E* in time constitutes weak evidence for a direct or indirect causal relation between them, as they can be two effects of a common prior cause or two phases of a preset developmental sequence. Occasionally, too, we are prepared to assert a causal ordering of events that take place, to all appearances, simultaneously.

Yet another interpretation connects the notion of causal direction to a hypothetical, contrary-to-fact conditional statement. If we just say "it rains, and Mr.
A puts up his umbrella," this is a simple statement of "fact." It may seem that
we can convert it to a causal assertion just by adding the claim that "if it had not
rained, Mr. A would not have put up his umbrella." Here we do not intend to
convert a sufficient condition—Mr. A puts up his umbrella if it rains—to a
necessary and sufficient condition—Mr. A puts up his umbrella if and only if it
rains. This may be true, and it would assert a symmetric relationship—it rains if
and only if Mr. A puts up his umbrella. But we do not intend to be understood as
saying "if Mr. A had not put up his umbrella, it would not have rained." On the
contrary, it is precisely this that we would deny! The reader will easily translate
all the examples into the contrary-to-fact conditional form (e.g., if Mr. B had not
smoked, he would not have contracted lung cancer). The form of the contrary-to-
fact conditional statement implies a controlled experiment to test the stated
hypothesis wherever this is practical, and it does seem to capture a large part of
the meaning of a causal assertion. On the face of it, we thus avoid the symmetry
of "E occurs if C occurs and E does not occur if C does not occur," which can
be written symmetrically as "E occurs if C occurs and C occurs if E occurs."
For "E occurred and C occurred, but E would not have occurred if C had not
occurred" is not equivalent to "C occurred and E occurred, but C would not
have occurred if E had not occurred." It seems clear that "E does not occur if C
does not occur" differs from "E would not have occurred if C had not occurred"
and that the first of these statements represents an observable regularity of
association, whereas the second is in some sense hypothetical. Perhaps this is all
that can be said as a general distinction or perhaps it merely postpones the real
difficulty, because it appears hard to say in general what is captured in the
contrary-to-fact conditional statement beyond the fact of association.

This formulation of the causal relation might also seem open to the objection
that it still includes relations that we might not regard as causal. Suppose, for
example, that educational attainment is shown by purely correlational methods to
covary in the obvious way with amount of schooling and with a measure of
intelligence, which we shall for the moment pretend, for the sake of discussion,
is largely a stable, genetically based property of the examinees. We can easily
suppose, contrary to fact, that the same examinees could have been given more
or less schooling. But it is not obvious whether we can legitimately suppose,
contrary to fact, that the same examinees could have had their intelligence
altered. It might be claimed that we cannot, because by definition they would not
then be the same examinees. Thus, on this view, we must be careful to rule out
statements that might seem to be of the form "if event C had not occurred, event
E would not have occurred in S" but are actually of the form "if S had not had
the stable property C (and therefore, properly speaking, were not the given S), it
would not have had the property E." Perhaps the greatest danger in the causal
analysis of multivariate social science data is the danger of falling into this

confusion. A possible way to avoid it is to conceptualize causal events as imping-ing on a system from the outside, where *outside* can be literal in cases where the system is a person or a country both of which have clear boundaries separating inside and outside, or metaphorical yet clearly understandable in other cases, as where the system is a social class. It is as though the classical paradigm of all causal inquiry would be Newton's first law of motion, the statement that a body continues in a state of rest or uniform motion except when acted on by external, impressed force. The counterpart in causal analysis is the variable that is *exogenous* to (outside) the system.

We come close at this point to a paradigm for the causal relation given by a physicist, Campbell. Suppose we have an effectively isolated system S. If, whenever event C, outside S, is arbitrarily applied to it, event E takes place in S; and whenever event C is arbitrarily withheld from S, event E does not take place in S, then C is the cause of E. This conception is specialized, idealized, and open to the charge of circularity. We know that the system is effectively isolated from other causes, if it emits an effect only in response to C. Event C is applied arbitrarily if it is not applied as the consequence of some other prior causal event. In spite of such obvious defects, however, Campbell's paradigm seems close in intention to the way we conceptualize any supposed causal relation, and it actually describes the thought experiment or actual experiment by which we verify it. Rain is not random. It is meteorologically predictable, though still with regrettable uncertainty. But it functions as an arbitrary external event in relation to Mr. A's use of his umbrella. The decision to smoke or not smoke presumably has its personality correlates. Any uncertainty we might have as to the causal direction in the statistical association between smoking and lung cancer stems from considering an alternative hypothesis that some unidentified psycho-physiological correlate predestines both the decision to smoke and the later onset of lung cancer. Under this alternative hypothesis, cigarette smoke does not impinge arbitrarily on some lungs and not on others.

Although some types of causal relation do not seem to allow manipulation of causal events—it is easier to control Mr. A's umbrella than it is to control the rain—a very large class of such relations would allow human manipulation at least in principle. Intervention can help individuals stop smoking, drastic penal-ties may reduce drunk driving, international agreements can control oil prices, and so on. Where manipulation is possible, Campbell's paradigm can be convert-ed into the fully respectable experimental paradigm in which manipulation of C controls the occurrence of E in S. In an experiment we "replicate" S as a sample of S's, randomly assign them to C and to not-C, or to two or more levels of C, and usually compare the mean effects. Random assignment is certainly arbitrary. Commonly, individual differences in the properties of the systems we are using as "replicates" yield variability in the size of a measurable effect or some uncertainty as to the occurrence of a qualitative effect. In discussions of sophisti-cated causal models for multivariate data this elementary fact is sometimes neglected, and we are left with the impression that all statistical variability is due to external impressed *random shocks, disturbances,* or as yet unknown imping- ing causes and that the systems have no stable individual properties of their own.

The systems we study (countries, communities, human individuals) not only possess stable individual properties but they can also, for some purposes, be articulated into subsystems, so that an event taking place within a system can be thought of as taking place within one subsystem and impinging externally upon another subsystem. The subsystems may be obvious or may take quite subtle forms. An obvious case is the sequence from the oil-exporting country through the oil-importing company to the gas station to the consumer in example (b). In a contrasting case from the history of psychology, where we commonly say that "I" ran away because "I" was afraid, the extreme form of the classical James– Lange theory of emotion stated that "I" was afraid because "I" ran away, or, more precisely, fear in my "mind" was caused by the flight response in my "body." In the systems we study, recognizing the subsystems and their inter- connections might seem to be the major task of theory.

These remarks seem to lead us to the suggestion that in any particular attempt at causal modeling we can hope to have a particular theoretical understanding of the system, in terms of its properties and subsystems, so that we know which events are external to the system or its subsystems and which events are changes in properties of the system or its subsystems. If any of these changes can be described in turn as changes in a subsystem impinging externally on another subsystem and producing further effects, they are links in a causal chain or network in an obvious sense. In most cases, this implies a fairly detailed the- oretical understanding of the system under study, especially in the absence of experimental manipulation of causal variables. And we must be able to imagine the contrary-to-fact behavior of the same system in the absence of the causal event (or with a different value of the causal variable).

It is not claimed that a satisfactory account of causal statements has been offered here, but some of the main problems have been noted, and a possible perspective on them has been indicated. We begin now to focus more narrowly on our objective in this chapter, an account of linear structural models for multivariate data, partly motivated by notions of causal modeling.

Where both the causal event C and the effect E are measurable changes, we can describe C as a change ΔX in the value of a variable X and E as a change ΔY in the value of a variable Y. Obviously, the statement that a change ΔX in X causes a change ΔY in Y implies that the value of Y is causally dependent on the value of X (i.e., that the value of Y is at least in part determined by the value of X in a sense in which we do not therefore assert that the value of X is at least in part determined by the value of Y). For example, we say that price and demand for gasoline are dependent on oil prices in the oil-exporting country but not therefore conversely. Accordingly, in the context of linear relations between measurable variables, Blalock, for example, defines X as a direct cause of Y if, other things equal (except previous values of Y itself), a change in X produces a change in the conditional mean of Y.[1]

In the case where we can manipulate the values of X and randomly assign S's (Systems or, in particular, Subjects) to them, we can as a rule obtain a quantitative estimate of the effect of X by the use of classical analysis of variance designs. With the use of two or more levels of X chosen by the experimenter, and S's randomly assigned to each, the usual F test determines whether a change in X produces a significant change in the mean of Y. If a linear regression fits the data, the regression weight of Y on X literally gives the amount of change ΔY of Y resulting from a change ΔX in X. Unlike the correlation between Y and X or the ratio of the variance due to X to the total variance of Y (the squared correlation ratio), both of which are dependent on the experimenter's choice of the range of X, the regression weight (with X and Y not standardized) should, under reasonable conditions, be invariant under choices of the range of X. (See Chapter 6.) But most important is the fact that by random assignment of S's to the levels of X, the experimenter gets estimates of the effect of X, expressed in the regression weight (the mean change in Y divided by the corresponding change in X), unconfounded with the effects of any other causal variable whose uncontrolled variation might also cause changes in Y. Thus, suppose one experimenter postulates that a manipulable variable X_1 has an effect on variable Y and tests the relationship by random assignment of S's to a set of levels of X_1. Suppose then that a second experimenter postulates that in addition to variable X_1 a second manipulable variable X_2 has an effect on Y and combines both in an experiment. In the usual carefully designed analysis of variance, with balanced numbers of S's randomly assigned to the combinations of levels of X_1 and X_2, their main effects and interaction are uncorrelated (orthogonal). The important result is that the second experimenter should, under mild assumptions, confirm the first experimenter's conclusions about the effect of X, in particular obtaining the same value, within sampling error, of the rate of change of Y with X_1 and also perhaps finding a significant effect of X_2 and a significant interaction (multiplicative effect) of the two causal variables. Thus by experimental assignment of S's to levels of the causal variables, we can keep the effects of one, two, or more such variables unconfounded and therefore determine invariant regression slopes for each of them. This fact gives the experiment a second major advantage over mere observation of uncontrolled covariation of measures, beyond the primary advantage that we arbitrarily assign the values of the causal variables to the S's and thus eliminate possible effects of prior causes.

In contrast, whenever we study the rate of change of a dependent variable Y and a postulated causal variable X_1, on the basis of their uncontrolled covariation across a sample of S's, we cannot expect the obtained rate of change of Y with X_1 to remain invariant if we add other causal variables $X_2, X_3, \ldots$ to the analysis,

---

[1]See Blalock (1964).

because in general these will be correlated with X_1 and their effects accordingly confounded. That is, in general as we add correlated variables, all the regression weights will change. Indeed, the regression weight of Y on X_1 can change from positive and significant to zero or to negative and significant by the addition, at any stage, of just one further causal variable. Consequently, non experimental causal modeling has to rest upon the assumption that all causal variables, known or as yet unknown, that are omitted from a study are uncorrelated with all causal variables included in the study (whereas those we have happened to include may be mutually correlated). This is a very strong assumption, generally unlikely to be true, and it is untestable except in the sense that a given study can be tested for invariance of its parameters by a more comprehensive study that includes all its variables and more.

There are several distinct ways to describe the problem just noted. Suppose we know and study just two causal variables X_1, X_2 that have an effect on a variable Y. We suspect that there are other as yet unknown causal variables. We write the relation between Y and X_1, X_2 as

$$Y = p_{y1}X_1 + p_{y2}X_2 + d \tag{4.1.1}$$

where p_{y1}, p_{y2} are rates of change of Y with changes in X_1, X_2, respectively. In causal analysis, we wish to think of d, a random errorlike term in the determination of Y by the two known causes, as containing the effects of the as yet unknown causes. That is,

$$d = p_{y3}X_3 + p_{y4}X_4 + \cdots + \delta \tag{4.1.2}$$

where δ is a residual, after all causal variables have been accounted for. We then wish to think of the coefficients p_{y1}, p_{y2} as representing the rates of change of Y with X_1 and with X_2, respectively, in the context of these as yet unknown causes X_3, X_4, ... They are indeed regression weights in the complete, unknown causal specification

$$Y = p_{y1}X_1 + p_{y2}X_2 + p_{y3}X_3 + p_{y4}X_4 + \cdots + \delta \tag{4.1.3}$$

If we assume that X_3, X_4, . . . are each uncorrelated with X_1 and with X_2 (which may be correlated with each other), then d is uncorrelated with X_1 and X_2. Equation (4.1.1) can then be identified with the ordinary regression equation in just the two variables X_1, X_2, namely,

$$Y = \beta_{y1}X_1 + \beta_{y2}X_2 + e \tag{4.1.4}$$

in which the residual e is uncorrelated with the two independent variables by definition of the regression function. The conventional estimators of the regression coefficients β_{y1}, β_{y2} are then estimators of p_{y1}, p_{y2}, the first two terms in the "complete" causal model. If it is not true that the omitted causes X_3, X_4, . . . are each uncorrelated with X_1, X_2, then we can say, as before, that the regression weights in (4.1.4) are not invariant under the addition of one or more of the initially omitted variables. We can also say that the usual estimators of the regression weights in (4.1.4) are inconsistent (asymptotically biased) estimators of the coefficients in the complete causal model. That is, no matter how large the sample becomes, the estimates will converge on incorrect parameter values. The simplest way to say this, however, is to say that unless the omitted variables are uncorrelated with the included variables and hence the disturbance term d in (4.1.1) is uncorrelated with them, estimates of the regression coefficients on the included variables are not estimates of the *coefficients* p_{y1}, p_{y2}. And generally we do not then have a procedure for estimating these coefficients.

There are two main ways in which users of causal modeling wish to go beyond regression analysis. We have just considered the first way, namely the desire to obtain regression coefficients on one or more independent variables that would prove invariant under the addition of further independent variables, so that we may interpret them as measures of the strength of causal influence. The second is the desire to postulate and, in some sense confirm, causal sequences or chains of three or more members of a set of covarying measures on a population of S's. That is, instead of having one or more dependent variables causally dependent on one or more independent variables, we may have intermediate variables that are dependent with respect to certain variables and independent with respect to certain other variables.

Thus, in example (b), writing X_e for the export price of oil, X_i for its import price, X_g for the price of gasoline at the pump, and X_c for consumption of gasoline by motorists, we imagine a pure causal chain in which

$$X_i = p_{ie}X_e + d_i$$
$$X_g = p_{gi}X_i + d_g$$
$$X_c = p_{cg}X_g + d_c \tag{4.1.5}$$

with obvious notation. Here we suppose that the oil-export price affects gas price only through the oil-import price, and in turn the oil-import price affects gas consumption only through the retail price of gas. This will seem reasonable enough, and the example serves to show that plausible causal sequences, beyond the ordering of two variables, can sometimes be postulated. In the terminology adopted in causal modeling, originally introduced by economists, the oil-export price is an *exogenous* variable (literally *outside* the economic system under study). The other variables are *endogenous* (inside the system) and of these only consumption is a pure dependent variable, whereas oil-import price and retail gas price function both as dependent and independent variables. It may seem desirable to imagine the system as articulated into subsystems, consisting of the oil companies, the gas stations, and the consumers, so that each variable in turn is exogenous with respect to the next subsystem.

In formulating the simple chain model (4.1.5) we are rejecting as implausible a more general model in which we might have

$$X_i = p_{ie}X_e + d_i$$
$$X_g = p_{gi}X_i + p_{ge}X_e + d_g$$
$$X_c = p_{cg}X_g + p_{ci}X_i + p_{ce}X_e + d_c \qquad (4.1.6)$$

That is, in (4.1.5) we chose not to suppose that oil-export price has a direct effect on gas price, which in contrast is included in (4.1.6) as $p_{ge}X_c$, or that oil-export price and oil-import price have direct effects on consumption effects, which are included in (4.1.6) as $p_{ci}X_i + p_{ce}X_e$.

Both sets of equations (4.1.5) and (4.1.6) are examples of a recursive causal model. The model is recursive in the sense that the paths of causal influence run back (*re-* = back, *cursum* = run) in a single direction from the dependent variable to the exogenous variable. There is no circuit whereby variations in one variable cause variations in another and also conversely. If we suppose that a drop in consumption causes a drop in oil-export prices and add to (4.1.5) the equation

$$X_e = p_{ec}X_c + d_e \qquad (4.1.7)$$

we close a causal circuit and introduce a *nonrecursive* model in which the paths of causal influence do not run in just a single direction. In this version of the model, negative feedback (a drop in consumption following a rise in gas price) drops the oil-export price and acts to stabilize it, so a stable system of reciprocal causation may result. A good example of an unstable system of reciprocal causation based on positive feedback would be an arms race, in which each side increases its arsenal in response to an increase in the other's arsenal (perhaps in order to negotiate arms reduction "from strength").

The set of equations (4.1.6) illustrates the *fully recursive* model, an important general case in causal modeling, in which all the variables are placed in a postulated causal order, and it is supposed that each variable is directly influenced by all variables preceding it. That is, every coefficient in (4.1.6) is permitted to be nonzero. If any of these causal links were omitted, the model would be recursive but not fully recursive.

In one terminology, causal analysis is known as *path analysis,* due originally to a biologist, Sewell Wright, and the coefficients p_{jk} represented in equations (4.1.5) and (4.1.6) are known as *path coefficients,* measuring the strength associated with each path by which one variable influences another. It has been traditional to provide a *path diagram,* a graphical representation of a postulated set of relationships in a path-analysis model. In it, a set of variables $X_1, \ldots, X_n$ is represented by a corresponding set of symbols, usually a square for an observable or manifest variable and a circle for an unobservable or latent variable arranged in a two-dimensional space, and every nonzero path coefficient p_{jk} indicating causal dependence of X_j on X_k is represented by a *directed path*, a line from X_k to X_j with an arrowhead indicating that the direction of causal action is from X_k to X_j. Because not all relationships between the variables are necessarily explained by the causal model, we may also add *undirected paths*, connecting lines (usually curved) with arrowheads at both ends, to indicate any nonzero residual covariances expected after fitting the model. Unfortunately, nothing in the causal models dictates the arrangement in the diagram of the symbols representing the variables. This arrangement is an arbitrary choice on the part of the person drawing the path diagram, and it often seems to depend on aesthetic considerations. For example, model (4.1.5) can be represented by Fig. 4.1.1(a), (b), or (c) and model (4.1.6) can be represented by Fig. 4.1.2(a), (b), or (c), as well as in other ways. Of these, versions 4.1.1(a) and 4.1.2(a) seem most intelligible. We can see immediately that the models are indeed recursive, that literally all the relationships go in one direction. However, aesthetic considerations might tend to rule out this choice in favor of alternatives in which not even the recursive property is visually compelling. However, those whose topological ability is strong enough to override their conventional visual response may find path diagrams useful.

The basic assumption of causal modeling, as we have seen, is that the disturbance term (perhaps representing omitted causal variables) in a causal equation is uncorrelated with the causal variables included in that equation. In a recursive model this takes the form of an assumption that the disturbance component of each variable is uncorrelated with all preceding causal variables. In both (4.1.5) and (4.1.6), for example, writing $\rho(x, y)$ for the correlation between x and y, we assume that

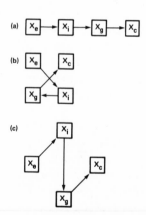

FIG. 4.1.1. Path diagrams for chain model.

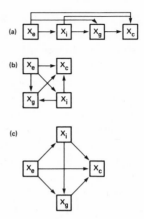

FIG. 4.1.2.   Path diagrams for fully recursive model.

$$\rho(d_i, x_e) = 0$$

$$\rho(d_g, x_i) = \rho(d_g, x_e) = 0 \tag{4.1.8}$$

$$\rho(d_c, x_g) = \rho(d_g, x_i) = \rho(d_c, x_e) = 0$$

[But we do not assume, for example, that $\rho(d_i, x_i) = 0$, which in fact is mathematically impossible.)

Under assumptions such as these the traditional treatment of the estimation of sets of recursive causal equations such as (4.1.5) or (4.1.6) has been the obvious one, namely to fit each equation separately by the standard least-squares procedure for fitting the regression of one dependent variable on one or more independent variables. (This supposes that all the variables in the set are observable. Later we consider cases where some of them are unobservable or *latent variables,* being common factors or true scores.)

Once the set has been fitted, the question then arises of confirming the postulated structure. It turns out that a fully recursive model such as (4.1.6) is unrestrictive in the sense that it is perfectly consistent with any set of variables, whatever values their covariances and variances might take and whatever causal ordering we might propose for them. In this respect it is very like a common factor model with as many common factors as tests. Restrictive, hence falsifiable, models are obtainable by postulating that one or more paths of causal influence are absent [i.e., that one or more of the coefficients p_{jk} in (4.1.6) are zero].

Corresponding to the piecemeal method of fitting a recursive model by fitting the individual regression functions, we can test for the existence of all postulated paths by applying the conventional t-test to each estimated (unstandardized) regression coefficient and by showing that it departs significantly from zero at our preferred level of significance. (And perhaps we should make an adjustment to this level to allow for the fact that we are repeatedly applying the t-test to a number of regression weights.) Failure of a regression coefficient to be significant is failure to justify a postulated path at the available sample size. Conversely, if we deliberately fit an alternative model, estimating path coefficients as possibly nonzero that we originally hypothesized to be zero, we confirm our hypothesis about these by establishing that the corresponding estimated regression weights are nonsignificant at the available sample size. The same situation arises here as in the common factor model, that we wish to declare that a restrictive hypothesis gives a reasonable approximation to the data even if, for a large enough sample size, we would be forced to reject it on statistical criteria. The traditional approach to this problem is to use the model equations to obtain mathematical expressions for the expected covariances (correlations) of the observed variables as functions of the restricted set of path coefficients, just as we derive expressions for the correlations as functions of the common factor loadings (and factor correlations) when working with the common factor model. In a very similar way, restrictions in the form of omitted paths create restrictions on the correlations of the variables. For example, in the simple chain model of equation (4.1.5), with all variables standardized, we find that the six correlations between X_e, X_i, X_g, and X_c are given by

$$\rho(X_e, X_i) = p_{ie}$$

$$\rho(X_e, X_g) = p_{gi}p_{ie}$$

$$\rho(X_e, X_c) = p_{cg}p_{gi}p_{ie}$$

$$\rho(X_i, X_g) = p_{gi} \qquad\qquad\qquad (4.1.9)$$

$$\rho(X_i, X_c) = p_{cg}p_{gi}$$

$$\rho(X_g, X_c) = p_{cg}$$

That is, the six correlations are all functions of the three path coefficients. This is a restrictive law of formation that recalls the parsimony of the Spearman case (Section 1.5), though not closely resembling it in mathematical form. After obtaining estimates of the path coefficients by least-squares estimation of each equation separately, we can calculate the correlations reproduced from (4.1.9), subtract these from the given sample correlations, and decide whether or not the residuals are satisfactorily small. The general process of obtaining expressions for the correlations, such as in (4.1.9), as expressions in the nonzero path coefficients involves straightforward but tedious algebra when approached in a piecemeal fashion as an exercise based on particular sets of causal equations. We can regard it as superseded by general treatments of the analysis of covariance structures such as the general model described in Section 4.2. The piecemeal estimation of separate regression equations has the general defects that it fails to make use of all the information contained in the covariance (correlation) matrix of the variables, and it is unusable if the model is nonrecursive or if any of the variables are unobservable.

Actually, it is questionable whether causal models in which all the variables are observable can ever give a satisfactory fit to empirical data. Just as we cannot in practice expect to find observable variables that behave like common factors (i.e., we cannot find observable variables which, if partialled out, reduce the correlations of other variables to zero), so we cannot in practice expect to find observable variables that behave like links in a causal chain. This is because in practice measurements in social science data are subject to nonnegligible errors. It is easy to show that if we were able to measure quantities such as X_e, X_i, X_g, and X_c in the model (4.1.5) without any error and the true measures behaved according to the model, then the corresponding quantities including their errors of measurement would not do so. That is, if the true parts of the variables obey the restrictive law (4.1.9), the observed variables will not obey the law and can at best only approximate it. Given reliabilities of the four measures, we can use formulas from classical test theory to correct the correlations for attenuation by error (i.e., to estimate the correlations between their true parts). However, it is usually not necessary to resort to such procedures, because with the multiple measures of the variables in a causal model that would be necessary to estimate the errors of measurement in each we can use a general model for the analysis of linear structural relations to fit a causal model with unobservable variables to the multiple measures, using all the information in their covariance (correlation) matrix simultaneously.

A simple and very general model developed by McArdle is described in Section 4.2. McArdle's model looks as though it was designed just for the path analysis or causal analysis of a set of variables containing both observables and unobservables (true scores, common factors). It turns out that it also contains, as special cases, many models for the analysis of linear structural relations between variables that would not have been conceived of originally in terms of path analysis. Accordingly, an attempt will be made to convey an impression of the range of possibilities encompassed by the model as well as its applicability to causal modeling as outlined in this section.

4.2. MCARDLE'S MODEL FOR LINEAR STRUCTURAL RELATIONS

Very general models for linear structural relations have been obtained by combining concepts from confirmatory factor analysis as described in Chapter 3 with concepts from path analysis as described in Section 4.1. Probably the best known of these models is the LISREL model, which was introduced by Keesling and Wiley and developed for practical use by Jöreskog. A very complex model, COSAN, misleadingly titled "a simple comprehensive model for the analysis of covariance structures" has been developed by McDonald. McArdle has found an extremely simple formulation of a path-analytic model, the *reticular action model* (where *reticular* = network) that contains apparently much more complex models, such as LISREL and COSAN as in a sense special cases. The reticular action model (RAM) is easy to describe and can be used to introduce the other models in a simple fashion.

A RAM model is specified by three steps. (1) We write down a complete set of regression equations, in which every variable, observable or unobservable, dependent, intermediate or exogenous, is regressed on all the variables. (2) We specify the pattern of the residual covariance matrix of all the variables. That is, we specify which residuals are restricted to have zero covariances and which have possibly nonzero covariances. (3) We label each of the variables as directly measured, observable, *manifest* variables or as unobservable, *latent* variables.

Fitting the RAM model can be achieved by the use of existing computer programs for the analysis of covariance structures, such as the LISREL series or COSAN. Let n be the total number of variables, manifest or latent; let m be the number of manifest variables; and let l be the number of latent variables. (Of course, $n = l + m$). The system of n regression equations of the n variables on the n variables can be solved to express the variables as n linear combinations of the residuals. (If the system is recursive, this is always possible. In some non-recursive models the system of equations may not be capable of being solved as required.) Once we have the variables as linear functions of the residuals, their covariances (correlations) can be expressed as functions of the residual covariances, and we can select out of these the submatrix of covariances (correlations) of observed variables. We thus have a specification, usually chosen to be restrictive, of the structure of the covariance matrix of the manifest variables as a function of the nonzero regression weights and the nonzero residual covariances of all the variables, manifest or latent. A not infallible guide to determine whether or not the model is restrictive is to count the number of parameters to be estimated in the regression weight matrix and the residual covariance matrix and subtract it from $m(m + 1)/2$, the number of variances and covariances (allowing for symmetry) in the covariance matrix of the manifest variables. If the resulting difference, d, is positive, the model is restrictive, with d df for a test of significance of the hypothesis under the usual assumptions of multivariate normality. If d is zero, there are just as many "knowns" as "unknowns," and we expect the model to fit any data set exactly. If d is negative, there are too many unknowns, and the model can fit any data set exactly and not even yield unique values of the fitted parameters. It has been the custom in econometric theory to refer to these cases as *overidentified,* when there are fewer parameters than variances and covariances from which to determine them, as *just identified* when "knowns" equal "unknowns" in number, and as *underidentified* when there are too many parameters and they are not uniquely determined by the variances and covariances. This rule of determining whether the model is restrictive and the parameters are identified, uniquely estimable quantities can fail us. It fails (see following) in a model that contains a multiple factor model as part of its structure if we do not fix enough zeros, suitably placed, to prevent rotation. It also fails, in a manner too technical to describe here, at special singular values of the parameters (usually when one or more of them is in fact zero) that we could regard as degenerate cases. Given a restrictive model, with positive degrees of freedom, the misfit of the model to a sample covariance or correlation matrix can be minimized in the usual way, with the use of a computer program to minimize the appropriate functions to yield least-squares or maximum likelihood estimates of the parameters.

These steps are now described and illustrated in some detail. Generally we shall label the variables $v_1, v_2, \ldots, v_n$. If the model is recursive, it is desirable to list the variables in an order that corresponds to the postulated sequence. If it is nonrecursive, as a rule there will still be a main recursive sequence with just one or two closed causal loops, so again the variables should be ordered so as to correspond with the main recursive sequence. For example, we would write a fully recursive model in four variables as

$$
\begin{aligned}
v_1 &= & + e_1 \\
v_2 &= p_{21}v_1 & + e_2 \\
v_3 &= p_{31}v_1 + p_{32}v_2 & + e_3 \\
v_4 &= p_{41}v_1 + p_{42}v_2 + p_{43}v_3 & + e_4
\end{aligned}
\tag{4.2.1}
$$

Terms with fixed zero coefficients are omitted. Notice that we do not regress a variable upon itself (i.e., there are no terms of the type p_{jj}). Notice also that the exogenous variable v_1 is included in the set of regression equations, but because it has no nonzero regression coefficients in its regression on the other variables, it is identical with its own residual. As pointed out earlier, the model (4.2.1) is nonrestrictive and can always be fitted to any data set. To obtain a restrictive model we would fix one or more additional coefficients in (4.2.1) to be zero.

If on the other hand we allow the model to have a closed loop, in which variable v_1 is in turn regressed on variable v_4 [as in the oil-price example when we turn a causal chain into a closed loop by adding (4.1.7) to (4.1.5)], we modify the system (4.2.1) by adding a further term and obtain

$$
\begin{aligned}
v_1 &= & p_{14}v_4 + e_1 \\
v_2 &= p_{21}v_1 & + e_2
\end{aligned}
$$

$$
\tag{4.2.2}
$$

$$v_3 = p_{31}v_1 + p_{32}v_2 \qquad\qquad\qquad\qquad\qquad + e_3$$
$$v_4 = p_{41}v_1 + p_{42}v_2 + p_{43}v_3 \qquad\qquad\qquad + e_4$$

(This example is then underidentified, with too many unknown parameters to be determined from the variances and covariances.)

To complete the specification of a model such as (4.2.1), we need two more steps. First we need to indicate which residual covariances are fixed zeros and which are possibly nonzero parameters to be estimated. In the case of the fully recursive model (4.2.1), by the classical assumption of causal modeling that each residual is a disturbance, uncorrelated with prior causal variables, we must assume that the four residuals are mutually uncorrelated.

To simplify the presentation of the models, we adopt a convention like the one employed in confirmatory factor analysis for describing a simple structure (Section 2.4). We draw up an $n \times n$ matrix, with the subscripts of the variables labeling both rows and columns. We enter a cross at the point of intersection corresponding to a nonzero regression weight of a row variable on a column variable, and we leave it blank if it is a fixed zero. Thus, the models (4.2.1) and (4.2.2) would be represented as in Table 4.2.1.

We note that in the case of (4.2.1) all the nonzero regression weights are in the lower triangle of the matrix, lying below the blank diagonal. This contrasts

TABLE 4.2.1

(a) Regression Weight Pattern
of Fully Recursive Model

	1	2	3	4
1				
2	X			
3	X	X		
4	X	X	X	

(b) Regression Weight Pattern
of Chain Model

	1	2	3	4
1				
2	X			
3		X		
4			X	

TABLE 4.2.2
Regression Weight Pattern of
Fully Recursive Model, Reordered

	2	1	4	3
2		X		
1				
4	X	X		X
3	X	X		

with the case of (4.2.2), and indeed in the latter case we cannot find a different order of the variables in which all the crosses lie in the lower triangle. This is the basic test whether a model is recursive, containing no paths of reciprocal causation, or whether it is nonrecursive, with closed "feedback" loops. It is recursive if we can put the variables in an order such that all the nonzero regression weights lie below the diagonal of the regression weight matrix. Otherwise it is nonrecursive. But we have to find the right order. For example, (4.2.1) can be represented as in Table 4.2.2. In this form it is not lower triangular. If we invent a very complex model by drawing a path diagram, it may take a little trial and error to get the variables in the right order to prove or disprove recursiveness, but as a rule the right order will suggest itself readily enough.

We shall represent the pattern of the residual covariance matrix in the same way as the regression matrix, recognizing that it will always be symmetric, with a cross in the (k, j)th position if there is one in the (j, k)th position and conversely. Thus, the residual covariance matrix of (4.2.1) can be represented by Table 4.2.3.

TABLE 4.2.3
Residual Pattern of
Fully Recursive Model

	1	2	3	4
1	X			
2		X		
3			X	
4				X

As we examine a series of specialized models, general principles will emerge for setting down one or more patterns for the residual covariance matrix to complete the expression of the hypothesis or hypotheses of interest to us in the case of recursive models. It seems difficult, in the present state of knowledge, to state any general principles governing the choice of appropriate hypotheses for the pattern of residual covariances in a nonrecursive model. Nonrecursive models also yield other special problems concerning stability or instability of the causal system and the conditions under which the parameters will be identified, uniquely estimable quantities. Having pointed to the existence of such models, we shall regard further discussion of them as beyond the scope of this book. In reading any published account of a nonrecursive model, we should take particular care to note the argument by which the author derives expectations in respect of the residual covariances. If there is no explicit treatment of this question, a valid overall test of the model may not have been provided.

Given the first two steps, specifying the pattern of the regression coefficient matrix and specifying the pattern of the residual covariance matrix, we complete the specification of a RAM model by indicating the latent variables, if any, in the model. In the tables we shall adopt the simple convention of placing parentheses around the row and column labels of the latent variables. In the path diagrams the usual convention is followed of putting squares around observed variables and circles around latent variables.[2]

It would not be easy to provide an exhaustive list of all the varieties of linear structural models that have been used or that might be worth using. Most such models will contain components of one or more of the variants we now consider. All of them are special cases of the fully recursive model, obtained by setting to zero one or more of its regression coefficients and, possibly, estimating as nonzero one or more of its residual covariances. Except for cases considered later, in which we constrain certain parameters to be equal to other parameters, these models can be regarded as free from problems of scaling and can be fitted, as suits our convenience, to a sample covariance matrix or to a sample correlation matrix. Most commonly, if a variable is specified to be latent, we fix its scale by standardizing it. This will be represented in the tables showing residual covariance matrices by writing a unity in place of the diagonal cross for the fixed unit variance of a latent variable. Each case will be illustrated by a small number of variables. Usually it will be obvious how to generalize from the example to other cases of the same type.

---

[2]To be strictly correct, the path diagrams should include for each variable an undirected path from the variable to itself, representing the nonzero residual variance of the variable in just the same way that the nonzero residual covariances of distinct variables are represented. These have been omitted to avoid overloading the diagrams. If they are added, the correspondence between the path diagram and the model in its algebraic form is complete, with a directed path for every nonzero regression weight and an undirected path for every nonzero residual.

TABLE 4.2.4
Univariate Regression

Regression Pattern				Residual Pattern				
1	2	3	4		1	2	3	4
1				1	X	X	X	
2				2	X	X	X	
3				3	X	X	X	
4	X	X	X	4				X

(a) Univariate Regression

The pattern matrices of this case are shown in Table 4.2.4, and the path diagram is given in Fig. 4.2.1. Variable v_4 is the single dependent variable in a regression on variables v_1, v_2, v_3. There is no assignment of causal priority between v_1, v_2, and v_3, and the model cannot explain the correlations of these variables. By the basic regression principle the three correlations between these and the residuals of the dependent variable must be zero. There are 10 parameters, namely three regression weights and seven residual variances and covariances to estimate from the 10 variances and covariances of the four variables, so the model is just identified, giving an exact fit to any sample covariance (correlation) matrix. Apart from the three regression weights, the only parameter of interest is the residual variance of variable v_4. The squared multiple correlation of v_4 with v_1, v_2, v_3 is computed by subtracting its residual variance from unity if sample correlations are fitted or by subtracting it from the variance of v_4 and dividing by the latter if sample covariances are fitted.

(b) Partial Covariance

We recognize two versions of the model. In version (i), as in Table 4.2.5 and Fig. 4.2.2, variables v_2, v_3, v_4, v_5 are four dependent variables, each regressed on v_1, and all five variables are manifest variables. We wish to compute the six partial covariances of v_2, v_3, v_4, v_5 (and thence, by dividing by the square roots

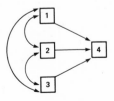

FIG. 4.2.1. Univariate Regression.

TABLE 4.2.5
Partial Covariance (i)

	Regression Pattern						Residual Pattern				
	1	2	3	4	5		1	2	3	4	5
1						1	X				
2	X					2		X	X	X	X
3	X					3		X	X	X	X
4	X					4		X	X	X	X
5	X					5		X	X	X	X

of the products of their residual variances, the six partial correlations), and we do not assume that these quantities are fixed zeros. In this version, variable v_1 is necessarily manifest. The partial covariances of v_2, v_3, v_4, v_5 with v_1 must be zero by the basic principle of regression theory. We can also declare that variable v_1 is "causally prior" to v_2, v_3, v_4, and v_5. The number of parameters to be estimated is 15, namely four regression weights and 11 nonzero residual variances and covariances, the same as the number of independent pieces of information in the covariance matrix of the five manifest variables.

In version (ii), we postulate that variable v_1 precisely explains the correlations of v_2, v_3, v_4, v_5. Because we can hardly hope to find a measurable variable that will in fact do this, usually in this version v_1 is a latent variable. We then have the pattern matrices in Table 4.2.6 and path diagram as in Fig. 4.2.3. This is the classical general-factor model of Spearman, as discussed in Section 1.5. In this version the parameters to be estimated are the four regression weights (common factor loadings) of the manifest variables on the latent variable and the four residual variances (unique variances) of the manifest variables. There are 10

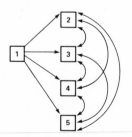

FIG. 4.2.2. Partial Covariance (i).

TABLE 4.2.6
Partial Covariance (ii)

	Regression Pattern						Residual Pattern				
	(1)	2	3	4	5		(1)	2	3	4	5
(1)						(1)	X				
2	X					2		X			
3	X					3			X		
4	X					4				X	
5	X					5					X

independent pieces of information in the covariance matrix of the manifest variables, so the model is overidentified, yielding a restrictive hypothesis with 2 df to test it if it is fitted by maximum likelihood.

(c) Chain Model

This is the case illustrated by the oil-price example of (4.1.5). The pattern matrices are given in Table 4.2.7 and the path diagram in Fig. 4.2.4. All six residual covariances are expected to be zero by the basic principle of causal priority. Given that all the variables are manifest variables, we have seven parameters (three regression weights and four residual variances) to explain 10 pieces of information, so the model is overidentified, yielding a restrictive hypothesis with 3 df. As indicated earlier, such a hypothesis is extremely unlikely to be true, though it might provide a not unreasonable approximation to reality, because errors of measurement would prevent the observed variables from behaving like a chain if their true parts do so.

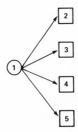

FIG. 4.2.3.   Partial Covariance (ii).

TABLE 4.2.7
Chain Model

Regression Pattern					Residual Pattern			
	1	2	3	4		1	2	3	4
1					1	X			
2	X				2		X		
3		X			3			X	
4			X		4				X

(d) Multivariate Regression

This is actually a combination of case (a) and case (b). Variables 3, 4, 5, 6, and 7 are regressed on variables 1 and 2. In version (i), as in Table 4.2.8 and Fig. 4.2.5, all are manifest variables and we have a just-identified, nonrestrictive model in which the number of parameters and the number of pieces of independent information in the covariance matrix of the manifest variables are each 15. The parameters of interest are the regression weights of the five dependent variables on each of the two independent variables and the residual variances and covariances of the dependent variables, from which their partial correlations and their multiple correlations with the two independent variables can be computed.

In version (ii) variables 1 and 2 are common factors. Remembering that these variables are the same as their residuals, because they are not regressed on further variables, we see that the residual covariance of v_1 and v_2 represents the actual covariance of these two common factors. Because the factors are not observable, it is necessary to fix their scale of measurement. We fix their variances equal to unity. The patterns and path diagram for this version are shown in Table 4.2.9 and Fig. 4.2.6. The unit variances are indicated by unities in the pattern matrix for the residual covariances. In the regression weight pattern matrix we have also set the regression weight of variable v_3 on common factor v_2 equal to zero. This is in order to eliminate the rotational indeterminacy of the exploratory factor model. Correspondingly we have fixed the correlation between the factors at zero, thus setting up the orthogonal, exploratory factor model. We have 15 independent variances and covariances in the covariance matrix of the five manifest variables, and 14 parameters, consisting of nine factor loadings and five unique variances, to estimate, leaving 1 df to test what is an

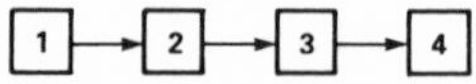

FIG. 4.2.4.   Chain Model.

TABLE 4.2.8
Multivariate Regression
(i) All Variables Manifest

	Regression Pattern								Residual Pattern						
	1	2	3	4	5	6	7		1	2	3	4	5	6	7
1								1	X	X					
2								2	X	X					
3	X	X						3			X	X	X	X	X
4	X	X						4			X	X	X	X	X
5	X	X						5			X	X	X	X	X
6	X	X						6			X	X	X	X	X
7	X	X						7			X	X	X	X	X

overidentified, restrictive model. [This result is consistent, as we would expect, with the formula (2.2.3).]

$$df = \tfrac{1}{2}[(5 - 2)^2 - (5 + 2)]$$

in Section 2.2.

As version (iii) of this model we consider a confirmatory multiple factor model with simple structure, as in Table 4.2.10 and Fig. 4.2.7. Here we have chosen an oblique simple structure model, fixing 4 of the 10 factor loadings equal to zero and allowing the two common factors to be correlated. This yields an overidentified model with 3 df to test the restrictive hypothesis.

As version (iv) of this model we consider a higher-order factor model with simple structure, containing one second-order factor, variable v_1, three first-order factors, variables v_2, v_3, v_4, regressed on v_1; and five manifest variables, v_5, v_6, v_7, v_8, v_9, regressed on the three first-order factors, as shown in Table 4.2.11 and Fig. 4.2.8. From another point of view this is a case (e) model (see

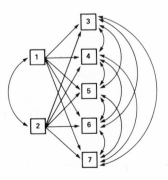

FIG. 4.2.5. Multivariate Regression (i).

TABLE 4.2.9
Multivariate Regression
(ii) Two Common Factors (exploratory)

	Regression Pattern								Residual Pattern						
	(1)	(2)	3	4	5	6	7		(1)	(2)	3	4	5	6	7
(1)								(1)	1						
(2)								(2)		1					
3	X							3			X				
4	X	X						4				X			
5	X	X						5					X		
6	X	X						6						X	
7	X	X						7							X

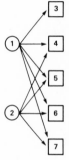

FIG. 4.2.6. Multivariate Regression (ii).

TABLE 4.2.10
Multivariate Regression
(iii) Two Common Factors (Confirmatory)

	Regression Pattern								Residual Pattern						
	(1)	(2)	3	4	5	6	7		(1)	(2)	3	4	5	6	7
(1)								(1)	1	X					
(2)								(2)	X	1					
3	X							3			X				
4	X							4				X			
5	X	X						5					X		
6		X						6						X	
7		X						7							X

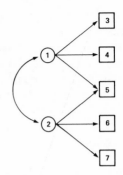

FIG. 4.2.7. Multivariate Regression (iii).

TABLE 4.2.11
Multivariate Regression
(iv) Higher-Order Factors

	Regression Pattern										Residual Pattern								
	(1)	(2)	(3)	(4)	5	6	7	8	9		(1)	(2)	(3)	(4)	5	6	7	8	9
(1)										(1)	1								
(2)	X									(2)		1							
(3)	X									(3)			1						
(4)	X									(4)				1					
5		X								5					X				
6		X								6						X			
7			X							7							X		
8			X	X						8								X	
9				X						9									X

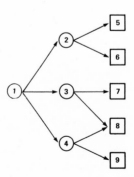

FIG. 4.2.8. Multivariate Regression (iv).

following). Note that variable v_8 is the only factorially complex variable. Note also that this example would probably give a Heywood case (Section 2.3) because the first-order factors are defined by less than three manifest variables, so in practice we would seek to add more variables to define each factor.

At this point a general comment is in order about the relationship between causal modeling and factor modeling. Here we are rewriting common factor models as though they are causal models. As in the main example running through Chapters 2 and 3, let us imagine that the higher-order factor in the last case is general intelligence and the first-order factors are Thurstone's verbal ability, word fluency, and reasoning factors. The position taken in this book has been that common factors are, quite precisely, common abstractive attributes of which the tests are specific measures. This amounts to a denial, for example, of the simple reading of the last path diagram as declaring that variations in general intelligence *cause* variations in verbal ability, word fluency, and reasoning and that these in turn *cause* variations in scores on tests designed to measure them. The discussion in Section 4.1 should have made it clear that we cannot regard a common factor as a cause of a test measurement in any intelligible sense of the word *cause*. The fact that the path diagrams and the regression representations do not distinguish between common factors and prior causal variables is simply another reflection of the fact that the inference of causal ordering rests upon theoretical considerations that are not themselves expressed in statements of models for linear structural relations. We may have good reason to distinguish in theory between the measurement (common factor) part and the structural (causal) part of a linear structural model for multivariate data, although the distinction does not correspond to any clear-cut mathematical properties of the model.

(e) Block Recursive Model

This case is illustrated by Table 4.2.12 and Fig. 4.2.9. Again we have a combination of cases (a) and (b), but with a different pattern and a different logical

TABLE 4.2.12
Block Recursive Model

Regression Pattern					Residual Pattern			
	1	2	3	4		1	2	3	4
1					1	X			
2	X				2		X	X	
3	X				2		X	X	
4		X	X		4				X

FIG. 4.2.9. Block Recursive Model.

character. Variable v_1 causally influences both v_2 and v_3 and is imagined to have a further effect on v_4 but only through the intermediate agency of both v_2 and v_3. By the rule that each disturbance is uncorrelated with the disturbances of causally prior variables, all residual covariances are fixed zeros except that of v_2 and v_3, where causal priority does not determine the question. We might make the additional assumption that this covariance is zero (i.e., that v_2 and v_3 are correlated only because each is an effect of v_1). But as a rule this is not a reasonable expectation if all variables are observable.

The general principle illustrated by this case should be clear. We can have a *block recursive* model in which one or more groups, or *blocks,* of variables behave like the group formed here by variables v_2 and v_3, intermediating as a block between other variables or blocks of variables. In specifying the pattern of the residual covariance matrix, we set residual covariances equal to zero by the causal priority rule, leaving nonzero residuals within the blocks, because no internal causal priority has been assigned, that is, unless the investigator has special reasons to believe that some of these should also be zero. The block recursive model is to be distinguished, as we shall see, from a model in which the intermediary between, say, a final dependent variable and an exogenous variable is a common factor of the variables in a block. The investigator makes an important theoretical commitment in choosing between the block recursive model and a causal latent-variable model such as we consider next.

(f) A Causal Model with a Latent Variable

This case is illustrated in Table 4.2.13 and Fig. 4.2.10 in a variant in which latent variable v_2 is a common factor of manifest variables v_3, v_4, or, if we believe the latter variables to be parallel forms, v_2 is the true score that each of them measures plus error. (Again we should have more manifest variables to define the factor.) Here all the residual covariances are zero except between v_3 and v_5 and between v_4 and v_5. We do not expect v_2 to explain these two relationships because in contrast to the variant on this model that we shall consider next, variable v_5 is not thought of as another measure of (factor) variable v_2, along with v_3 and v_4, but is thought of as a further effect of variable v_2. At the same time, although v_3 and v_4 are not ordered in the recursive sequence,

TABLE 4.2.13
Causal Model with Latent Variable
(i) Variable 2 as Factor of 3 and 4

	Regression Pattern						Residual Pattern				
	1	(2)	3	4	5		1	(2)	3	4	5
1						1	X				
(2)	X					(2)		1			
3		X				3			X		X
4		X				4				X	X
5		X				5			X	X	X

because v_2 is their common factor it explains their correlation by definition, so the residual covariance of v_3 and v_4 is fixed to be zero.

Notice the contrast with case (e) in which the two intermediate variables are taken to have separate influences on the final dependent variable, where here it is only what they have in common that influences the dependent variable.

A second variant on this case is illustrated in Table 4.2.14 and Fig. 4.2.11. The pattern of the regression weight matrix is unchanged, but here variable v_2 is the common factor of v_3, v_4, and v_5 and therefore explains their mutual correlations.

We should also compare these two variants with the parallel case where all the variables are manifest variables. This is illustrated in Table 4.2.15 and Fig. 4.2.12. Again the regression pattern is unaltered, but v_3, v_4, v_5 are not causally ordered, and because v_2 is not a common factor, it does not explain their correlations.

The general principles for prescribing a reticular action model for multivariate data should now be clear. Perhaps with the aid of a path diagram we list the variables in a recursive sequence and prescribe the pattern of fixed zero regression weights and regression weights to be estimated. We identify the manifest and latent variables. We then prescribe the corresponding pattern of the residual covariance matrix by operating two rules. The recursive priority rule states that a

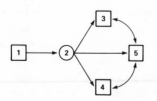

FIG. 4.2.10. Causal model with latent variable (i).

TABLE 4.2.14
(iii) Variable 2 as Factor of 3,4, and 5

Regression Pattern						Residual Pattern				
	1	2	3	4	5		1	(2)	3	4	5
1						1	X				
(2)	X					(2)		1			
3		X				3			X		
4		X				4				X	
5		X				5					X

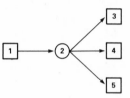

FIG. 4.2.11.   Causal Model (ii).

TABLE 4.2.15
(iii) Causal Model with All Variables Manifest

Regression Pattern						Residual Pattern				
	1	2	3	4	5		1	2	3	4	5
1						1	X				
2						2		X			
3		X				3			X	X	X
4		X				4			X	X	X
5		X				5			X	X	X

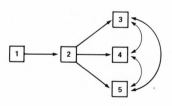

FIG. 4.2.12.   Causal Model (iii).

residual covariance of two variables is zero if one of them precedes the other in a recursive sequence. The latent-variable rule states that a residual covariance of two variables is zero if they are both regressed on one or more of the same group of latent variables (common factors or true scores). If the model contains latent variables, it may be necessary to invoke the usual principles of exploratory or confirmatory factor analysis, preferably the latter, to prevent rotational indeterminacy, and typically we shall fix the variance of each latent variable to be unity to eliminate indeterminacy due to arbitrariness of scale.

Once the model is completely prescribed, it can be fitted by a program for the analysis of covariance structures such as LISREL or COSAN. This step requires a deeper technical understanding of the model, which has been left to the mathematical notes in Section 4.3. The reader who chooses to bypass the mathematical notes in this book should be content to be told that the logic of the models has been described fully enough, but advice of a technical nature would be needed if he or she wished to analyze data in terms of a linear structural model.

At this point, a brief account can be given of the Keesling–Wiley–Jöreskog model, LISREL, in terms of the RAM model. The LISREL model consists of two *measurement* models (latent-variable models) relating two sets of manifest variables to two corresponding sets of latent variables and a *structural model* linking the members of one set of latent variables to the other set and to other members of its own set. We have a common factor, or latent-variable model,

$$y_j = \sum_{q=1}^{t} \lambda_{jq}\eta_q + \epsilon_j \tag{4.2.3}$$

relating manifest dependent variables y_j to latent dependent variables η_q through a patterned matrix of common factor loadings $[\lambda_{jq}]$ with the usual assumption that the residuals (unique parts) ϵ_j are uncorrelated. We also have a common factor model

$$x_l = \sum_{m=1}^{u} \mu_{lm}\xi_m + \delta_l \tag{4.2.4}$$

relating manifest independent variables x_l to latent independent variables ξ_m through a patterned matrix of factor loadings $[\mu_{lm}]$ with uncorrelated residuals (unique parts) δ_l. Finally we have a structural ("causal") model

$$\eta_p = \sum_{q=1}^{v} \beta_{pq}\eta_q + \sum_{s=1}^{w} \gamma_{ps}\xi_s + \zeta_p \tag{4.2.5}$$

in which each latent dependent variable η_p is regressed, through a patterned matrix of regression weights $[\beta_{pq}]$, on other latent dependent variables η_q and through a patterned matrix of regression weights $[\gamma_{ps}]$ on one or more of the latent independent variables ξ_s. Equation (4.2.5) is commonly written in the form

$$\sum_{q=1}^{v} \beta_{pq}^{*} \eta_q = \sum_{s=1}^{w} \gamma_{ps} \xi_s + \zeta_p \qquad (4.2.6)$$

where $\beta_{pq}^{*} = -\beta_{pq}$ if q is not equal to p and $\beta_{pp}^{*} = 1$ (if, as in any rational application of the model, $\beta_{pp} = 0$). In this form, the model lacks a direct path–analytic interpretation. The patterns of the residual covariance matrices in LISREL follow the basic recursive priority and common factor rules. These are indicated shortly.

At first sight the LISREL model is more complex than the simple RAM model. However, it is easy to represent the former model as a special case of the latter. We describe LISREL as though it were a model for eight variables, ξ_r, ξ_s, η_p, η_q, x_l, x_m, y_j, y_k. A pair of variables of each kind is enough to represent all pairwise relationships and it is easy to see how to write the representation for a larger number of variables of each type. Here we write in the actual symbols for the regression coefficients in the regression weight matrix, using the notation of equations (4.2.3), (4.2.4), and (4.2.5). See Fig. 4.2.13 and Table 4.2.16.

We note that the LISREL model is nonrecursive if and only if there are nonzero coefficients β_{pq} above the diagonal in the regression weight matrix. Otherwise it is a block–recursive model. We can make the parameters identifiable, and thus uniquely estimable and hopefully interpretable, by invoking the patterning principles of confirmatory factor analysis to fix zeros within the sub-matrices of the two measurement models (i.e., set certain coefficients λ_{jp} and μ_{lm} to zero). At the same time we use path-analytic principles to set coefficients γ_{ps} or β_{pq} equal to zero to give restrictive hypotheses declaring the absence of certain paths whereby the latent exogenous variables ξ_s influence the latent variables η_p and whereby the latter influence each other.

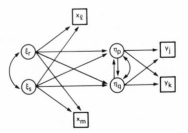

FIG. 4.2.13.   LISREL Model.

A further provision of LISREL allows the user to constrain parameters of the model to be equal to each other. Loosely and broadly speaking, this provision enables us to express hypotheses of parallelism, equivalence, or interchangeability between variables and is particularly suitable for expressing concepts from true-score theory. When this provision is used, care is needed over the scaling of the model and the variables, and as a rule we cannot indifferently fit the model to a sample correlation matrix or a sample covariance matrix, because (as pointed out in Chapter 3) if two correlations are equal, the corresponding covariances may not be and conversely. In applications, the investigator may choose to regard the multiple measurements x_l and the multiple measurements y_j as parallel or, in some sense, equivalent forms of a single test, and the latent variables ξ_r and η_p on which they are regressed as *true scores* in which case the residuals ϵ_j, δ_l are thought of as pure errors of measurement, containing no stable specific component, conceptually unique to each test. There is no mathematical basis for this distinction, and the choice in practice can look totally arbitrary. The view taken here is that unless the measures are literally retests with the same instrument, it will seldom be reasonable to suppose that the "error" term does not contain a conceptually unique and stable component.

The final model to be discussed in this section is McDonald's COSAN model. Although it was not originally conceptualized this way, we shall find it convenient to regard the COSAN model as a block–recursive model obtained by indefinitely repeating a simplified version of LISREL in a block–recursive sequence. First we shall recognize that the LISREL model can be simplified by dropping the distinction between the independent variables ξ_r, x_l and the dependent variables η_p, y_j and writing the model as two equations; namely

$$v_j = \sum_{q=1}^{t} \lambda_{jq} u_q + \epsilon_j \tag{4.2.7}$$

for the measurement model, and

$$u_p = \sum_{s=1}^{w} \beta_{pq} u_q + \zeta_p \tag{4.2.8}$$

for the structural model. For if we take four each of the variables v_j and u_p and label them in conformity with the eight subscripts of LISREL in Table 4.2.16, we obtain the specification in Table 4.2.17, from which the LISREL model is obtained by setting the coefficients in brackets equal to zero. The path diagram of this simplified version is shown in Fig. 4.2.14, in which, in most applications, we have a recursive model with no reciprocal paths between latent variables u_p, u_q.

The COSAN model corresponds to a block–recursive model with some number b of blocks in which the simplified LISREL model is the basic block

TABLE 4.2.16
LISREL Model

Regression Weights

	(ξ_r)	(ξ_s)	(η_p)	(η_q)	x_l	x_m	y_j	y_k
(ξ_r)								
(ξ_s)								
(η_p)	γ_{pr}	γ_{ps}		β_{pq}				
(η_q)	γ_{qr}	γ_{qs}	β_{qp}					
x_l	μ_{lr}	μ_{ls}						
x_m	μ_{mr}	μ_{ms}						
y_j			λ_{jp}	λ_{jq}				
y_k			λ_{kp}	λ_{kq}				

Residual Pattern

	(ξ_r)	(ξ_s)	η_p	η_q	x_l	x_m	y_j	y_k
(ξ_r)	1	X						
(ξ_s)	X	1						
(η_p)			X	X				
(η_q)			X	X				
x_l					X			
x_m						X		
y_j							X	
y_k								X

unit. We have b sets of variables, which we shall label $\{v_j^{(1)}\}$, $\{v_j^{(2)}\}$, . . . , $\{v_j^{(b)}\}$, with n_s variables in the sth set. The variables in the sth set are regressed on each other (usually without reciprocal, nonrecursive paths) and on the variables in the $(s - 1)$th set. That is, the one basic model equation is

$$v_j^{(s)} = \sum_k \beta_{jk}^{(s)} v_k^{(s)} + \sum_l \gamma_{jl}^{(s)} v_l^{(s-1)} + e_j^{(s)} \qquad (4.2.9)$$

All the variables in the model are latent except the final set of dependent variables, the bth set $\{v_j^{(b)}\}$. The path diagram for the model consists of a sequence

TABLE 4.2.17
Simplified LISREL Model

Regression Weights

	(u_r)	(u_s)	(u_p)	(u_q)	v_l	v_m	v_j	v_k
(u_r)		(β_{rs})	(β_{rp})	(β_{rq})				
(u_s)	β_{sr}		(β_{sp})	(β_{sq})				
(u_p)	β_{pr}	β_{ps}		β_{pq}				
(u_q)	β_{qr}	β_{qs}	β_{qp}					
v_l	λ_{lr}	λ_{ls}	(λ_{lp})	(λ_{lq})				
v_m	λ_{mr}	λ_{ms}	(λ_{mp})	(λ_{mq})				
v_j	(λ_{jr})	(λ_{js})	λ_{jp}	λ_{jq}				
v_k	(λ_{lr})	(λ_{ls})	λ_{kp}	λ_{kq}				

containing repetitions of the simplified LISREL path diagram, as shown in Fig. 4.2.15 (omitting undirected paths).

Instead of just controlling the patterns of the regression coefficient and residual covariance matrices by specifying that certain parameters are fixed zeros or that some parameters are equal to others, the COSAN model and program allow the user to declare that any parameter in these matrices is a function, possibly nonlinear, of one or more fundamental parameters. This allows a number of devices to be introduced, to constrain parameters to be positive, or to require inequalities to be satisfied. For example, we may believe that one test should have a larger factor loading on a given factor than another test. Such a hypothesis is easily incorporated in the COSAN model.

Again we must recognize that the COSAN model can be described as a special case of the RAM model, as shown in Table 4.2.18, where again we use just two variables from each set to exhibit the pairwise relationships.

FIG. 4.2.14.   Simplified LISREL Model.

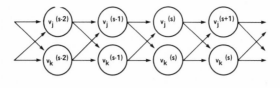

FIG. 4.2.15.   COSAN Model.

Although the RAM model is clearly practically and algebraically simpler than the COSAN model, there are technical reasons for retaining the COSAN formulation and program for applications and using the RAM model as a conceptual simplifier and organizer for the handling of input and output in fitting a linear structural model. This is because a computer program written directly to embody the RAM model will be likely to run into difficulties if we have a block–recursive model in which the number of blocks in the recursive sequence is considerable. The same is true of LISREL. For example, a model for longitudinal data, with three tests each given on three occasions yielding nine manifest variables, has been fitted by COSAN with 19 regression weights and 18 residual variances and covariances to be estimated from the 45 independent pieces of information in the data. Expressed as a RAM model, it becomes a model in 236 variables, 9 manifest and 227 latent, with 236 rows and columns in the regression weight matrix and the residual covariance matrix, most of whose contents are zeros. We refer to a matrix containing many zeros as a *sparse matrix,* in an obvious sense of the word. Such a data set would be difficult to analyze using LISREL or a direct enbodiment of RAM because of the arithmetic to be performed on the 236×236 matrix of regression weights. (Technically, it requires to be inverted many times.) It is easily analyzed by COSAN because the COSAN model was specifically designed to capitalize on the properties of sparse matrices.

However, for the intended reader of this book, the simple conceptualization of linear models for structural relations afforded by McArdle's reticular action model should serve as a general organizer of the field and a first introduction to the more complex models that have been proposed. As already implied, most applications of any of these models for the analysis of linear structural relations arise from path analysis or from confirmatory factor analysis or from a combination of the two. The provision in programs such as LISREL and COSAN for specifying that parameters in the model are constrained to be equal also enables us to express hypotheses of equivalence or interchangeability of variables, as when we construct parallel forms of a test and we wish to imagine that they differ only by an error of measurement.

Actually, models such as LISREL and COSAN and their associated computer programs have applicability beyond the fitting of path-analytic, factor-analytic,

TABLE 4.2.18
COSAN MODEL

Regression Weights

	$(v_j^{(1)})$	$(v_k^{(1)})$	$(v_j^{(2)})$	$(v_k^{(2)})$	...	$(v_j^{(b-1)})$	$(v_k^{(b-1)})$	$(v_j^{(b)})$	$(v_k^{(b)})$
$(v_j^{(1)})$	X	X							
$(v_k^{(1)})$	X	X		X					
$(v_j^{(2)})$	X	X	X						
$(v_k^{(2)})$									
....									
$(v_j^{(b-1)})$						X	X		
$(v_k^{(b-1)})$						X	X		X
$(v_j^{(b)})$						X	X	X	
$(v_k^{(b)})$									

and true-score hypotheses. They can also be used to incorporate transformations of scale of variables for which neither path analysis nor factor analysis provide a natural interpretation. (See Section 6.3 for an example from multimode data analysis.) They can further be used to fit certain nonlinear models. (See Section 7.2 for the treatment of the normal ogive model.) The range of such applications is not yet even approximately known and therefore cannot be indicated here.

4.3. MATHEMATICAL NOTES ON CHAPTER 4

Here we outline the treatment of McArdle's reticular action model and relate it to the Keesling–Wiley–Jöreskog LISREL model and to McDonald's COSAN model.

Let $\mathbf{v}' = [v_1, \ldots, v_n]$ be a vector of $n = l + m$ random variables, of which l are latent and m are manifest. We write

$$\mathbf{v} = \mathbf{Pv} + \mathbf{e} \tag{4.3.1}$$

where $\mathbf{P}$, $n \times n$ is a patterned matrix of regression weights with zeros in the diagonal in all cases. If the model is recursive, we so order the components of $\mathbf{v}$ that $\mathbf{P}$ is lower triangular. We assume that

$$E\{\mathbf{e}\} = \mathbf{0} \qquad E\{\mathbf{ve}'\} = \mathbf{0} \tag{4.3.2}$$

and we write

$$\mathbf{U} = E\{\mathbf{ee}'\} \tag{4.3.3}$$

for the (symmetric) patterned residual covariance matrix. Notice that we do not generally assume that $E\{\mathbf{v}\} = \mathbf{0}$.

General Note: The discussion of causal relations in Section 4.1 is based on contributions from philosophers of science (see, in particular, Campbell, 1957) as well as introductory remarks made by various writers in their accounts of causal modeling. The following references given to the latter should be sufficient for further reading on causality. The account of the fundamental postulate of causal models, in respect of omitted causes, is perhaps formulated a little differently from other accounts that the reader will find. Further reading for this chapter would naturally include Duncan (1975), who gives more information about nonrecursive models, and James and Mulaik (1982) for a recent account of causal modeling that is relatively nontechnical. The reader should be advised that the transition from fitting linear structural models by fitting individual regressions to fitting the entire model, with the prescribed pattern for the residual covariances, is relatively recent. The most recent treatments of the topic are still in the form of very technical journal articles.

McArdle (1978) described the simple RAM model on which the discussion in Section 4.2 is based, and McArdle and McDonald (in press) treat the algebra summarized in equations (4.3.22)–(4.3.23). The Keesling–Wiley–Jöreskog model LISREL is described in Jöreskog (1973). The theory and computer program have been repeatedly updated. McDonald's COSAN is described technically in McDonald (1978b) and slightly less technically in McDonald (1980). A variant on the RAM model has been described by Bentler and Weeks (1980).

We define an $m \times n$ selection matrix $\mathbf{J}$, each of whose elements is either zero or unity, the effect of which is to operate on v to select out the subset of m manifest variables from the $n = l + m$ latent and manifest variables. That is, we write

$$\mathbf{v}^* = \mathbf{J}\mathbf{v} \tag{4.3.4}$$

where $\mathbf{v}^{*'} = [v_j, v_k, \ldots, v_l, v_m]$ is the subset of components of $\mathbf{v}$ that are manifest variables. As an exercise, the reader may verify by trial with small examples or by finding a general algebraic proof that $\mathbf{J}$ contains just m unities, with just one unity in each of m columns and that a unity in the jth row and kth column copies the kth component of $\mathbf{v}$ as the jth component of $\mathbf{v}^*$.

We rewrite (4.3.1) as

$$(\mathbf{I}_n - \mathbf{P})\,\mathbf{v} = \mathbf{e} \tag{4.3.5}$$

and note that if $(\mathbf{I}_n - \mathbf{P})$ is nonsingular (which is certainly true in recursive models because $\mathbf{I}_n - \mathbf{P}$ in lower triangular with unities in the diagonal), then, further, we have

$$\mathbf{v} = \mathbf{J}(\mathbf{I}_n - \mathbf{P})^{-1}\,\mathbf{e}. \tag{4.3.6}$$

Equation (4.3.6) is the fundamental equation of the RAM model, and from it, using (4.3.3), we immediately have the covariance structure, or rather, in general, the raw product-moment structure of the model; namely,

$$\mathbf{c} = E\{\mathbf{v}^*\mathbf{v}^{*'}\} = \mathbf{J}(\mathbf{I}_n - \mathbf{P})^{'-1}\,\mathbf{U}(\mathbf{I}_n - \mathbf{P})^{'-1}\mathbf{J}'. \tag{4.3.7}$$

In general $\mathbf{C}$ is a matrix of raw mean squares and mean products of the components of $\mathbf{v}^*$, not "corrected for means," and it becomes a covariance matrix if and only if we suppose that $\mathbf{v}^*$ is rescaled so that $E\{\mathbf{v}^*\} = \mathbf{0}$. We do this from here on. Not making this assumption enables us to combine hypotheses restricting the means of the variables with the usual hypotheses restricting their covariance. This feature will not be discussed further here. The covariance structure (4.3.7) can immediately be fitted by an application of such general-purpose programs such as LISREL or COSAN, because the very general RAM model is, somewhat paradoxically, a special case of the former, whereas the former are both special cases of the RAM model.

We write the LISREL model with obvious matrix notation as

$$\mathbf{y} = \mathbf{L}\boldsymbol{\eta} + \boldsymbol{\varepsilon} \tag{4.3.8}$$

corresponding to (4.2.3), where $\mathbf{L} = [\lambda_{jp}]$, with

$$\mathbf{x} = \mathbf{M}\boldsymbol{\xi} + \boldsymbol{\delta} \tag{4.3.9}$$

corresponding to (4.2.4), where $\mathbf{M} = [\mu_{lm}]$ and

$$\boldsymbol{\eta} = \mathbf{B}\boldsymbol{\eta} + \mathbf{G}\boldsymbol{\xi} + \boldsymbol{\zeta} \tag{4.3.10}$$

corresponding to (4.2.5), where $\mathbf{B} = [\beta_{pq}]$ and $\mathbf{G} = [\gamma_{ps}]$. We define the diagonal matrices

$$\mathbf{\Theta}_\varepsilon^2 = E\{\boldsymbol{\varepsilon\varepsilon}\} \qquad \mathbf{\Theta}_\delta^2 = E\{\boldsymbol{\delta\delta}'\} \tag{4.3.11}$$

and the symmetric matrices

$$\mathbf{\Phi} = E\{\boldsymbol{\xi\xi}'\} \qquad \mathbf{\Psi} = E\{\boldsymbol{\zeta\zeta}'\} \tag{4.3.12}$$

Equation (4.3.10) may be rewritten in its *reduced form*

$$\boldsymbol{\eta} = (\mathbf{I} - \mathbf{B})^{-1}[\mathbf{G\xi} + \boldsymbol{\zeta}] \tag{4.3.13}$$

The reader should be able to verify thence that

$$\mathbf{C}_{yy} = E\{\mathbf{yy}'\} = \mathbf{L}(\mathbf{I} - \mathbf{B})^{-1}(\mathbf{G\Phi G}' + \mathbf{\Psi})\,(\mathbf{I} - \mathbf{B})'^{-1}\mathbf{L} + \mathbf{\Theta}_\varepsilon^2 \tag{4.3.14}$$

$$\mathbf{C}_{xx} = E\{\mathbf{xx}'\} = \mathbf{M\Phi M}' + \mathbf{\Theta}_\delta^2 \tag{4.3.15}$$

and

$$\mathbf{C}_{yx} = \mathbf{L}(\mathbf{I} - \mathbf{B})^{-1}\mathbf{G\Phi M}. \tag{4.3.16}$$

To express the LISREL model as a RAM model, we write

$$
\begin{bmatrix} (\xi) \\ (\eta) \\ \mathbf{x} \\ \mathbf{y} \end{bmatrix} =
\begin{bmatrix}
\mathbf{0} & \mathbf{0} & \mathbf{0} & \mathbf{0} \\
\mathbf{G} & \mathbf{B} & \mathbf{0} & \mathbf{0} \\
\mathbf{M} & \mathbf{0} & \mathbf{0} & \mathbf{0} \\
\mathbf{0} & \mathbf{L} & \mathbf{0} & \mathbf{0}
\end{bmatrix}
\begin{bmatrix} (\xi) \\ (\eta) \\ \mathbf{x} \\ \mathbf{y} \end{bmatrix} +
\begin{bmatrix} \xi \\ \zeta \\ \varepsilon \\ \delta \end{bmatrix} \tag{4.3.17}
$$

which yields the covariance structure of the manifest variables.

$$
\begin{bmatrix} \mathbf{C}_{yy} & \mathbf{C}_{xy} \\ \mathbf{C}_{yx} & \mathbf{C}_{xx} \end{bmatrix} = \mathbf{J}
\begin{bmatrix}
\mathbf{I} & \mathbf{0} & \mathbf{0} & \mathbf{0} \\
-\mathbf{G} & \mathbf{I} - \mathbf{B} & \mathbf{0} & \mathbf{0} \\
-\mathbf{M} & \mathbf{0} & \mathbf{I} & \mathbf{0} \\
-\mathbf{0} & -\mathbf{L} & \mathbf{0} & \mathbf{I}
\end{bmatrix}^{-1}
\begin{bmatrix}
\mathbf{\Phi} & & & \\
& \mathbf{\Psi} & & \\
& & \mathbf{\Theta}_\varepsilon^2 & \\
& & & \mathbf{\Theta}_\delta^2
\end{bmatrix}
$$

$$
\begin{bmatrix}
\mathbf{I} & \mathbf{0} & \mathbf{0} & \mathbf{0} \\
-\mathbf{G} & \mathbf{I} - \mathbf{B} & \mathbf{0} & \mathbf{0} \\
-\mathbf{M} & \mathbf{0} & \mathbf{I} & \mathbf{0} \\
\mathbf{0} & \mathbf{L} & \mathbf{0} & \mathbf{I}
\end{bmatrix}^{'-1}
\mathbf{J}' \tag{4.3.18}
$$

which yields the covariance structure of the manifest variables. where, in this case

$$\mathbf{J} = \begin{bmatrix} \mathbf{0} & \mathbf{0} & \mathbf{I} & \mathbf{0} \\ \mathbf{0} & \mathbf{0} & \mathbf{0} & \mathbf{I} \end{bmatrix}. \tag{4.3.19}$$

The equivalence of the expressions in (4.3.18) and (4.3.14)–(4.3.18) is proved essentially by verifying the algebraic identity

$$
\begin{bmatrix}
\mathbf{I} & \mathbf{0} & \mathbf{0} & \mathbf{0} \\
-\mathbf{G} & \mathbf{I} - \mathbf{B} & \mathbf{0} & \mathbf{0} \\
-\mathbf{L} & \mathbf{0} & \mathbf{I} & \mathbf{0} \\
 & -\mathbf{M} & \mathbf{0} & \mathbf{I}
\end{bmatrix}^{1}
=
\begin{bmatrix}
\mathbf{I} & & & \\
(\mathbf{I} - \mathbf{B})\mathbf{G} & (\mathbf{I} - \mathbf{B})^{-1} & & \\
\mathbf{M} & \mathbf{0} & \mathbf{I} & \\
\mathbf{L}(\mathbf{I} - \mathbf{B})\mathbf{G} & \mathbf{L}(\mathbf{I} - \mathbf{B})^{-1} & \mathbf{0} & \mathbf{I}
\end{bmatrix}
\tag{4.3.20}
$$

This is easily done by multiplying these two matrices together according to the rules for multiplying partitioned matrices and thus obtaining an identity matrix. On substituting the matrix on the right in (4.3.20) into (4.3.18), we obtain the usual LISREL expressions for the covariance matrices.

Thus, LISREL is a special case of RAM. Conversely, RAM from another point of view is a special case of LISREL. We can write the RAM model as a LISREL model by setting $\mathbf{L} = \mathbf{J}$, $\mathbf{B} = \mathbf{P}$, $\mathbf{G} = \mathbf{I}$, $\mathbf{\Phi} = \mathbf{U}$, and the other matrices null.

The COSAN model can be described in a number of ways. In one matrix representation of it, following from (4.2.9), we write the covariance structure as

$$
\mathbf{C} = (\mathbf{I} - \mathbf{B}_b)^{-1}\mathbf{G}_b(\mathbf{I} - \mathbf{B}_{b-1})^{-1}\mathbf{G}_{b-1}
$$
$$
\cdots (\mathbf{I} - \mathbf{B}_1)^{-1}\mathbf{G}_1\mathbf{\Phi}\mathbf{G}_1' \cdots (\mathbf{I} - \mathbf{B}_b)'
\tag{4.3.21}
$$

where the matrices $\mathbf{B}_s = [\beta_{jk}^{(s)}]$ are patterned square matrices and the matrices $\mathbf{G}_s = [\gamma_{ji}^{(s)}]$ are patterned rectangular matrices. In terms of the RAM model, this structure can be written as

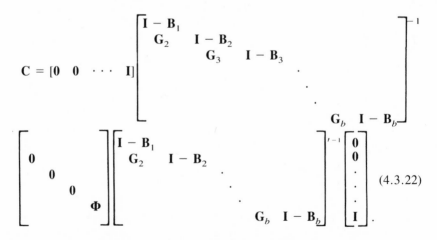

$$\tag{4.3.22}$$

Conversely, we can write the RAM model as a COSAN model by choosing $b = 2$, setting $\mathbf{B}_1 = \mathbf{I}$, $\mathbf{G}_1 = \mathbf{J}$, $\mathbf{B}_2 = \mathbf{P}$, $\mathbf{G}_2 = \mathbf{I}$, and

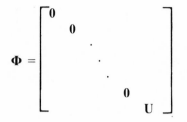

$$\boldsymbol{\Phi} = \begin{bmatrix} 0 & & & & \\ & 0 & & & \\ & & \cdot & & \\ & & & \cdot & \\ & & & \cdot & \\ & & & 0 & \\ & & & & U \end{bmatrix}$$

In practical applications, if a RAM model contains a block–recursive sequence whose extent b is large, we shall expect to translate the RAM model into a COSAN model to avoid the computing problems involved in storing and repeatedly inverting a very large matrix, most of whose elements would be zero as would be required in using LISREL or a program written to embody the RAM model directly.

5 The Problem of Factor Scores

5.1. FACTOR ANALYSIS AS A TEST CONSTRUCTION DEVICE

It might seem that a factor-analytic study would be painfully incomplete if we did not obtain some assessment of the common factors themselves (i.e., of the common factor scores, or factor values, of the individual subjects in the study) as well as estimates of factor loadings. One reason why a factor-analytic study can give the appearance of leading nowhere while it actually leads somewhere is that it may serve as a guide to the construction of homogeneous tests of the traits or generic properties identified in the analysis. Because there may be a time gap between the publication of the factor analysis and the appearance of the consequent invented test, we may fail to notice the follow-up work that adds a practical justification to the earlier study.

For example, Thurstone's work yielding a set of correlated "primary mental abilities" led, through a series of refinements of sets of items, to a battery of standardized and easily usable tests of those abilities. The simple sum scores (total number of right answers—the "number right" score) on these developed cognitive tests can reasonably be thought of as the ultimate result of the factor-analytic work and as good "practical" measures of the factors identified. In the case of Thurstone's primary mental abilities, it is an open question whether the outcome of the whole enterprise was worthwhile. McNemar[1] (as mentioned previously) has surveyed evidence in support of a conclusion that the measures of general intelligence favored in Britain that stem naturally from the earliest factor-

---

[1]See McNemar (1964).

analytic tradition prove more effective in further research than the primary abilities that stem from Thurstone's oblique simple structure notions. If this issue remains controversial, it still serves to show that the effectiveness of research based on mental tests can rest on the effectiveness of the prior analysis on which the test construction was based.

The phrase "construction of homogeneous tests" was used as though its meaning is already quite obvious. Intuitively, we would expect that a set of measures that were indicators of just one generic property that they shared in common would be scored collectively to give a single measure of that property, and we would regard them as a *homogeneous* set of indicators (homogeneous = of the same kind). In the context of psychological or educational testing, such a combination of measures is said to yield a homogeneous test. The theory of tests and test construction tends to be dealt with rather separately from the theory of factor analysis. One reason for this lies in doubts as to whether the common factor model can be applied to dichotomous items. Crude practical devices have been developed for selecting and combining items intended to form homogeneous tests, and there have been some conceptual confusions about the meaning and the assessment of test homogeneity. But it seems reasonable to recognize that the primary theoretical conception of a homogeneous test (or set of measures) is one whose items measure only one (generic) property in common. When that property is held constant, the measures are statistically independent and certainly uncorrelated. In the context of this kind of thinking, we call the generic property a *latent trait*. The view taken here is that common factors and latent traits are essentially the same quantities—they are quantities that explain the relations among our measures. However, dichotomous items do not meet the usual assumptions of common factor analysis (e.g., we cannot assume their regressions on the factors are linear). Hence theory for items has, regrettably, been developed separately from factor theory, and their essential unity is not always recognized. More will be said about this in Chapter 7. The point here is that factor analysis, or closely related techniques, does provide a very good way to construct homogeneous tests of interesting generic properties of the subjects we study, though its role as a test construction device is not always recognized.

To repeat the central point of this section, although the connections are not always obvious from the literature, a usual sequel to factor analysis is the construction of a test intended to measure a common factor that has been "identified," "discovered," or "invented." Where such tests are produced, we do not need factor scoring procedures as such.

5.2. THE ESTIMATION OF COMMON FACTORS

Suppose that we know the population parameters of the common factor model in some application of it. That is, we know the nm factor loadings in the factor pattern and the n residual variances, and, if the factors are correlated, we know their correlations. We can draw a subject from the population and measure his or her values of the n variables. The question is, what can we say about the m factor "scores" of the individual, corresponding to the n observed scores? It should be immediately clear that the factor scores are not uniquely determined by the observed scores. This fact has worried some workers in the field and is sometimes perceived as a basic fault of the model, justifying its abandonment in favor of, for example, principal components or images (Section 2.3). The position taken here is that we should not expect factor scores, measures of generic properties, to be exactly determined by means of a small number of empirical measures, each with its specific property and error of measurement, any more than we expect a population parameter to be precisely determined by statistics from a small sample of subjects. If the measures are drawn from a well-defined, appropriate behavior domain, they tend to yield estimates of factors that become increasingly precise as the number of measures is increased, just as the subjects drawn from a well-defined population tend to yield estimates of the model parameters that become increasingly precise as the number of subjects is increased. If we adopt a conception of our field of inquiry as a behavior domain, we may think of the factor score as a limit of its estimate as we draw all possible variables from the behavior domain. (See Section 5.2.)

To return to our question: We know the regression weights of the n observed variables on the m common factors, and we assumed at the outset that the regressions are linear. It is natural to ask if we can now reverse the roles of the observed variables and the factors. That is, we wish to estimate the factors by determining their regressions on the observed variables. We want m linear combinations $\hat{x}_p$ of the n observed variables that will have maximum correlations with the unknown factors in the population, or, with the right scaling of variables and factors, we want m linear combinations $\hat{x}_p$ whose discrepancies $(x_p - \hat{x}_p)$ from the unknown factors x_p in the population are as small as possible (i.e., have minimum variance). Let us write

$$\hat{x}_p = \sum_{j=1}^{n} b_{pj} y_j \qquad p = 1, \ldots, m \qquad (5.2.1)$$

to represent a general expression for the *regression estimates* $\hat{x}_p$ of the factor scores x_p. We need a procedure for computing the factor-variable (f–v) regression weights b_{pj} (i.e., the regression weights of the factors on the tests). The f–v regression weights, b_{pj}, can be computed by the standard formulas of regression theory from knowledge of the correlations between the factors and the variables and the correlations between the variables. As usual we assume that a computer program is looking after this problem for us. The f–v regression weights are always necessarily different from the v–f regression weights (i.e., the factor lqadings). (They would be the same theoretically if the observed variables were uncorrelated, but then all the regression weights would be zero; there would be no common factors, and the whole case would have degenerated into triviality.) We can arrange the f–v regression weights b_{pj} in either an $(m \times n)$ matrix as the order of its coefficients suggests or transpose it as is usually convenient and have the computer print it out as an $(n \times m)$ matrix, of which the pth column contains the n regression weights of the pth factor on the n variables. This matrix would be unambiguously recognizable in computer printout or in a program write up, if it is described as "regression weights for estimating factors," "weights for least-squares estimation of factor scores," or a clearly equivalent phrase. It is desirable to have in the printout also the multiple correlation between each factor and the n variables. This is a fundamental quantity, as we can think of it as an index of the precision of the estimates. We would not feel that we had used enough measures to estimate their generic property if this coefficient were low. (See following for typical coefficients). Table 5.2.1 gives the f–v regression weights calculated for the Thurstone case, from (1) the orthogonal factor pattern in Table 2.2.6; and (2) the oblique factor pattern in Table 3.2.2 and also gives the multiple correlation of each factor with the variables. The estimates $\hat{x}_p$ are

TABLE 5.2.1
Regression Weights for Thurstone Case

	(a) From Orthogonal Pattern			(b) From Oblique Pattern		
	I	II	III	I	II	III
1	.451	-.135	-.028	.353	.044	.064
2	.485	-.013	-.133	.391	.049	.071
3	.263	-.025	-.054	.226	.028	.041
4	-.152	.572	-.072	.025	.406	.056
5	-.110	.347	.013	.020	.319	.044
6	-.019	.224	-.072	.012	.203	.028
7	-.126	-.139	.650	.025	.041	.359
8	.027	-.072	.197	.019	.031	.269
9	-.095	.023	.286	.017	.029	.250

	(c) Correlation Matrix of Estimates From Orthogonal Pattern			(d) Cross-Correlation Matrix of Estimates and Factors From Orthogonal Pattern		
	$\hat{x}_1$	$\hat{x}_2$	$\hat{x}_3$	x_1	x_2	x_3
$\hat{x}_1$	1.000	-.072	-.069	.927	-.062	-.059
$\hat{x}_2$	-.072	1.000	-.098	.066	.872	-.084
$\hat{x}_3$	-.069	-.098	1.000	-.064	-.086	.855

computed by combining the standard scores of each subject, using (5.2.1), with these regression coefficients.

The mathematical theory of the problem reveals the following further properties of regression estimators:

1. By definition, each estimator $\hat{x}_p$ is uncorrelated with its own residual $x_p - \hat{x}_p$, but also each estimator $\hat{x}_p$ is uncorrelated with the residual $x_q - \hat{x}_q$ of every other estimate.

2. In general, when the common factors x_p in the model are uncorrelated (i.e., when we have used the orthogonal model) the estimates $\hat{x}_p$ are mutually correlated. The correlation matrix of the estimates for the Thurstone matrix is given in Table 5.2.1.

3. In general, when the common factors x_p are uncorrelated, the estimator $\hat{x}_p$ of one factor can be correlated with the other $m-1$ factors x_q $(q \neq p)$. The cross-correlation matrix of estimators and factors for the Thurstone case is shown in Table 5.2.1.

4. The regression estimators are biased, in the sense that *if* we could select a subpopulation of subjects all having the same factor score x_p, the mean of the estimator for the selected subpopulation would not be the same as the factor score on the basis of which they were selected. This causes a worry that if we had groups of subjects selected on the basis of experimental treatments and we wished to compare their mean factor scores, we *might* be misled by a comparison of means of regression estimators.

The properties 2 and 3 are rightly thought of as unfortunate defects of the regression estimators. In practice, these correlations tend to be low, so perhaps only theoretical purists should worry about them.

In practice and as already illustrated, we do not know the parameters of the model but have to estimate them. In practice, therefore, we use estimated correlations in the formulas for regression weights in place of the population values.

By definition, the regression estimators yield best estimators in the sense of least squares and have maximum correlations with the factors in the given population. They are based on one clear notion of a "best" choice for the population as a whole.

An alternative to regression estimation arises when we consider just one subject drawn from the population, not necessarily at random, and we want "best" estimates of just that subject's factor scores. We have no concern now with any other individual and certainly not with the population as a whole. There are two recognized ways to get best estimates of just one individual's factor scores, which yield the same answer so it can be encountered under two distinct headings. The first way is to get maximum likelihood (ML) estimates of the factor scores. That is, given the model itself, which states that, for this and other individuals,

$$y_j = \sum_{p=1}^{m} f_{jp}x_p + e_j \qquad j = 1, \ldots, n$$

we will assume that the subject's n unique factors $e_1, \ldots, e_n$ are normally distributed variables and choose values of $x_1, \ldots, x_m$ that make the obtained values of $y_1, \ldots, y_n$ maximally probable. The second way is known in the literature as *weighted least squares*, but to avoid ambiguity (as this sounds like a variation of the regression estimates) and for another reason it would be better to call it specifically *weighted least-squared residuals* (WLSR). We choose values of $x_1, \ldots, x_m$ for our individual to minimize the quantity

$$\phi = \sum_{j=1}^{n} \frac{e_j^2}{u_j^2} \tag{5.2.2}$$

where

$$e_j = y_j - \sum_{j=1}^{m} f_{jp}x_p \tag{5.2.3}$$

That is, we choose numbers $x_1, \ldots, x_m$ that minimize the sum of the ratios of the squares of the n unique scores to the variances of those unique scores. (This is what is meant by *weighted least-squared residuals*.)

The mathematician, on being presented with the task of finding an expression for the ML estimator of our individual's factor scores and with the task of finding an expression for the WLSR estimator, announces that the same solution applies to both problems. Again the problem yields an expression for a set of coefficients, let us say t_{pj}, calculated from knowledge of the factor loadings and residual variances from which we shall compute the ML/WLSR estimators, denoted by $\tilde{x}_1, \ldots, \tilde{x}_m$, as

$$\tilde{x}_p = \sum_{j=1}^{n} t_{pj}y_j. \tag{5.2.4}$$

[Note that we use a caret (^) for the regression estimators and a tilde (~) for the ML/WLSR estimators.]

The expression for ML/WLSR estimates was first given by Bartlett, and these estimates are often referred to in the literature as the *Bartlett estimates* of factor scores. We shall call them ML/WLSR estimates. As in the case of the regression estimates, we can expect to find the weights t_{pj} printed out by a computer program either as an $(m \times n)$ matrix or transposed into an $(n \times m)$ matrix. Unambiguous titles or descriptions would include ''weights for maximum likelihood/weighted least-squares estimators of factor scores'' and ''Bartlett scoring weights.'' Table 5.2.2 gives the ML weights for the Thurstone case (from Tables 2.2.2 and 3.2.2).

Although we have discussed this estimation method as though it is for just one individual, obviously we can apply it to each of many individuals drawn from the population, and we can in fact ask what properties the ML estimates have in the population. We find the following:

1. Necessarily, they have lower correlations with the common factors than do the regression estimates. In practice, the difference would usually be small.

2. Like the regression estimates, the ML estimates are correlated with each other even when the factors themselves are uncorrelated.

3. Unlike the regression estimates, the ML estimates have zero correlations with noncorresponding factors. Thus they are unambiguously related to ''the right'' factors and unrelated to ''the wrong'' factors.

4. Unlike the regression estimates, the ML estimates are unbiased. That is, if

TABLE 5.2.2
ML/WLSR Weights for Thurstone Case

	(a) From Orthogonal Pattern			(b) From Oblique Pattern		
	I	II	III	I	II	III
1	.546	-.222	-.064	.405	.0	.0
2	.553	-.044	-.228	.449	.0	.0
3	.317	-.052	-.097	.260	.0	.0
4	-.229	.790	-.167	.0	.551	.0
5	-.165	.473	-.020	.0	.434	.0
6	-.038	.312	-.130	.0	.275	.0
7	-.198	-.266	.937	.0	.0	.553
8	.019	-.127	.282	.0	.0	.414
9	.142	-.001	.404	.0	.0	.385

(c) Correlation Matrix of Estimates from Orthogonal Pattern				(d) Cross-Correlation Matrix of Estimates and Factors from Orthogonal Pattern			
	$\tilde{x}_1$	$\tilde{x}_2$	$\tilde{x}_3$		x_1	x_2	x_3
$\tilde{x}_1$	1.000	.079	.007	$\tilde{x}_1$	.992		
$\tilde{x}_2$	.079	1.000	.104	$\tilde{x}_2$		.865	
$\tilde{x}_3$	.077	.104	1.000	$\tilde{x}_3$			.848

we could select a subpopulation of subjects all having the same factor score x_p, the mean of the estimator over the subpopulation selected would be x_p. It rather seems that properties 3 and 4 of ML estimators, compared with the regression estimates, give the advantage to the ML estimates for both individual purposes and research on groups. Given an individual drawn from the population, certainly we would use the ML estimator, and we can use the normal distribution to put confidence bounds on the true values in the usual way. For group comparisons, unambiguous and unbiased estimates would generally seem desirable.

A small technical point should be noted in passing. By the usual principles of regression theory, the regression estimation procedure divides the factor score x_p into two uncorrelated parts, the regression part $\hat{x}_p$ and the residual $x_p - \hat{x}_p$. That is, we have

$$x_p = x_p + d_p \tag{5.2.5}$$

say, where

$$d_p = x_p - \hat{x}_p \tag{5.2.6}$$

and $\hat{x}_p$ and d_p are uncorrelated. It turns out that the ML estimator $\tilde{x}_p$ itself can be written as the sum of the factor score x_p and a discrepancy that are uncorrelated. That is, we have

$$\tilde{x}_p = x_p + \delta_p \tag{5.2.7}$$

say, where

$$\delta_p = \tilde{x}_p - x_p \tag{5.2.8}$$

and x_p and δ_p are uncorrelated. The result is that the variance of $\tilde{x}_p$ is the sum of the (unit) variance of x_p and the variance of δ_p, the error about the true value. If the computer program prints out the variances of the ML estimators, these must be greater than one, and we can compute the standard deviation of the error term and hence get confidence bounds. If the computer program prints out the variances of the regression estimators, these must be less than one, and of course we cannot obtain confidence bounds, which are meaningless for biased estimators. This paragraph is a technical aside that can be ignored, except that the reader should note the implied device for deciding whether given factor score estimates, inadequately labeled, are regression estimates or ML estimates. If their variances are less than one, they are regression scores. If their variances are greater than one, they are ML scores. To apply this test, it is necessary to know that they are one of these two, however.

Other estimators have been described in the literature but do not seem to have anything to recommend them. Package programs often contain estimates that cannot be recommended without enough information for one to be able to tell what device is being employed. In particular, the factor pattern itself, the v–f regression weight matrix, is sometimes used as though it were the f–v regression weight matrix. There is absolutely no foundation for this procedure in theory. It does not produce nonsensical results in general, however. In multivariate statistical methods, crude weighting methods have a way of giving results that are not at all horrible in comparison with optimal methods.

From one point of view, we could describe the process discussed in Section 5.1 of developing a test out of factor-analytic work as the process of assigning weights to a set of items equal to $+1$, -1, or 0, according to whether their factor loadings are "high positive," "high negative," or "low." Such crude but convenient scoring systems tend to yield sums of variables that are very highly correlated with combinations of them that employ "best" weights, in some precise sense of the word *best*, so it often may not seem worthwhile to work with optimal weights.

We can gain a sense of the typical numerical properties of factor score estimates by considering the special case of just one factor with equal factor loadings yielding equally correlated variables. In this case, the square of the correlation between the factor and its estimate from the n tests, whether regression or ML, is given by

$$\rho^2(x, \hat{x}) = \frac{nr}{1 + (n - 1)r} \tag{5.2.9}$$

where r is the correlation between any two variables y_j, y_k. (This expression is the same as the Spearman–Brown formula for the effect of test length on reliability. Here it is just a special case of factor score estimation theory. Whether or not true scores are factor scores depends on nonmathematical considerations.) By prevailing standards, in social science research, we might feel content with a correlation of about .85 or more between our estimate and that which we are estimating. By such a standard, it seems that 5 variables whose average correlation is above .4 or 2 with a correlation above .6 or 10 with an average above .2 will serve to determine a factor adequately.

The results on regression estimates and ML/WLSR estimates of common factor scores generalize, though not without complications, to models for linear structural relations as discussed in Chapter 4. In such models, if we wish to estimate the latent variables from the corresponding observed variables, we can do so with expressions that are of the same form as the ones used in the common factor model. However, in order to apply them it is necessary to do some extra manipulations of the parameter values obtained by fitting the model in order to compute the residual covariances of the observed variables about their regressions on the unobserved variables, to get ML/WLSR estimates, and to compute the covariances of the unobserved variables in order to get the regression estimates. A description of these manipulations without the language of matrix algebra would be quite uninformative.[2]

5.3. THE INDETERMINACY OF COMMON FACTORS

A number of investigators working on the mathematical theory of factor analysis have become convinced that common factor scores are seriously indeterminate quantities. As shown in equation (5.2.5), the unknown factor score x_p is the sum of its computable estimate $\hat{x}_p$ and the unknown residual d_p. It turns out that we can always invent arbitrary numbers d_p to add to $\hat{x}_p$ that yield arbitrary numbers x_p that have all the required properties of factor scores. There has been disagreement about the interpretation of the arbitrariness of the numbers x_p. We can work out the correlation between two sets of possible factor scores (estimates plus or minus invented numbers) that are chosen to be as dissimilar as possible. (This is a purely mathematical exercise, given the factor loadings.) The minimum possible correlation between alternative factor scores is given by $2\rho^2(x, \hat{x}) - 1$, where, as before, $\rho^2(x, \hat{x})$ is the square of the multiple correlation between the factor x and the n tests. If $\rho(x, \hat{x})$ is $1/\sqrt{2}$ (approximately .707), which does not seem a very low correlation, then $\rho^2(x, \hat{x})$ is $\frac{1}{2}$, and the correlation between the most dissimilar alternative factor scores that we can arbitrarily construct is zero.

The implications of this mathematical result are perhaps not yet fully understood and are still subject to disagreement. Some investigators have taken it to mean that the common factor model is subject to such a serious indeterminacy in its fundamental measurements that it should not be used, even if we have no interest in the factor scores themselves. The notion seems to be that if the factor scores of a set of examinees are not well determined by their scores on a set of tests, then the abstractive attributes that these scores serve to measure are not well defined by the characteristics of the tests in the set. That is, if the scores on a small number of items measuring a common property do not yield a unique score for the property, then correlatively the common features of the items do not provide a unique interpretation of the common property itself. Indeed, there is a sense in which this can be true.

As implied earlier, if we can imagine that the tests in a factor analysis are drawn from an infinite set of tests comprising a behavior domain, in which every

---

[2]See McDonald and Burr (1967) for a review of these and further results on factor score estimation. The importance of these results is probably diminishing as new, more general, models for linear structural analysis are developed. In research work on groups of examinees, we would now be likely to incorporate hypotheses about mean factor scores in models for simultaneous analysis in several populations (Section 6.2) or for repeated-measures, multimode data (Section 6.3), with no need to estimate individual factor scores and compare the means of the estimates across groups of examinees or across conditions.

common factor has infinitely many tests with nonzero loadings on it, then in the domain the common factor scores are correlated unity with their estimates from the infinity of tests. Suppose two investigators independently draw nonoverlapping subsets of tests from what is understood to be this behavior domain. Then the correlation between their factor score estimates will be equal to the product of the correlations of their estimates with the factor scores, as defined by the entire behavior domain. This correlation must be positive. As each augments the given set of tests to improve their estimates of the factor scores, the correlation between their factor score estimates must increase until in the limit the estimates coincide with each other and with the factor scores uniquely defined by the behavior domain they are both, by agreement, drawing from.

On the other hand, suppose that two investigators were to begin with the same set of tests, already factor analyzed, but with no idea of a defined behavior domain to draw from. Each then independently chooses further tests to add to the initial set to improve the estimation of the factors but with no concept of a defined behavior domain to draw them from. The augmented sets of tests are subject only to the requirement that the new tests have nonzero loadings on the same factors as the initial set. In such a case, there is no mathematical or logical reason why the two investigators should improve the agreement in their factor score estimates as they increase the number of their tests. Indeed, as this number becomes very large, the correlation between their estimates can be anything between unity and the quantity $2\rho^2(x, \hat{x}) - 1$, the minimum correlation between arbitrary mathematical constructions of factor scores, where $\rho^2(x, \hat{x})$ is calculated on the basis of the original, perhaps quite small, set of tests that both investigators started from. If the squared multiple correlation between the factor and the original tests is less than a half, then the correlation between their estimates can become and remain negative.

The mathematical theory just summarized in English is based on an extreme idealization of the process of inventing usable tests. Such idealizations are common in fields like classical physics, where the behavior of infinite homogeneous entities is commonly worked out as a theoretical approximation to the behavior of finite inhomogeneous entities. For the relation in our case between theory and practice, we must first make a further examination of the concept of a behavior domain.

We can imagine an exploratory factor analysis of a given, extremely large and thus virtually infinite collection of tests, whose extension (the range of its members) is defined by simple enumeration of its contents. In it, each factor score is determined almost certainly by scores on extremely large subsets of the tests. Given the tests and the factor analysis, the factor scores are measures of factor attributes that are definable *post facto* by abstraction of the common properties of the tests in those subsets. However, the collection of tests has not been supposed to have a clear denotation, a set of defining characteristics that distinguish tests that belong (and should belong) to the collection from those that do not (and should not). This means that two investigators cannot be conceived of as independently drawing tests from this one collection, except in the literal sense that they share a list of all the tests and agree to choose tests out of that list. This will not happen in practice, because there is just no reason why they should wish to do such a thing. And if there is no agreed list, there is no reason, as we have seen, why the investigators should approach agreement with each other.

On the other hand, if a behavior domain is a set of tests with a stated denotation of their attributes, enabling us to distinguish tests that have these attributes from tests that do not, then two investigators can be conceived of as drawing tests from this one behavior domain whenever they invent a set of tests that possess the required denotation. We can then reasonably hope that as they augment their sets of tests to improve the measures of their defined common attributes, measures that in this case follow naturally from a confirmatory rather than an exploratory factor analysis, they will approach agreement in their measurements of these. The question of disagreement about the "interpretation" of the factors cannot arise as such in this case.

The conclusion we draw is that common factor scores appear to be centrally and essentially defined on the basis of the generalizability of the tests we use to tests we have not used that are in a clear sense of the same kind, in the sense that factor score estimates from the tests we have used are estimates of the scores defined by all the tests of that kind. As a special case of this, in classical test theory, the score on a test of finite length estimates the "true score" that would be obtained by augmenting the test to make one of infinite length. But unless the items in the imagined test of infinite length have a clear denotation in terms of their content, we can in theory find more than one test of infinite length that contains a given finite test and more than one "true score" that it is estimating.

In practice, the idealized theory described here can fail to approximate reality well for a number of reasons. There can be and no doubt will be hidden ambiguities in the denotation of the behavior domain, leading to distinct realizations of it in the constructed tests (e.g., hidden ambiguities in the concept of *extraversion* or of *clinical anxiety*). Also, it can be difficult or impossible to find many exemplars of a concept that do not form groups on the basis of other characteristics, which cause the number of common factors to multiply rapidly.

Whatever the difficulties of implementing behavior domain concepts in practice, we can use these concepts as a framework for examining a common alternative view of the problem of factor score indeterminacy. Some of those who regard this problem as indicating a serious flaw in the common factor model have suggested that we abandon the model in favor of other methods of analysis that yield very similar results, yet with all their quantities ("loadings" and "scores") uniquely determined by the test scores even from a quite small number of tests. For example, as shown in Chapter 2, principal component theory and image analysis give close approximations to common factor loadings. They also give close approximations to common factor score estimates. It has therefore been argued that, for example, principal component scores are preferable to common factor scores because they are determinate and known and also that the methods are preferable to common factor analysis because they contain no indeterminate, unknown quantities. This argument, however, does not take into account the complementary facts that (1) the common factor score estimates are also determinate, so there is no reason to substitute principal component scores, for example, for estimates of common factor scores; (2) the principal component scores cannot have higher correlations with the corresponding principal component scores in a defined behavior domain from which the tests are drawn than do common factor score estimates with their corresponding factor scores in the domain. That is, principal components, images, and the like suffer a greater problem of indeterminacy than do common factors, in the sense that they have lower correlations with their counterparts in a defined behavior domain.

Some writers assert, then, that the common factor model has a serious indeterminacy problem in respect to its factor scores. Some further suggest that we should therefore use component theory, image theory, or even ad hoc adaptations of multidimensional scaling to the analysis of correlation coefficients as substitutes for the common factor model to achieve its intended purpose. In the present state of knowledge, the reader need not feel coerced by these assertions. Such alternative devices may be useful for certain purposes, but they have not been shown to be improvements on common factor analysis, preferably in its confirmatory form, for the purpose of investigating the generic properties of tests.[3]

5.4.   MATHEMATICAL NOTES ON CHAPTER 5

By the theory of regression already given in Section 1.6, given the $(n \times m)$ matrix of regression weights $\mathbf{F}$ of the observed variables $\mathbf{y}$ on the factors $\mathbf{x}$, the $(m \times m)$ correlation matrix of the factors, $\mathbf{P}$, and the $(n \times n)$ correlation matrix of the observed variables, $\mathbf{R}$, we know that the correlation matrix $\mathbf{S}$, of order $(n \times m)$, of $\mathbf{y}$ and $\mathbf{x}$ is given by

$$\mathbf{S} = \mathbf{FP}.$$

Then by (1.6.16), applied to the present problem, the vector of regression estimates $\hat{\mathbf{x}}$ of $\mathbf{x}$, required in (5.2.1), is given by

$$\hat{\mathbf{x}} = \mathbf{B}'\mathbf{y} \tag{5.4.1}$$

---

[3]In a penetrating article, Guttman (1955) extended earlier results of Kestelman and used them to raise the problem discussed in this section. Mulaik and McDonald (1978) and McDonald (1977) give technical discussions of the issue, and McDonald and Mulaik (1979) give a nontechnical review of the question.

where

$$B = R^{-1}S \tag{5.4.2}$$

or, alternatively,

$$B = R^{-1}FP. \tag{5.4.3}$$

In the special case of uncorrelated factors, (5.4.3) reduces to

$$B = R^{-1}F. \tag{5.4.4}$$

To obtain the ML/WLSR estimates $\tilde{x}$, we minimize the quantity

$$\phi = (y - Fx)'U^{-2}(y - Fx) \tag{5.4.5}$$

where, as usual, U^2 is the diagonal matrix of uniquenesses. The idea is to minimize the sum of squares of an individual's residuals but weighted proportionally to the variance of each residual in the population. The alternative approach via maximum likelihood leads us to maximize

$$\phi^* = \frac{1}{(2\pi|U^2|)^{1/2}} \exp - \frac{1}{2}(y - Fx)'U^{-2}(y - Fx) \tag{5.4.6}$$

and, by inspection, the two problems must have the same solution. The ML/WLSR estimator $\tilde{x}$ of x turns out to be

$$\hat{x} = (F'U^{-2}F)^{-1}F'U^{-2}y \tag{5.4.7}$$

a result obtained by methods outside the scope of the algebra introduced in Appendix A1.

In a computer program designed to produce factor scores after completing estimation of the factor pattern and so on, we would expect to find that the observed scores, formed into an $(n \times N)$ matrix Y, are put into standard measure in the sample and stored on scratch tape while the main computations are going on; then, after F and U have been estimated, the estimates are employed to obtain the matrices required by (5.4.3) or (5.4.7). Finally, the scores on scratch tape would be called in, one subject at a time, and the estimates computed.

For the rest of these remarks we assume the model with uncorrelated factors. From (5.4.1) we find that

$$E\{\hat{x}\hat{x}'\} = B'E\{yy'\}B$$
$$= B'RB \tag{5.4.8}$$

hence, with (5.4.4)

$$E\{\hat{x}\hat{x}'\} = F'R^{-1}F \tag{5.4.9}$$

which in general is not a diagonal matrix. That is, in general the regression estimators are mutually correlated even when the "true" values are assumed uncorrelated.

Further,

$$E\{x\hat{x}'\} = E\{xy'R^{-1}F\}$$
$$= E\{xy'\}R^{-1}F$$

or

$$E\{x\hat{x}'\} = F'R^{-1}F \tag{5.4.10}$$

That is, in general the regression estimators are correlated with noncorresponding "true" values as well as with the corresponding "true" values.

In contrast,

$$E\{\hat{x}\hat{x}\} = (F'U^{-2}F)^{-1}F'U^{-2} E\{yy'\}U^{-2}F(F'U^{-2}F)^{-1}$$
$$= (F'U^{-2}F)^{-1}F'U^{-2}RU^{-2}F(F'U^{-2}F)^{-1}$$
$$= (F'U^{-2}F)^{-1}F'U^{-2}(FF' + U^2)U^{-2}F(F'U^{-2}F)^{-1}$$

from which we obtain

$$E\{\tilde{x}\tilde{x}'\} = I_m + (F'U^{-2}F)^{-1} \tag{5.4.11}$$

and similarly

$$E\{x\tilde{x}'\} = E\{xy'U^{-2}F(F'U^{-2}F)^{-1}\}$$
$$= F'U^{-2}F(F'U^{-2}F)^{-1}$$
$$= I_m$$

that is, the ML/WLSR estimators are uncorrelated with noncorresponding true factors.

It should also be noted that we can express (5.3.3) in the form

$$B = R^{-1}FP = U^{-2}F[F'U^{-2}F + P^{-1}]^{-1} \tag{5.4.12}$$

This is a well-known "shortcut" expression for computing the regression weights, due originally to Ledermann. It has been used in Table 5.2.1. It requires the inversion of an $m \times m$ matrix instead of an $n \times n$ matrix, thus saving arithmetic. The reader may prove the identity of the expressions in (5.4.12) by multiplying on the left by R in the form $FPF' + U^2$.

6

Problems of Relationship Between Factor Analyses

6.1. THE COMPARISON OF SEPARATE ANALYSES

So far we have considered factor-analytic hypotheses relating to a single-sample correlation matrix drawn from a single population. In this and Section 6.2 we consider the problem that arises when we wish to compare and contrast sets of factor-analytic results from two or more populations. In section 6.3 we consider the distinct but similar problem in repeated-measures designs where we compare factor-analytic results from the same measures repeatedly administered to the same subjects in two or more conditions. The first problem in its most general form arises when we have multivariate data from two or more samples of subjects, based on variables that might be the same or might be overlapping sets or different yet similar in what is deemed to be measured, and we wish to make comparative judgments. The comparison may be based on raw data matrices, or it may be based on our own data relative to published, possibly quite ancient, correlation matrices or published factor patterns whose origins in data have been left a total mystery.

Here we briefly consider a list of problems; then in Section 6.2 we describe a general system, due to Jöreskog, that handles a number of situations very well.

(a) Factorial Invariance

The question is, to what extent will a variable retain its *factorial description* (i.e., the list of factor loadings on the m factors that describes the variable as a mixture of factors) independently of the set of other variables in the matrix and independently of the population sample? It seems just obvious that we should not expect absolute invariance of such a description. If we think of the problem from a content-analysis point of view, the same variable in different contexts of other variables will be a joint indicator of different generic properties. Moved from one context to another, its specific content may become content in common with the other variables, and its previous generic content may now be unique to it, out of all the variables in the set we have moved it to. This does not mean that factor-analytic results do not point at all to realities of the world of social science data. It just means that there are many ways to classify the materials of that world. Also, our freedom to invent tests in psychology and education means a freedom to emphasize and, up to a certain point, to create particular generic properties by the redundancy we ourselves put into our "distinct" measures. To the extent that we have a well-defined behavior domain, we may manage to get reasonably invariant results by staying within that domain and selecting from it systematically. If we step outside it, knowingly, we expect our factors to change and the classification of the variables to change.

It has particularly been claimed for simple structure that the pattern of zero and nonzero factor loadings for a given variable tends to remain unchanged as other variables are added or deleted. There may be something to this claim, though like all tendency statements it is hard to prove or falsify. We can, of course, perversely and deliberately produce cases where it is not true and could even turn this into a game. That is, B can "prove" that A was wrong in supposing that, say, extraversion is a single factor, by inventing enough groups of similar variables to define subgeneric properties as special facets of extraversion. More rarely, A may "prove" that B was wrong in supposing the concept to be multifactor, by making sure that different facets of the concept are not represented by more than one measure. A sufficiently careful content analysis should enable us to discover what is going on in these cases. Commonly we might wish to treat A's general factor as a higher-order factor explaining the correlations among B's multiple factors.

From these remarks, the reader will understand how delicate an art is involved in the surveys we find from time to time, in which the attempt is made to identify factors discovered or invented by different investigators, using different measures, at least some of which might be thought to be measures of "similar" properties. (Note that the phrase *discovered or invented* leaves open the question whether, when we invent tests, we invent the generic properties of the tests or we discover generic properties of the behavior we are investigating, i.e., properties of a behavior domain that exists independently of our decision to make measurements.)

(b) The Effects of Selection

One year after the basic theory of correlation was worked out, Pearson in 1896 gave formulas for the effects on correlation coefficients of selecting a subpopulation differing from a "parent" population in the variances of one or more variables. We expect, for example, that when we select a subgroup of students for university, their range of talent will be narrower than in the population from which they are selected. We would not be surprised if the correlations of cognitive measures in such a group dropped below those in the general population. Such a selection is like the case of partial correlation, which is just what we get when we select a subpopulation to have zero variance on one variable—the one partialled out. Thus, selection formulas are more general versions of partial correlation formulas.

A simple and powerful principle from which the Pearson formulas may be derived is the principle that a regression function, by definition, is independent of the distribution of the independent variables. That is, a regression function is a mathematical function giving the mean of the dependent variable for any *fixed* values of the independent variables and hence must be the same in any subpopulation selected on the basis of the independent variables. From this, the mathematician is able to reverse the mathematical logic that gives regression weights as a function of the correlations to give the changes in the correlations that would be consistent with unaltered regression weights.

Meredith (1964) applied Pearson's selection theorem to the effects of selection on factor analysis. Meredith concludes that it is reasonable to expect to obtain a factor pattern that is invariant over subpopulations derived from a parent population by selection on the basis of some variable external to those in the analysis. This conclusion actually follows immediately from the definition of the factor pattern as a matrix of v–f regression weights. Care is needed over scaling to make the statement true. Obviously, we could not expect to put either the variables or the factors into standard measure (mean zero, variance unity) in more than one subpopulation simultaneously. It is necessary to find a common scale for all the populations, for variables and factors, to obtain invariant factor patterns. If we do choose to write the factor pattern for each subpopulation as though the variables and the factors were in standard measure in that subpopulation, then the factor patterns for different populations are related by scale transformations of rows and columns. It also turns out that the correlations between the variables and the factors change from one subpopulation to another. It is the invariance of the factor loadings that suggests we should regard the factor pattern as the fundamental, interpretable set of numbers arising from factor analysis rather than the quite alterable correlations of the variables with the factors. Also, the advantage of uncorrelated factors seems a little less attractive when we note that factors that are uncorrelated in one population will generally be correlated in another.

(c) Indices of Factor Congruence

Attempts have been made to define an index measuring the "resemblance" of two factors. Suppose we are comparing a single column $[f_1^{(1)}, \ldots, f_n^{(1)}]$ of factor loadings from one population or treatment condition with another column

$[f_1^{(2)}, \ldots, f_n^{(2)}]$ of factor loadings from a second population or treatment condition with the same n measures. If the paired numbers in the two columns are exactly the same, both factors—the generic properties x_1 and x_2 of which our n measures are weighted combinations with these weights—would perforce receive the same interpretation, because our interpretation is based solely on the nature of each of the n measures and their regression weights on the factor. Hence we go beyond the mathematical truism that the two sets of factor loadings are the same, to the nonmathematical statement that x_1 and x_2 are the same (i.e., they are the same measurable generic property).

Now suppose that instead of being the same, the columns are proportional. That is, each number in the second list is the corresponding number in the first list multiplied by a common constant. In such a case, the investigator need not interpret the factors in the same way. If we followed the oldest tradition of interpretation, we would interpret them alike, because the strategy was to identify the generic property on the basis of the conceptual contrast between the measures whose loadings show the most extreme numerical contrast. On the other hand, in the set of practices associated with approximate simple structure whereby a factor is identified by the variables with loadings above a certain value (perhaps .3), a change in proportionality constant could carry a critical number of variables above or below the magic threshold for regarding them as *salient* (to introduce further, self-explanatory jargon) and cause a change in interpretation. In practice, some investigators seem content to check for proportionality when comparing factors while working with the actual sizes of the loadings when interpreting the factors. This *should* create inconsistencies.

One argument for the notion of proportionality as identifying factors was given by Cattell (1944) under the title *parallel proportional profiles*. He argued that factor loadings should change proportionally under selection or under experimental manipulation if they are "real psychological entities." Actually, from the argument based on Pearson's selection theorem, we would expect factor loadings from correlation matrices to change proportionally when the effect of selection is to change the variance of each factor score and we fit the model with factor scores in standard measure. On the other hand, one might suppose that the typical effect of experimental selection would be to change the mean of the factor score rather than its variance.

Basically, two measures of the resemblance of factors have been employed, one measuring departure from equality of the factor loadings, the other measuring their closeness to proportionality. It is unclear what we should use such indices for. That is, if two factors are not the same in two populations and yet they "resemble each other," it is unclear what we should do about them in further research. Hence it might seem pointless to contemplate the measured degree of a resemblance that is less than complete. One proper motive for introducing such indices appears under heading (d).

The measures of resemblance have come to be known as measures of *congruence*. The measure based on departures from equality is the usual "distance" or squared discrepancy measure, namely, just a sum of squares of the differences between corresponding factor loadings. The measure based on closeness to proportionality is much more popular. It is known as the *coefficient of factorial congruence*. It is due to Burt (1948) and is sometimes attributed to Tucker (1951). It is given by

$$\rho_1 = \frac{\displaystyle\sum_{j=1}^{n} f_j^{(1)} f_j^{(2)}}{\left[\displaystyle\sum_{j=1}^{n} f_j^{(1)2}\right]\left[\displaystyle\sum_{j=1}^{n} f_j^{(2)2}\right]} \tag{6.1.1}$$

It is a quantity resembling a correlation coefficient (without a "correction" for means). It reaches a maximum of unity when the loadings are proportional. If negative, its sign could always be changed by changing the signs of all the loadings in one column. Because of its resemblance to a correlation coefficient, it will probably appeal to those social scientists who take comfort from contemplating indices that give them a sense of closure and the right to regard their research as finished. It might be said, however, that these quantities are of little value in themselves and of little use if one goes beyond them.

(d) Transformations to Maximize Resemblance

If we have two (or more) factor patterns based on the same variables whose columns do not resemble each other closely, it may be that a further transformation will reveal a resemblance that was initially concealed by the arbitrariness of the rotations in the separate exploratory analyses. A number of methods have been suggested for transforming factor patterns to make one or more or all their columns maximally similar.

The methods result from four basic choices. (i) *Procrustean* or *target* methods transform one pattern to maximize its similarity to a fixed *target* matrix, which may be another given pattern or may be a theoretical matrix containing prescribed zero and nonzero numbers. *Mutual congruence* methods transform two or more factor patterns to maximize mutual similarity. (ii) The transformations may be orthogonal or oblique. (iii) The similarity sought may be *pairwise* or *entire*. That is, we may seek to build up transformations that successively optimize the pairwise similarity of individual columns of the factor patterns (which may contain different numbers of factors), or we may seek to optimize the overall similarity of the nm loadings in the entire matrices. (iv) Measures of similarity chosen to solve these problems include: first, the *discrepancy* measure already discussed; second, the coefficient of factorial congruence in (6.1.1); third, a *sum of products* measure,

$$\Pi = \sum_{j=1}^{n} f_j^{(1)} f_j^{(2)} \tag{6.1.2}$$

obtained, in effect, by leaving out the normalizing denominator from (6.1.1); and, fourth, a *test-congruence* measure, which is a sum of measures of congruence of the factor loadings of the same tests across samples, given by

$$\tau = \sum_{j=1}^{n} \left\{ \frac{\sum_{p=1}^{m} f_{jp}^{(1)} f_{jp}^{(2)}}{\sqrt{\left[\sum_{p=1}^{m} f_{jp}^{(1)2} \right] \left[\sum_{p=1}^{m} f_{jp}^{(2)2} \right]}} \right\} \tag{6.1.3}$$

where $f_{jp}^{(1)}, f_{jp}^{(2)}$ represent the factor loading of test j on factor p in samples 1 and 2, respectively. [Notice that the test-congruence coefficient in (6.1.3) is based on row sums of squares and products of m factor loadings, whereas the factorial congruence coefficient in (6.1.1) is based on column sums of squares and products of n factor loadings.]

Not all possible combinations of choices (i)–(iv) have been treated. Most theorists working on them have faced the mathematical challenge of finding an algebraic solution rather than simply using a numerical optimization technique, and some combinations yield seemingly intractable problems in matrix algebra. In particular, the choice of a measure of similarity may be made in order to create a solvable algebra problem rather than because it is the desired criterion. Accordingly, a coefficient of factorial congruence may be calculated and quoted when it is not in fact the criterion that has been optimized. This is a reasonable strategy, but it should be noted that it contains an element of compromise.

Evans (1971) has compared and illustrated a number of methods (including his own contribution). Our numerical examples are directly taken from his work. Eighteen cognitive tests were given by Flores to samples of Canadian and Filipino children in Grades 6 and 8, yielding four samples for comparison. The tests are measures of Thurstone's primary mental abilities, including tests of verbal ability (V), word fluency (W), reasoning (R) as in the much-studied example of Chapters 2 and 3, plus spatial ability (S), perceptual ability (P), numerical ability (N), and memory (M). The four sample correlation matrices were separately factor analyzed by an exploratory least-squares method ("principal axes with iterations"), with six factors prescribed in each sample. The resulting factor patterns were transformed by varimax to approximate orthogonal simple structure. The resulting factor patterns, just for the two Grade 8 samples, are given in Table 6.1.1. The mutual agreement between the matrices and the agreement of each with the "known" classification of the tests is not what we could regard as very satisfactory. Table 6.1.2 gives the factor pattern matrices resulting from rotating the varimax matrices to maximize the factorial congruence coefficient for each factor in turn, while keeping the transformation orthogonal. Table 6.1.3

TABLE 6.1.1*

Independent Varimax Factor Matrices

	Canadian Grade 8 Factors						Filipino Grade 8 Factors					
	I	II	III	IV	V	VI	I	II	III	IV	V	VI
1. Verbal Meaning (V)	.65	.05	.17	.27	.22	-.02	.65	.03	.14	-.02	.26	.15
2. Vocabulary (V)	.89	.22	.10	.02	.06	.06	.47	.44	.07	.00	.03	.13
3. Word Endings (W)	.26	.13	.59	.03	-.05	.24	.32	-.07	.00	.06	.19	.57
4. Word Beginnings (W)	.36	.05	.58	.26	-.01	-.15	.12	.03	-.07	-.10	.29	.54
5. Spatial Relations (S)	.17	.84	.05	-.10	.08	.04	.17	.13	.61	.18	.15	-.19
6. Card Rotation (S)	.15	.82	.06	.03	-.03	.07	.11	-.01	.94	.13	.05	.06
7. Identical Pictures (P)	-.01	.29	.21	.12	.43	-.08	.35	-.18	.22	.40	.36	.23
8. Maze Tracing (P)	.02	.45	.40	-.21	.23	-.10	.05	-.07	.30	.69	.10	.04
9. Finding A's (P)	-.15	.15	.11	-.10	.41	.13	.31	-.15	.15	.01	-.04	.50
10. Arithmetic (N)	.32	.26	.20	.13	.22	-.02	.56	.09	.09	.18	.27	.01
11. Subtr. Mult. (N)	.10	-.18	.04	.82	-.07	.03	.64	-.13	.18	.03	.00	.14
12. Division (N)	.03	.11	.01	.73	.11	.05	.81	.09	.10	.15	.01	-.06
13. Letter Series (R)	.17	-.03	-.06	.06	.77	.15	.06	.02	.08	.16	.76	.07
14. Word Grouping (R)	.40	.16	.34	-.17	.24	-.02	.43	.25	.35	-.01	.23	.02
15. Number Series (R)	.34	.14	-.08	.07	.33	.52	.10	.05	.15	.05	.61	-.08
16. Raven's P.M. (R)	.29	.16	.39	-.26	.52	-.05	.28	.30	.21	.54	.26	.12
17. Picture-Number (M)	.03	.18	-.03	.33	.06	.38	-.22	.12	.10	.15	-.07	.64
18. Object-Number (M)	-.10	.11	.28	.14	.19	.44	.04	.05	-.08	.08	-.04	.62

*From Table 2 in Evans (1971).

TABLE 6.1.2
Congruent Matrices for Groups C8 and F8
Maximum Congruence Coefficients Method

	Canadian Grade 8 Factors						Filipino Grade 8 Factors					
	I	II	III	IV	V	VI	I	II	III	IV	V	VI
1. Verbal Meaning (V)	.54	.00	.51	-.01	-.02	-.13	.50	.01	.33	.18	.02	.38
2. Vocabulary (V)	.43	.12	.64	-.03	.09	-.49	.44	.02	.39	.13	-.26	-.03
3. Word Endings (W)	.43	-.10	-.03	.38	-.01	-.39	.50	-.10	-.05	.41	.19	.08
4. Word Beginnings (W)	.49	-.07	.22	.36	-.33	-.17	.46	-.19	-.02	.23	.30	-.10
5. Spatial Relations (S)	.23	.75	-.03	.09	.12	-.34	.22	.61	.15	-.17	-.07	.19
6. Card Rotation (S)	.20	.72	.02	.23	.15	-.26	.22	.90	.12	.09	.16	.33
7. Identical Pictures (P)	.46	.27	-.14	-.08	-.11	.07	.52	.19	-.22	.12	.04	.41
8. Maze Tracing (P)	.35	.35	-.27	.02	-.22	-.32	.29	.43	-.45	.02	-.25	.23
9. Finding A's (P)	.29	.11	-.33	-.20	.07	.00	.29	.06	.01	.52	.17	.10
10. Arithmetic (N)	.44	.20	.17	.03	-.04	-.13	.48	.03	.18	.03	-.16	.38
11. Subtr. Mult. (N)	.27	-.17	.39	.40	.07	.55	.28	.09	.26	.37	-.04	.43
12. Division (N)	.37	.12	.23	.30	.12	.50	.37	.05	.38	.23	-.34	.50
13. Letter Series (R)	.58	-.01	-.03	-.52	.17	.13	.58	.00	-.15	-.38	.26	.21
14. Word Grouping (R)	.43	.06	.08	-.09	-.14	-.41	.44	.26	.36	-.02	-.04	.16
15. Number Series (R)	.42	.03	.11	-.15	.54	-.14	.42	.07	.02	-.39	.19	.22
16. Raven's P.M. (R)	.57	.08	-.11	-.29	-.20	-.37	.61	.27	-.13	-.04	-.33	.12
17. Picture-Number (M)	.24	.09	.03	.20	.40	.14	.28	.11	-.29	.37	.12	-.43
18. Object-Number (M)	.38	-.05	-.28	.19	.29	-.01	.33	-.11	-.17	.44	.09	-.23
Root Mean Square Discrepancies							.04	.12	.18	.23	.25	.40
Congruence Coefficients							1.00	.91	.74	.62	.27	.05

*From Table 5 in Evans (1971).

178

TABLE 6.1.3*

Maximally Similar Factor Matrices (Least Squares Method)

	Canadian Grade 8 Factors						Filipino Grade 8 Factors					
	I	II	III	IV	V	VI	I	II	III	IV	V	VI
1. Verbal Meaning (V)	.44	-.55	-.14	-.13	-.14	.15	.43	-.49	-.00	-.02	-.33	.03
2. Vocabulary (V)	.50	-.56	-.07	-.48	.07	.24	.46	-.34	-.05	-.17	.06	.27
3. Word Endings (W)	.40	-.32	.31	.17	.28	.17	.39	-.37	.22	.32	.00	-.16
4. Word Beginnings (W)	.45	-.34	.05	.26	-.01	.42	.31	-.34	.11	.21	.18	-.32
5. Spatial Relations (S)	-.05	-.26	.63	-.44	-.15	.27	-.08	-.29	.34	-.45	-.26	.20
6. Card Rotations (S)	.08	-.16	.64	-.40	-.20	.25	.03	-.20	.74	-.48	-.31	.05
7. Identical Pictures (P)	-.13	-.42	.23	.13	-.25	.09	.01	-.56	.32	.21	-.28	.05
8. Maze Tracing (P)	-.18	-.37	.42	.03	.07	.34	-.29	-.34	.46	.15	-.13	.36
9. Finding A's (P)	-.26	-.31	.23	.11	-.02	-.15	.42	-.15	.34	.24	-.11	-.10
10. Arithmetic (N)	.17	-.42	.14	-.07	-.13	.17	.22	-.52	-.03	-.01	-.28	.19
11. Subtr. Mult. (N)	.58	.05	-.15	.29	-.57	-.14	.43	-.25	.12	.08	-.44	.12
12. Division (N)	.39	-.09	.09	.18	-.59	-.13	.44	-.38	-.07	-.01	-.45	.40
13. Letter Series (R)	-.18	-.68	-.10	.01	-.19	-.33	-.22	-.71	.00	-.03	-.02	-.25
14. Word Grouping (R)	.08	-.52	.08	-.07	.18	.25	.28	-.43	.10	-.32	-.18	.11
15. Number Series (R)	.21	-.46	.16	-.26	.01	-.42	-.17	.55	-.04	-.18	-.11	-.18
16. Raven's P.M. (R)	-.15	-.71	.10	.04	.17	.20	-.00	-.61	.25	-.01	.04	.39
17. Picture-Number (M)	.28	-.09	.27	-.04	-.19	-.31	.17	-.06	.48	.22	.44	-.09
18. Object-Number (M)	.15	-.23	.38	.22	.05	-.29	.33	-.12	.27	.34	.29	-.09
Congruence Coefficients	.93	.97	.96	.93	.79	.94	.92	.99	.92	.89	.84	.56
R.M.S. Discrepancies	.12	.09	.08	.08	.15	.10	.12	.07	.12	.11	.14	.20

*From Table 6 in Evans (1971).

gives the factor pattern matrices, for the same two samples only, that result when all four factor patterns are orthogonally transformed to minimize the discrepancy measure between each of them and a matrix containing the average of the four factor loadings of each test on each factor. Table 6.1.4 gives the results of a further varimax transformation, which we are free to apply, that is chosen to yield approximate simple structure for the average factor loadings (as already transformed to minimize discrepancies) and then applied to the Canadian and Filipino Grade 8 matrices (as transformed to minimize discrepancies). Note that the measures of congruence and discrepancy are calculated between each of the given matrices and the average factor loading matrix of the four samples (not shown here).

Clearly the transformation methods improve the resemblance between the columns of the matrices. But from this example it is also clear that different methods do not necessarily agree with each other closely and that the resulting matrices may not yield clear, interpretable structure. Such exploratory analyses and rotations to improve congruence are perhaps best regarded as preliminary steps to aid in the formulation of suitable hypotheses for Section 6.2, in cases where the investigator feels quite unable to formulate such hypotheses on substantive grounds. We may hope that such cases will be uncommon. It should also be noted that most of these methods were developed before those of Section 6.2 became available. Perhaps the need for congruence-transformation methods can be considered to be less than in earlier times.

6.2. SIMULTANEOUS FACTOR ANALYSIS IN SEVERAL POPULATIONS

Jöreskog (1971) presented an extremely general system for the analysis of samples from l distinct populations, measured on possibly different variables (and different numbers of variables). We suppose that within the gth population we have the usual form of the common factor model for n_g variables and m_g factors. We write it as

$$y_j^{(g)} = \sum_{p=1}^{m_g} f_{jp}^{(g)} x_p^{(g)} + e_j^{(g)} \qquad \begin{aligned} j &= 1, \ldots, n_g \\ g &= 1, \ldots, l \end{aligned} \qquad (6.2.1)$$

We have a superscript (g) in addition to the usual subscripts. As before, the correlation (covariance) of two measures in the gth population is given by

$$c_{jk}^{(g)} = \sum_{p=1}^{m_g} \sum_{q=1}^{m_g} f_{jp}^{(g)} \rho_{pq}^{(g)} f_{kq}^{(g)} \qquad (6.2.2)$$

TABLE 6.1.4*
Varimax Rotated Maximally Similar Factor Matrices

	Canadian Grade 8 Factors						Filipino Grade 8 Factors					
	I	II	III	IV	V	VI	I	II	III	IV	V	VI
1. Verbal Meaning (V)	.64	.09	.03	.32	.22	-.01	.44	.09	.08	.50	.27	.09
2. Vocabulary (V)	.89	-.07	.22	.09	.11	.03	.63	.10	.08	.15	-.05	-.04
3. Word Endings (W)	.37	.41	.11	.01	-.05	.42	.19	.31	-.07	.28	.20	.46
4. Word Beginnings (W)	.44	.51	.05	.29	-.09	.06	.20	.15	-.21	.07	.25	.48
5. Special Relations (S)	.17	-.03	.84	.00	.09	.12	.19	-.13	.64	.08	.19	-.07
6. Card Rotation (S)	.15	-.05	.80	.12	-.02	.18	.06	-.20	.87	.17	.13	.28
7. Identical Pictures (P)	-.00	.28	.30	.18	.37	-.01	.08	.37	.30	.30	.45	.14
8. Maze Tracing (P)	.09	.41	.50	-.14	.16	.04	-.09	.47	.55	-.02	.21	-.05
9. Finding A's (P)	-.14	.15	.16	-.09	.40	.12	.08	.20	.06	.37	.00	.46
10. Arithmetic (N)	.33	.16	.25	.19	.20	.04	.40	.20	.15	.35	.29	-.10
11. Subtr. Mult. (N)	.07	.00	-.28	.78	-.09	.12	.25	.13	.15	.61	.06	.08
12. Division (N)	-.01	-.01	.01	.73	.09	.13	.48	.21	.18	.59	.04	-.19
13. Letter Series (R)	.12	.01	-.03	.09	.79	-.00	.17	.08	.06	-.08	.76	.05
14. Word Grouping (R)	.45	.29	.20	-.12	.22	.02	.48	-.07	.30	.22	.20	.05
15. Number Series (R)	.31	-.24	.08	.06	.45	.40	.19	-.07	.11	-.02	.60	-.05
16. Raven's P.M. (R)	.34	.41	.22	-.19	.48	-.03	.38	.44	.41	-.03	.27	-.02
17. Picture-Number (M)	.01	-.15	.09	.30	.13	.39	.01	.29	.08	-.23	-.09	.60
18. Object Number (M)	-.05	.16	.05	.09	.23	.51	.10	.34	-.11	.01	-.05	.51
Factor Content	V	P/F	S	N	R_s	M	V	P	S	N	R_s	M
Congruence Coefficients	.98	.92	.95	.88	.94	.90	.92	.79	.95	.88	.93	.87
R.M.S. Discrepancies	.08	.10	.10	.14	.10	.10	.13	.15	.10	.14	.11	.14

*From Table 7 in Evans (1971).

where $\rho_{pq}^{(g)}$ is the correlation between factors $x_p^{(g)}$ and $x_q^{(g)}$ in the gth population. The $v-f$ regression weights (factor loadings) $f_{jp}^{(g)}$; the correlations between factors, $\rho_{pq}^{(g)}$ in each population; and, implicitly, a set of n_g residual variances, $u_j^{(g)2}$, of the residuals $e_j^{(g)}$, are the parameters of the model that we would have to estimate from samples. It is not assumed to begin with that we have the same number of variables or factors in each population or, indeed, that the variables or the factors are the same. Some overlap of variables and factors in distinct populations would be necessary to motivate a simultaneous and comparative analysis; otherwise we might as well just do l separate analyses, one for each population. (For simplicity, we are assuming, incorrectly, that the variables are in deviation measure in each of the l populations. In a correct but more complicated account, we would describe the model in raw measure, introducing population means for the tests and the factors.)

Now suppose we draw a sample from each of the l populations. The samples need not be of the same size, and we shall say that we draw N_g subjects from the gth population. We compute the sample covariance matrix from each sample. (Here, the correlation matrices do not contain all the relevant information. We can always think about the covariances as correlations multiplied by the two standard deviations of the variables, if we want to have a "meaning" for each such number). Note that the l samples are independently drawn with no subjects in common. Then we are able to obtain a quantity for this case that again has the properties of the LRC (likelihood ratio criterion) that was taken for granted in previous uses of ML estimation. That is, we compute an LRC whose minimum gives in large samples a chi-square (assuming normality of the l population distributions) for a test of the hypothesis that the l sets of covariances are given by (6.2.2) against the alternative hypothesis that they are any possible values. The quantity computed is also an algebraic, distribution-free measure of the fit of the hypothesis to the l samples, being zero only if it is possible to describe each sample precisely by the model and becoming larger as the discrepancies between the sample covariances and the fitted values increase. The degrees of freedom for the chi-square are given by the number of independent covariances in the l covariance matrices, less the number of factor loadings $f_{jp}^{(g)}$, and correlations $\rho_{pq}^{(g)}$ between factors that are to be estimated.

As in the models for confirmatory factor analysis, it is possible to prescribe where there will be zero factor loadings in the factor patterns for each of the l populations and to have equalities linking them. For most purposes, this is all we need to know about the theory. The technical part of it is contained in the definition of the LRC for the problem and the computing arithmetic for minimizing it.

The description so far would give no idea of the flexibility and generality of this model in use for comparative factor analysis. The following illustrations should help to do this.

1. We might wish to test the hypothesis that the covariance matrices of the l populations are all equal. (This includes the requirement that the number of variables be equal, and usually the measures would be the same in each population.) This particular case is well-known to be solved quite simply. The LRC becomes a function of the sample covariance matrices and of the average covariance matrix of all the samples (their determinants) taking into account their sample sizes. The problem can also be treated as a special case of Jöreskog's model. Possibly we should test this hypothesis before we take seriously any hypothesis of specific differences in factor composition between the populations, at least in exploratory work.

2. We might wish to test the hypothesis that the correlation matrices of the l populations are all equal. This is not, of course, the same as the preceding hypothesis. It seems quite likely that the variance of a set of variables will change from one condition to another, thus changing their entire covariance matrices while their correlations remain unchanged. So the hypothesis here is that the correlations are unchanged, and the populations differ, if at all, only in the variances of the variables. This hypothesis can also be treated as a special case of Jöreskog's model. Again, failure to reject it would lead us to treat with extreme scepticism most hypotheses of specific differences between the populations in factor pattern, unique variances, or correlations between factors.

3. If, with samples on which the same n measures are studied, we have rejected the two previous hypotheses, we might test a sequence of hypotheses as to the common factor composition of the variables, each including the previous as part of its specification and each more constraining than the previous. These are: (a) the hypothesis that the number of common factors is the same, $m,$ for all populations; (b) the hypothesis that the ($n \times m$) factor pattern is the same for all populations; (c) the hypothesis that the ($n \times m$) factor pattern and the n unique variances are the same for all populations; (d) the hypothesis that the ($n \times$ m) factor pattern, the n unique variances, and the ($m \times m$) matrix of covariances between factors are the same for all populations. Hypothesis 3(d) looks as though it is the same as hypothesis 1, because certainly if 3(d) is true, 1 must be true. That is, if the covariance matrices have the same factor loadings, unique variances, and factor covariances, then they are the same. But if hypothesis (1) is true, hypothesis 3(d) may be false, if, for example, all the covariance matrices were the same, but they needed more than m factors to explain them. Hence, 3(d) is a much more detailed hypothesis.

4. Many other very detailed hypotheses can be set up and tested. For example, we may prescribe a hypothesis of the simple structure type for the overlapping part of the factor patterns of two populations with some variables the same and some variables different when we are supposing that some factors are the same and some factors are different. Exact hypotheses corresponding to the notion of congruent factors discussed in Section 6.1 can be expressed by the

requirement that "congruent" sets of factor loadings be the same and then choosing whether to have their factor variances the same (corresponding to the requirement of zero discrepancy for congruence) or different (corresponding to the requirement of proportionality for congruence).

Occasionally we would like to use the Jöreskog model to compare new results with results published in the literature, where we may not hope to recover the original data from the previous investigator's data bank, as through inadvertence or lapse of time they may not have been left on file. Provided that the publication gives the sample correlation matrix and also the standard deviations and of course the sample size (without which any published study if valueless), we have sufficient information to make the published data serve as one sample representing one population in a comparative analysis. This is perhaps a good place to urge researchers to request and journal editors to accept publication of such information, as it is surely the key to real communication and the development of knowledge. At least we should encourage researchers to deposit such information in a known documentary file so that it remains accessible for a century or so. It is questionable, of course, if data sets ripen like cheese or mature like wire, but at least their quality should not suffer immediate decay, surely, unless they were rotten before collection.

It is necessary to warn that in setting up many of the hypotheses of comparative factor analysis there may be severe problems about the identifiability of the parameters, similar to the so-called "rotational" problem of exploratory factor analysis but much more complicated and much harder to deal with. We shall obtain estimates, but we may not know to what extent it might be possible to obtain from these some distinct alternative numbers that fit the data equally well. When a detailed hypothesis of the simple structure type has been imposed on the factor patterns in all populations, we can feel confident that the parameters are identified. In other cases, we would have to proceed with caution in interpreting the results.

The model will be illustrated with a data set that has been modified for the purpose. Meyer and Bendig (1961) administered five of Thurstone's tests of primary mental abilities, namely verbal ability, spatial ability, reasoning ability, numerical ability, and word fluency, at age 8 and at age 11 to a sample of 49 boys and 51 girls. They published only the two correlation matrices at the two ages, the means for the tests for each sex, and t-values for sex differences in the means. Later the cross-correlations of the five tests between the two ages were published by Harris (1962). Fortunately, from this information, working backward from the t-values, we can reconstruct the 10×10 covariance matrix of the five tests on the two occasions. This matrix is given in Table 6.2.1.

For the present illustration, we contrive to ignore the fact that we have repeated-measures data. (In Section 6.3 we reanalyze the same data more appropriately.) Here we behave as though we have two 5×5 covariance matrices

TABLE 6.2.1
Covariance Matrix (Meyer and Bendig, 1961)

	V8	S8	R8	N8	W8	V11	S11	R11	N11	W11
V8	48.140									
S8	25.250	92.740								
R8	17.670	19.130	36.000							
N8	28.890	10.470	17.830	61.150						
W8	29.170	10.830	13.230	20.030	116.860					
V11	57.560	33.750	29.630	46.130	34.830	102.010				
S11	25.320	64.810	12.530	-2.900	12.680	35.540	105.880			
R11	17.750	18.490	26.930	21.400	17.190	27.690	10.830	36.000		
N11	25.410	11.810	21.210	51.230	18.190	50.170	5.710	28.110	80.100	
W11	20.050	17.270	12.020	13.750	54.600	28.170	18.450	13.850	16.990	137.360

from two independent samples of size 100. We fit the common factor model simultaneously to the two 5 × 5 covariance matrices, prescribing two common factors. We restrict the factor loadings to be the same in the two samples. To illustrate an exploratory analysis, we arbitrarily choose to fit an orthogonal model to the first covariance matrix, and we set one factor loading (the loading of the fifth test, word fluency, on the first factor) equal to zero, just to fix the model against rotational indeterminacy. We fit the model by the method of maximum likelihood, obtaining a chi-square value of 6.689 on 8 df, which has a probability value of 7.5, so we certainly cannot reject the hypothesis on the basis of the available data. The fitted factor loading matrix and unique variances are given in Table 6.2.2(a). The factor loadings are regression weights of unstandardized tests on factor scores that are standardized and uncorrelated in the first sample and have the covariance matrix given in Table 6.2.3 in the second sample. Dividing the factor loadings by the standard deviations of the tests as obtained in the first sample gives the standardized regression weights in Table 6.2.2(b). We can apply to these the habits of interpretation that have become ingrained in users

TABLE 6.2.2
Meyer and Bendig Data (Independent Samples)
Factor Loadings and Uniquenesses

(a)

	Unstandardized Factor Loadings		Uniquenesses	
	I	II	Age 8	Age 11
V	1.14	6.04	12.44	43.98
S	-1.61	4.54	69.42	72.15
R	1.10	2.84	26.20	22.14
N	4.80	3.96	21.83	.00
W		3.91	97.54	121.51

(b) Standardized Loadings Age 8		(c) Standardized Loadings Age 11	
I	II	I	II
.163	.862	.177	.700
-.167	.472	-.244	.516
.183	.473	.287	.553
.614	.507	.841	.518
	.362		.398

TABLE 6.2.3
Meyer and Bendig Data (Independent Samples)
Factor Score
Covariance Matrix - Age 11

	I	II
I	2.455	.052
II	.052	1.601

of the common factor model. We are free to apply a rotation to the factor loading matrix of the first sample to yield an improved approximation to orthogonal or oblique simple structure. The same transformation would then have to be applied to the covariance matrix of the factor scores in the second sample. Further rotation would not increase the interpretability of this data set. The second factor is clearly the general factor that we expect to find linking the primary mental abilities, whereas the first factor is essentially defined by numerical ability. There are insufficient tests in the set to yield a clearer definition of the first factor. We notice in Table 6.2.3 that the variances of both the general factor and the "numerical" factor increase with age, whereas the correlation between them remains small. The fact that the specialized "numerical" factor increases its variance more than the general factor does is consistent with an expectation that abilities will become specialized in the course of mental development, but the data set does not contain enough tests to provide real support for this expectation. Because the first factor is poorly defined, it is not surprising that the numerical ability test has an unacceptably small unique variance in the second sample. This is consistent with the explanation of Heywood cases offered in Section 2.3. A zero or negative unique variance may be obtained if one of the common factors is defined by less than three variables having substantial loadings on it.

It should be admitted that the device just suggested, illustratively, of aiding interpretation by standardizing the factor loadings in one of the samples invites the samples to contradict each other. Presumably we would be embarrassed to find that the effect of rescaling in different samples was to yield matrices of standardized regression coefficients that appear to indicate distinct interpretations. Table 6.2.2(c) shows the standardized factor loadings that we obtain if we standardize in the second sample by dividing the elements in each row of the loadings in Table 6.2.2(a) by the standard deviations of the tests in the second sample and multiplying the elements in each column by the standard deviations of the factor scores (square roots of the variances in the diagonal of Table 6.2.3). The differences between the numbers in Table 6.2.2(b) and the numbers in Table 6.2.2(c) do not suggest a difference in interpretation. However, we can certainly imagine that other cases might yield an embarrassing degree of inconsistency. This example simply illustrates a general observation that unstandardized regression weights have desirable invariance properties but do not accord with conventional factor-analytic habits of interpretation, whereas standardized regression weights fit traditional interpretive customs but they lack invariance and therefore may lack interpretive consistency. One solution would be to cut loose from those habits and learn to make comparative judgments of unstandardized regression coefficients, taking into account the units of measurement of the tests.

6.3.   REPEATED-MEASURES DESIGNS

In this section we consider some factor-analytic treatments of multivariate repeated measures, that is, of n measurements repeated l times on each member of a single sample of subjects. A common source of such data would be a longitudinal study in which we seek to understand the nature of cognitive growth by giving the same tests to a sample of examinees on two, three, or more occasions at suitably spaced time intervals. As indicated in the example in Section 6.2, we might wish to test some version of the well-known hypothesis that special abilities tend to differentiate out of a general cognitive ability with increasing age. Such a hypothesis could be demonstrated statistically by setting up the hierarchical model discussed in Section 3.2(d) with a general factor and several group factors and showing that the proportionate variance of the general factor declines with age while the proportionate variances of the more specialized group factors increase.

Another possible form of multivariate repeated measures would be scores of the same subjects on the same tests in a number of experimental conditions, possibly with randomized or balanced presentation of the order of the conditions from subject to subject, to eliminate any purely temporal effects. One conventional form of analysis for such data would be multivariate analysis of variance (MANOVA), testing the hypothesis that there are no changes in any of the n measures from condition to condition. If this hypothesis is rejected, we would seek to locate the sources of significant mean changes in particular measures and conditions. A factor-analytic treatment of such data would focus the interest of the investigation on changes across conditions in means of common factors, jointly measured by the n variables.

Generally, then, we wish to have an appropriate extension of common factor analysis (confirmatory or exploratory) to the case of n measures repeatedly applied over l conditions, the term we shall adopt for the occasions, experimental treatments, or combinations of situations we might consider.

In the terminology introduced by Tucker, data consisting of observations on subjects × tests × conditions is known as *three-mode* data, and each of the classification bases of the data, namely subjects, tests, and conditions, is referred to as a *mode*. More general *multimode* data sets can be obtained with four or more bases of classification of the observations. For example, we might give a hundred subjects five tests under two conditions (viz., an anxiety-provoking, testlike condition and an anxiety-reducing, gamelike condition) and repeat the entire testing procedure over a series of four occasions to study the development of their responses, yielding four-mode data consisting of 100 subjects × 5 tests × 2 test conditions × 4 occasions.

A number of psychometric models have been proposed for repeated-measures, or multimode data. We shall consider a very general model due to Tucker and a more specialized one due to Harshman. We shall then examine a model of intermediate generality, which provides a relatively simple extension of the common factor model to multimode data.

Suppose that we obtain n test scores from a subject, randomly drawn from a prescribed population, in each of l conditions. We represent the score of the subject on test j in condition c by y_{jc}. In Tucker's original model, the N subjects in a sample are thought of as fixed, not randomly sampled from a larger population, and the model was designed to describe the observations on N subjects × n tests × l conditions as combinations of scores of K (much less than N) idealized subject types × m (much less than n) idealized test types × s (much less than l) idealized condition types. Here we follow a modified version of the model described by Bloxom and write the model as

$$y_{jc} = \sum_{r=1}^{t} f_{jcr} x_r + e_{jc} \qquad (6.3.1)$$

where

$$f_{jcr} + \sum_{p=1}^{m} \sum_{q=1}^{s} a_{cq} b_{jp} g_{pqr}. \qquad (6.3.2)$$

In this model, test j is regressed on t variables $x_1, \ldots, x_t$, which can be regarded as common factors or components depending on the assumptions we make about the covariances of the residuals e_{jc}. Each of the regression coefficients f_{jcr} of y_{jc} on the t factors has the mathematically complicated structure indicated by (6.3.2). The parameters of the model are the nm test ''factor loadings'' b_{jq}, the cs condition ''factor loadings'' a_{cp}, and the mst core ''factor loadings,'' g_{pqr} (to use Tucker's terminology for these latter coefficients) and in addition the factor correlations (i.e., the correlations between the t factor scores $x_1, \ldots, x_t$) plus the residual variances (i.e., the variances of the nl residuals e_{jc}) if a common factor model is used. The model allows m, s, and t, the number of test factors, condition factors, and core factors, to be different from each other. Not surprisingly, the model in its general form is subject to severe problems of identifiability of the parameters with a combination of rotational and scaling indeterminacies. Indeed it may be questioned whether it can be fitted in an unrestricted, exploratory fashion to a reasonably constructed data set of known structure and made to return a reasonable approximation to the known parameters. It may yet turn out to be the case that Tucker's model is of interest mainly as a general model containing special cases that are usable and interpretable for particular applications.

Before we turn to more specialized models, we may find it useful to break down the structure of Tucker's model into more manageable parts. We can describe it as a third-order factor model, in the language of Chapter 3. We write

$$y_{jc} = \sum_{p=1}^{m} b_{jp} x_{pc}^{(1)} + e_{jc} \qquad \begin{array}{l} j = 1, \ldots, n \\ c = 1, \ldots, 1 \end{array} \qquad (6.3.3)$$

for the regression of the jth test in the cth condition on m first-order common factors $x_{pc}^{(1)}$, $p = 1, \ldots, m$. Notice that in any two distinct conditions c and d, say, we have the same regression coefficients b_{jp} on m factors, but the factors themselves, $x_{pc}^{(1)}$, $x_{pd}^{(1)}$, are on the face of it different variables. Next we regress the ml first-order factors on ms second-order factors, writing

$$x_{pc}^{(1)} = \sum_{q=1}^{s} a_{cq} x_{pq}^{(2)} . \qquad (6.3.4)$$

However, we do not include a residual term, so the ml first-order factors are, exactly, linear combinations of the ms second-order factors. As before, the second-order factors $x_{1q}^{(2)}, \ldots, x_{mq}^{(2)}$ have the same variables (first-order factors) with the same factor loadings defining them independent of the index p, but they are distinct variables. Finally we regress the ms second-order factors $x_{pq}^{(2)}$ on t third-order factors, writing

$$x_{pq}^{(2)} = \sum_{r=1}^{t} g_{pqr} x_r \qquad (6.3.5)$$

again with no residual terms. In contrast to the two previous equations, the regression coefficients g_{pqr} vary according to all three indices in the equation.

Expressed in these terms, Tucker's model can be recognized as a third-order common factor model. It differs from a more general third-order factor model, first, in having equality constraints in its regression coefficients from condition to condition for each test and from test factor to test factor for each condition, and, second, in having zero residuals in the regressions of factors on factors, so that the first-, second-, and third-order factors are actually related by transformations. Because of these two special properties the order of the breakdown of the model can be altered, and instead of (6.3.3) and (6.3.4) we may write

$$y_{jc} = \sum_{q=1}^{s} a_{cq} x_{qj}^{(1)} + e_{jc} \tag{6.3.6}$$

and

$$x_{qj}^{(1)} = \sum_{p=1}^{m} b_{jp} x_{pq}^{(2)} . \tag{6.3.7}$$

Putting (6.3.3) and (6.3.4) together with (6.3.5) or putting (6.3.6) and (6.3.7) together with (6.3.5) equally yield (6.3.1) and (6.3.2).

The model does, indeed, treat tests and conditions in the same way. Whether it allows or requires a corresponding symmetry in interpretation seems to remain an open question. Although, as noted earlier, there seem to remain some unsolved general problems of indeterminacy of rotation and scale in the model, it is at least possible to fit the model to some data sets with a very restricted pattern in each parameter matrix and be reasonably confident that the parameters are identified and hence uniquely estimated. What may seem to be lacking is a general theory of design that would enable us to prescribe not only a theoretically justified pattern for the test-factor loadings but also a theoretically justified pattern for the condition-factor loadings and the core-factor loadings. For example, with cognitive longitudinal data, it may well be clear how to prescribe a simple structure for the $n \times m$ matrix of factor loadings of the cognitive tests, but it is not generally clear how to assign zero and nonzero loadings to the regression of ages 6, 8, 10, 12, 14, 16, 18 years on the occasion factors or how to assign zero and nonzero loadings to the relation between the test-occasion factors and the core factors. Similarly, with data consisting of ratings of subjects on n personality traits $\times l$ raters, it may be clear how to arrange the traits in clusters on the basis of their common characteristics. However, it seems less clear how, in general, to cluster the raters, a priori, into theoretically justified groupings or how to prescribe simple structure for the relations between the trait-rater factors and the core factors. The intention of these remarks is to indicate general challenges to users of the general model. Particular applications of it may avoid these problems, and further research may yield a general interpretive methodology.

We turn now from the general model to a specialized case of it, the PARAFAC model due to Harshman. The PARAFAC model may be written as

$$y_{jc} = \sum_{p=1}^{t} a_{cp} b_{jp} x_p + e_{jc} . \tag{6.3.8}$$

It can be obtained from Tucker's model by setting $m = s = t$ and writing (6.3.3), (6.3.4), and (6.3.5) as

$$y_{jc} = \sum_{p=1}^{m} b_{jp} x_{pc}^{(1)} + e_{jc} \qquad (6.3.9)$$

$$x_{pc}^{(1)} = a_{cp} x_{pp}^{(2)} \qquad (6.3.10)$$

and

$$x_{pp}^{(2)} = x_p . \qquad (6.3.11)$$

An obvious reading of the model is that it embodies Cattell's principle of parallel proportional profiles, as discussed in Section 6.1, applying it to repeated measures rather than to independent populations. That is, we can think of the coefficient a_{cp} in (6.3.8) as a common multiplier for the cth condition, acting to change all n coefficients b_{jp} of the tests proportionally in their regressions on the pth factor. Thus a very natural interpretation of the model (consistent with the general framework of this book) is as a version of the classical common factor model with n tests regressed on m factors in which the sole effect of the l conditions is to alter the standard deviations of the m common factors. If, to fix scale, we set the m factor variances to unity, in one baseline condition, then the coefficient a_{cp} is the standard deviation of the pth factor in condition c. This interpretation of the model is asymmetric in the coefficients b_{jp}, a_{cp}, the former being regression weights, and the latter being standard deviations of factor scores. The model itself is mathematically symmetric in b_{jp} and a_{cp}, and in some applications it might not be at all obvious that we should interpret the two sets of coefficients in these quite distinct ways.

A central property of the PARAFAC model follows from the principle of parallel proportional profiles. In general, once we fix scale, the coefficients b_{jp} and a_{cp} are identifiable, which means in particular that they are not subject to rotational indeterminacy, and we are not free after fitting the model to rotate the estimated coefficients to approximate simple structure. It is possible to take at least two distinct attitudes toward this built-in restriction in the model. One is to take the view that the PARAFAC model, making use of the additional information in multimode data, has precisely the advantage over classical common factor analysis that it eliminates the unfortunate arbitrariness of the latter in respect of rotation. Indeed, it is possible to go further and claim, following Cattell's original suggestion, that if factors are real organic unities, they should change, as factors, from one condition to another so as to induce proportional changes in the factor loadings. On this view, multimode analysis with PARAFAC would be the method to prefer, if we wish to find real factors.

The alternative view is developed as follows: As already implied in Section 6.1, there is a degree of ambiguity in the notion of parallel proportional profiles. The most important effect of conditions on factor scores should be to change their means, an effect that will not show up at all in conventional analyses of covariance matrices or correlation matrices. From Pearson's selection formulas, we expect factor loadings to change proportionally from one condition to another if both (1) the conditions change the variances of the factor scores and (2) the conditions leave the correlations between the factors unchanged. As a matter of fact, it will commonly happen that the effect of selection is to change both the variances of the factor scores and their correlations. For example, there is evidence that correlations between abilities tend to decrease with increasing age. A longitudinal data set in which the tests show good simple structure with increasing differentiation (decreasing correlations) between abilities with age should not fit the PARAFAC model, and we would not be free within the constraints of the model to recover the true simple structure and corresponding clear interpretation of the data by rotation. One could thus take the view that the freedom of the PARAFAC model from rotational indeterminacy is a disadvantage rather than an advantage over the classical common factor model.

These last considerations at least suggest that in addition to PARAFAC we might wish to have a model that allows the factor scores to change both their variances and their correlations from condition to condition. The *invariant factors* model is designed to provide a natural extension of the classical common factor model to multimode data, using the principle that the regressions of the tests on their common factors should remain unaltered from one condition to another and that the effect of conditions should be (at most) to change the variances and the covariances of the common factors of the tests.

The invariant factors model is both mathematically and conceptually asymmetric. It is supposed that one mode consists of tests or at least of variables that can be readily understood as measuring one or more abstractive attributes in common, whereas the remaining modes do not. Only the test mode yields factor loadings, although the other modes yield changes in factor scores. This notion is in accord with the more general, prior assumption from which Cattell derived his principle of parallel proportional profiles. If factors are genuine unities, changes in test scores should result from changes in factor scores. But here we do not make the additional assumption that changes in factor scores leave their correlations unchanged.

The invariant factors model can be written as

$$y_{jc} = \sum_{p=1}^{m} b_{jp} x_{pc} + e_{jc} \qquad (6.3.12)$$

where

$$x_{pc} = \sum_{q=1}^{m} a_{cq}x_q + \mu_c \tag{6.3.13}$$

That is, the regressions of the tests on m factors remain invariant from condition to condition, but the factor scores in each condition are treated as linear combinations of a fundamental set of m factors (plus a constant μ_c for each condition which allows changes in factor score means). The coefficients a_{cq} in the transformation of the fundamental factor scores are not of interest in themselves but would be used, after the model has been fitted, to compute the factor score covariance matrix in each condition. To ensure that the parameters of the model are identified, we would choose one condition as a baseline, origin, control, or standard condition, in an obvious meaning of these terms, and fix the scale of the factor scores in this condition by setting their means equal to zero and their variance equal to unity. If in addition we fix enough zeros in the test factor loading matrix of coefficients b_{jp} to eliminate rotational indeterminacy, as in the conventional common factor model, the entire model will then be identified. If the model is fitted in an exploratory analysis without prescribed simple structure in the test factor loadings, these can be rotated to approximate simple structure and corresponding rotations applied to all the factor score covariance matrices. The invariant factors model restores the rotational indeterminacy that PARAFAC eliminates. It is consistent with the general position taken in this book to regard it as an advantage to be able to define common factors by prescribing simple structure in the broad sense of the term. However, the possibility remains open that in practice the additional assumption that eliminates rotational indeterminacy in PARAFAC will commonly yield interpretable and convincing results.

From the form of the equations (6.3.12) and (6.3.13), it should be clear that the invariant factors model is a special case of Tucker's model and that in turn it contains Harshman's PARAFAC as a further special case. Care is needed over the assumptions we make about the covariances of the residuals. In the invariant factors model it is natural to suppose that the residual covariances of distinct tests should be zero, both within the same condition and between two distinct conditions. But generally we cannot expect the common factors to account entirely for the correlations between repeated measures on the same test, because presumably the test will possess a stable specific property not accounted for by the common factors. It therefore seems appropriate in the invariant factors model, and also presumably in some applications of the PARAFAC model, to allow the residuals of repeated measures to be correlated. It is not clear in what circumstances it would be appropriate to have these residuals correlated in Tucker's general model, and it seems that Tucker's model has been used in practice either as a common factor model with all distinct residuals assumed uncorrelated or in a componentlike fashion with the residuals treated as errors of misfit between the model and the sample of data.

All three models discussed in this section generally require to be fitted to sample covariance matrices. (If changes in factor score means are to be allowed for, information in the sample means must also be used.) Fitting these models to sample correlation matrices would seem difficult to justify, as it is precisely by changes in the variances (and possibly covariances) of the factor scores that we can expect to explain changes in the variances as well as covariances of the tests. In the case of the invariant factors model, where it is convenient to pick out one condition as the standard, baseline condition and to scale the factor scores to have zero means and unit variances in that condition, it may also be convenient to divide the factor loadings by the standard deviations of the tests to obtain standardized regression weights for the standard condition, whose relative magnitudes can be interpeted as in the classical common factor model.

A partial analysis of the data in Table 6.2.1 was given in Section 6.2. It was pretended that we had only the two 5×5 covariance matrices from independent samples of a hundred subjects rather than the entire 10×10 covariance matrix of the repeated measures. The entire data set will now be analyzed by the invariant factors model. For simplicity, in this analysis we ignore the possibility of explaining changes in test means by changes in factor score means.

As in the previous analysis in Section 6.2, we postulate two factors. We treat the first occasion (age 8) as the baseline or standard condition for the analysis, and we fit the exploratory model orthogonal in the standard condition, prescribing only one zero loading, for word fluency on the first factor, as in the previous partial analysis, to fix the model against rotation. Because we do not expect the common factors to explain the correlation between repeated measures on any test, we allow the residual covariances of the repeated measures to be nonzero. Except for this fact, the analysis closely follows the previous one. The model was fitted by maximum likelihood, yielding a chi-square of 36.21 on 28 df, hence a probability of $>.1$. We have no good reason to reject the model. Table 6.3.1(a) gives the estimated factor loadings, and Table 6.3.2 gives the covariance matrix of the common factors in the second condition. Table 6.3.1(b) gives the standardized factor loadings for the standard condition, obtained by dividing the rows of Table 6.3.1(a) by the standard deviations of the tests at age 8. Table 6.3.1(c) shows the standardized factor loadings we would obtain if we divide the rows of Table 6.3.1(a) by the standard deviations of the tests at age 11 and multiply the columns by the standard deviations of the factor scores (the square roots of the variances in Table 6.3.2) at age 11.

Table 6.3.3 gives the fitted residual variances and covariances. Again, as in the partial analysis in Section 6.2, the residual variance of numerical ability on the second occasion is so small as to suggest a Heywood case due to the fact that we do not have enough high-loading tests defining the first factor. Generally, the repeated-measures analysis confirms the findings of the incorrect or incomplete analysis in terms of independent samples. We have a general factor and an ill-

TABLE 6.3.1
Meyer and Bendig Data (Repeated Measures)
Factor Loadings

	(a) Unstandardized		(b) Standardized Age 8		(c) Standardized Age 11	
	I	II	I	II	I	II
V	.832	6.650	.119	.949	.133	.732
S	-1.518	4.218	-.158	.438	.238	.462
R	.850	3.194	.142	.531	.230	.600
N	4.708	4.003	.602	.512	.853	.504
W		3.595		.333		.346

TABLE 6.3.2
Meyer and Bendig Data (Repeated Measures)
Factor Score Covariance Matrix - Age 11

	I	II
I	2.631	.054
II	.054	1.271

TABLE 6.3.3
Meyer and Bendig Data (Repeated Measures)
Fitted Residual Covariance Matrix

	V8	S8	R8	N8	W8	V11	S11	R11	N11	W11
V8	4.22					6.41				
S8		72.64					41.34			
R8			25.08					14.17		
N8				22.98					-3.25	
W8					103.94					40.04
V11	6.41					43.38				
S11		41.34					77.90			
R11			14.17					20.84		
N11				-3.25					.46	
W11					40.04					120.93

defined factor involving numerical ability with the proportionate variance of the latter increasing relative to the former from age 8 to age 11.[1]

---

[1]For further reading on this section the reader is referred to Law, Snyder, Hattie, and McDonald (in press), in which all of these models are discussed. The first accounts of these models are, respectively, Tucker (1964) for his general model, Harshman (1970) for PARAFAC, and McDonald in Law et al. (in press) for the invariant factors model.

7

Item Response Theory

7.1. THE PROBLEM OF BINARY (DICHOTOMOUS) DATA

The question whether common factor analysis is "applicable" to items or other attributes that yield only two alternative "states" or "values"—yes/no, true/false, right/wrong—has been the subject of much confusion.

In the 1940s, the view developed that factor analyzing such *binary* (two-valued) data would yield misleading artifacts, known as "difficulty factors." In the context of cognitive testing, where an item is scored "right" or "wrong," an accepted (inverse) measure of the "difficulty" of an item is the proportion of the population that passes the item. Obviously, the higher the proportion that passes an item, the easier, we would say, the item is. (It would be nicer to speak of the "easiness" of an item, measured directly by the proportion passing it, but tradition is against this.) The view was put that if the difficulty levels of a set of items varied widely, a common factor analysis would yield extra factors known as *difficulty factors* that are not generic properties of the items but are in some sense mathematical artifacts of the analysis. The belief grew that difficulty factors would appear because the *phi coefficient*—a name often given to the usual correlation coefficient in the case where it has been computed from two binary variables—was not a "correct" measure of the extent of association of binary variables. The problem was considered to be that the correlation coefficient between two binary variables can never be as much as unity when the binary variables have different difficulties and hence must be "misrepresenting" the extent of the relationship. A formal mathematical justification for this belief was never given, but the view has been widely held. It has only recently been made quite clear that there is no reason to expect factors "due to difficulty" as such, in binary data, but rather the problem concerns the assumption of linearity. That is, we can find cases where items differ in difficulty, yet do not have "mathematical artifacts." This is because their regressions on the factors are linear. We can find other cases where items do not differ in difficulty; yet they do have "mathematical artifacts" because their regressions on the factors are non-linear. The basic rule is that if items *or* quantitative measures are nonlinear functions of common factors, the linear analysis provided by the models for common factor analysis will yield both "factors of content" (i.e., factors to be thought of as generic properties of the measures) and also "factors of cur-vilinearity." Usable methods for nonlinear factor analysis have been developed, but they are very difficult to describe and must be regarded as beyond the scope of this book. Broadly, the reader can hope he or she will not need them for quantitative measures, if the evidence from their univariate distributions is that they are not too far from normality. Artificial experiments suggest that if we obtain extremely sharply discriminating items (see following), we need either nonlinear factor analysis or one of the methods of latent trait theory discussed in Section 7.2. If we obtain items whose characteristics are those typical of empirical social science data, in practice we can safely use all the methods for analysis so far described, except that we must omit as unjustified the likelihood-ratio chi-square test and substitute judgment of the residual covariance matrices based on experi-ence. This actually gives us a wider range of techniques to draw from than those that have so far been developed specifically for use with binary data.

The reader may be content with the assurance just offered, but it should be of some use to go a little deeper into these matters. The further remarks of this section serve both to clarify the meaning of a (linear) factor analysis of binary data and to form a link to the concepts of Section 7.2.

If a characteristic admits of just two states, A or not-A, a satisfactory numer-ical coding of the states is obtained by assigning the numbers 1 and 0 to the respective states. Suppose we have one characteristic, characteristic j, that has states A_j and not-A_j, and another, characteristic k, that has states A_k and not-A_k. For each of these we define a variable, respectively, y_j and y_k, and we code the states by writing $y_j = 1$ corresponding to A_j and $y_j = 0$ corresponding to not-A_j, and similarly $y_k = 1$ corresponding to A_k and $y_k = 0$ corresponding to not-A_k. Then it turns out that the means μ_j and μ_k of y_j and y_k are the same as the probability of A_j, $P\{A_j\}$, and the probability of A_k, $P\{A_k\}$, and that the covariance of y_j and y_k, say c_{jk}, is the same as the joint probability of A_j and A_k, minus the product of their separate probabilities. The reader who recalls basic probability theory will recognize, then, that the covariance of the items scored zero or unity is essentially a measure of their departure from independence in probability. Further, and a very fundamental result for our purposes, it turns out that if we obtain a regression curve of the coded variable y_j on some independent variable x, say

$$\hat{y}_j = \beta_j x + \alpha \qquad (7.1.1)$$

then $\hat{y}_j$ is the same as the conditional probability of occurrence of state A_j as a function of x. This fact provides a simple and important link between two ways of thinking that are often kept separate. We are already accustomed to the idea of the regression curve of some measure y_j on some measure x. For example, y_j might be an examination score and x a measure of intelligence. The regression curve (usually a straight line) gives us the mean of our dependent measure y_j for each possible value of our independent measure x. The slope indicates the general rate of change of y_j as x increases (i.e., how fast the mean examination score increases as we move to subjects with higher intelligence scores). These rates of change of observed score with factor score are what we use to interpret a factor analysis. Now we consider a binary item (e.g., an item in an examination to which the response can be "right" or "wrong"), and we consider drawing a graph of the probability of getting the right answer as a function of an independent variable such as intelligence. We expect this probability to increase with the intelligence of the respondent. It is a very satisfying simplification of thought when we realize that the curve giving the probability of a response (having one alternative state) as a function of an independent variable is the same as the regression curve, on that independent variable, of the score coded one for the given response and zero for the alternative. This closes a gap between binary, "qualitative" data and measured, "quantitative" data that would otherwise force us to develop separate theories for them.

As a matter of historical fact, there have been strong claims that theory for binary variables has to be different from theory for measured variables, just because the one is "qualitative" and the other is "quantitative." Although we can now recognize that these claims were very extreme, they did serve to motivate some interesting and desirable developments of theory. We now recognize that the important theoretical differences between binary data and measured data are (1) we more often have to assume nonlinear regressions on factors for items than for measured variables; (2) we certainly cannot assume normality for the joint distribution of binary variables, so theory for statistical estimation has to be quite different. There is, however, no deep theoretical importance to the distinction between "qualitative" and "quantitative" variables, and to insist on one destroys an available unity of theory.

Suppose, then, that we have n binary items, $y_1, \ldots, y_n$, scored zero and unity. It turns out that we can write the usual common factor model for these, either as

$$\hat{y}_j = \sum_{p=1}^{m} f_{jp} x_p + \alpha_j \qquad (7.1.2)$$

or as

$$P\{y_j = 1\} = \sum_{p=1}^{m} f_{jp}x_p + \alpha_j \tag{7.1.3}$$

The first of these implies that the conditional mean of y_j is a linear function of the factors (plus a regression constant α_j to allow for the fact that we have not put y_j in deviation measure). The second is the equivalent statement that the conditional probability of the response that is scored unity is a linear function of the factors. We assume, as before, that any two variables are uncorrelated for every fixed value of the factors $x_1, \ldots, x_m$. It then follows that their covariances, say c_{jk}, are given by

$$c_{jk} = \sum_{p=1}^{m} \sum_{q=1}^{m} f_{jp} \rho_{pq} f_{kg} \tag{7.1.4}$$

where as usual the ρ_{pq} are the correlations between the factors. That is, the fundamental factor theorem holds for binary variables, if we assume they have linear regressions on the factors. In the theories of Section 7.2, the regression curve of a binary variable on a common factor is renamed an item *characteristic curve*, or *trace line*. To the extent that it is safe to assume these functions are linear, we may use the methods of exploratory or confirmatory analysis given in Chapters 2 or 3 to give what we call *heuristic* analyses in which the estimates are adequate but not "best." The LS and LRC functions, in this application, are just algebraic, distribution-free measures of fit of the hypothesis to a given sample, and there will be no basis for a statistical decision to accept or reject the hypothesis fitted to the sample. Care is needed over scaling if we wish to interpret the regressions as curves of conditional probability. If the computer program used necessarily computes and works from sample correlation coefficients, we shall obtain regression coefficients that assume the variables are in standard measure, and the regression constants α_j are zero. We can turn these regressions back into raw measure by multiplying the regression coefficients of each variable on the factors by the standard deviation of the variable and adding as the regression constant the mean of the variable (which is the same as the proportion of responses scored unity). An important point to note is that the factor loadings (v–f regression coefficients) account for the item covariances, which typically are very small; hence these numbers are smaller than we might be used to from the conventional applications of common factor analysis.

There is an obvious theoretical difficulty with the linear regression model for binary variables. The linear function is not bounded by the numbers zero and unity. That is, we can find values of the independent variables for which the mean of the dependent variable is less than zero or values for which it is greater than unity. But this mean is also a probability, so we have a mathematical absurdity. We immediately conclude that linear regressions, which are curves of conditional probability, are just not appropriate for binary variables.

However, what is absurd in theory need not be unreasonable in practice. If the actual distributions of the factors were restricted in their ranges, it might be that no individual can be found who has a combination of factor values that yield an impossible "probability" value for any item. Indeed, we may often apply the earlier methods of this book to binary data as heuristic devices for data analysis that avoid both the complexity and the current limitations of the methods of Section 7.2. This is partly because artificial data studies suggest that with typical parameter values impossible "probabilities" are rare and negligible in practice. In fact, they occur less frequently when we have more than one factor. This is because they then require the coincidence of two or more high or low values of different factors, which makes a combined event of low probability, compared with the occurrence of one high or low value.[1]

7.2. ITEM RESPONSE THEORY—LATENT TRAIT THEORY

As mentioned at the beginning of Section 7.1, in the 1940s doubts arose over the propriety of using the common factor model for binary data. Some of the discussion was directed at the misconceived notion of "difficulty factors," an issue that seemed to lead into the further question of choosing "the right" coefficient of association between binary variables. Some of it became the more radical assertion (Guttman, 1950; Lazarsfeld, 1950) that the common factor model was simply the wrong model for binary data, and other models were required. Guttman (1950), in response to this need, made an intensive investigation of a concept due to Walker (1933) of an *ideal answer pattern* under the title *scalogram analysis*. Lazarsfeld (1950) began the development of a group of models under the title *latent structure analysis*. Because terminology in this area has not yet stabilized, we shall speak of the collection of models for binary data discussed in this section as constituting *latent trait theory* or, interchangeably, item response theory.

The general notion behind all latent trait models can be recognized as a stronger counterpart of the familiar idea of the common factor model that a limited number of common factors explains the correlations between observed variables in the sense that for any fixed values of the factors these correlations vanish. The basic principle of latent trait theory is that a limited number of *latent traits* explains *all* the relations between observed variables in the sense that for any fixed values of the latent traits the observed variables are mutually statis-

---

[1]A background to the discussion in Section 7.1 is supplied by McDonald (1967). McDonald and Ahlawat (1974) give the results on difficulty factors.

tically independent. Because it is possible for two variables to be uncorrelated and yet not entirely statistically independent, this principle is different from the factor analytic principle and more stringent (stronger). The term *latent trait* carries essentially the same meaning as the term *common factor*. The word *trait* comes, of course, from psychology and implies a feature (a generic property, indeed) in respect of which personalities may be distinguished. In this context it expresses our hope that the unobserved variables that explain relationships among the observations will be identifiable as traits (i.e., generic properties of the persons observed, if the application is to persons). The word *latent* simply means unobserved. As mathematical quantities, latent traits are defined by their role as explainers of statistical relationships. The basic principle of latent trait theory that for any fixed values of the latent traits the observed variables are mutually statistically independent has come to be known as the *principle of local independence*. That is, for any location in the space of variation of the latent traits (i.e., any set of values of all the traits), there is mutual independence of the observations.[2] This is, in fact, a stronger principle than that which defines common factors, for these only explain correlations between observed variables and leave it possible that there are other relations between them, not captured in the correlation coefficient, that are left unexplained. At the same time, it is reasonable to say that although factor analytic theory is based on the weak, correlational version of the principle, this is probably because of an implicit assumption of multivariate normality. Under such an assumption, zero correlations imply statistical independence as well as conversely. The view taken here is that common factor analysis is really a special case of latent trait theory, based on the principle of local independence, but one in which for convenience only the weak, zero-partial-correlation version of the principle is typically tested.

Recognition of a family of latent trait models having in common the use of the principle of local independence took time to develop. Even now most of these models are in a relatively primitive state of development compared with the common factor model.

Lazarsfeld (1950) introduced a number of new models under the title of *latent structure analysis*.[3] He was concerned with models for binary data, and initially he chose to work with models in a single latent trait whose conditional probability curves (item characteristic curves) are polynomials of some prescribed degree. These necessarily have the central defect of the linear latent trait models, as we may now call them, described by (7.1.1) and (7.1.3) that there must exist latent trait values for which the conditional probability of the designated "positive" response lies outside the permissible range of zero to unity. Further, the polynomial models seemed to be intractable mathematically, so Lazarsfeld substituted for these a *latent class model*, which initially he regarded as a good

---

[2]See McDonald (1962) for a general statement of this principle.
[3]The most convenient reference for these is Lazarsfeld and Henry (1968).

mathematical approximation to the polynomial models. In the latent class model it is supposed that there exist just m classes (point values of a latent trait, perhaps) within each of which the observed variables are mutually statistically independent. Suppose that we have n binary variables, $y_1, \ldots, y_n$, coded for convenience to take the values $y_j = 1$ for one "value" and $y_j = 0$ for the other value. We write g_l for the (unknown) probability that a subject we have drawn is a member of the lth class. We write $p_j|l$ for the conditional probability that observed variable $y_j = 1$ (in our agreed coding of responses to binary items), given that the subject is from the lth latent class. The m numbers $g_1, \ldots, g_k$ and nm numbers $p_j|l$, $j = 1, \ldots, n$; $l = 1, \ldots, m$ are the parameters of the model.

It is shown theoretically that the unconditional probability p_j, that $y_j = 1$, is given by

$$p_j = \sum_{l=1}^{m} (p_j|l)g_l. \tag{7.2.1}$$

That is, the unconditional probability of $y_j = 1$ is a sum of conditional probabilities within each of the mutually exclusive latent classes, weighted by the proportions of the population that lie within each class. By the principle of local independence within any class the joint probability that $y_j = 1$ and $y_k = 1$ is $(p_j|l)(p_k|l)$, so overall, for the unconditional joint probability p_{jk} that both $y_j = 1$ and $y_k = 1$, we have

$$p_{jk} = \sum_{l=1}^{m} (p_j|l)(p_k|l)g_l. \tag{7.2.2}$$

Similar expressions are written and employed in the theory for higher-order association between items (e.g., for the joint probability) for three items j, k, l, that $y_j = 1$, $y_k = 1$, and $y_l = 1$. Lazarsfeld (1950) called such equations the *accounting equations* of the model. The central task of latent class analysis is that of estimating the values of the parameters of the model, $p_j|l$, $j = 1, \ldots, n$; $l = 1, \ldots, \ldots, m$, and g_l, $l = 1, m$ from sample observations of relative frequencies corresponding to p_j, p_{jk}, and higher-order joint occurrences.

Although the latent class model is conceptually very interesting to the psychometric theorist, we may question its value to potential users. It was first introduced as an approximation to a model in which one latent trait is assumed, and the item characteristic curve is assumed to be a polynomial of appropriate degree. Early in the development of the model, investigators were pleased to note that it was free of the identifiability problems (rotational indeterminacy) that are characteristic of exploratory common factor analysis. However, in moving from a polynomial in one latent trait to a collection of latent classes, we actually run into difficulties that are worse than those of rotational indeterminacy. Nothing in the further analysis of the model corresponds to a notion of an ordering of the classes on a line or an arrangement of the classes in a space, and nothing in the model tests the correctness of the assumption that the latent trait is distributed on just a few points (values). If we generate data according to the linear latent trait model, with the latent trait x having a continuous, perhaps normal distribution, we find that we can account for the data so generated with just two latent classes, and so a danger is created that we may take the classes seriously as representing a genuine dichotomy of x. We might say that latent class analysis has no "rotation" problem because it is inherently nonspatial. But, in consequence, attempts to interpret the latent classes will quite probably fail for a lack of knowledge of their ordering or arrangement in relation to each other. It is not surprising, therefore, that published empirical applications of latent classes tend to suggest that the classes are concealing continuities. For example, a study by Miller, Sabagh, and Dingham (1962) of retarded children gave two "kinds" of children, "mildly retarded" and "severely retarded." A reanalysis of their data by McDonald (1967) using a different technique showed that the data were consistent with the linear latent trait model (7.1.1) rather than with just two latent classes. Broadly, McDonald (1967) recommended that in order to distinguish between latent classes arranged in order and latent classes arranged in a more complicated fashion or between subjects grouped into latent classes and subjects distributed continuously we need to use methods that amount to carrying out a common factor analysis and studying the distribution of the factor scores of subjects.

Actually, what seems to be the oldest latent trait model, is also possibly still the best current unidimensional latent trait model for binary data. If we attempt to invent a plausible form for an item characteristic curve for binary data, at least for a mental test item, we find the following requirements appealing: (1) The curve should be monotonic increasing; for if the latent trait is an ability, the probability of passing the item should increase with ability. (2) The curve should have a lower symptote that is zero or greater than zero and an upper asymptote of unity. If we exclude guessing, for a sufficiently small quantity of ability, the probability of passing the item should be zero (and certainly not less). If guessing can yield a correct answer by chance, the lower asymptote would be equal to the probability of being correct by pure guessing. For a sufficiently great amount of ability, the probability of passing the item should be unity and certainly not more. These considerations suggest, as a usable item characteristic curve, the cumulative normal density function graphed in Fig. 7.2.1. For this purpose, we regard it just as a mathematically specified curve, *not* as a cumulative statistical distribution. To emphasize this, we use the ancient name for such a curve, the *normal ogive*. The normal ogive model in latent trait theory is defined by the principle of local independence, together with the assumption that the jth item of a set of n items has a characteristic curve defined by

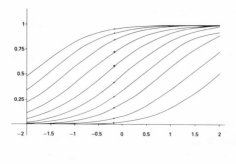

FIG. 7.2.1.   Normal Ogive Model.
Discrimination   fixed,   difficulty
varied.

$$P\{y_j = 1 | x = X\} = N\left\{\frac{X - \mu_j}{\sigma_j}\right\}$$ (7.2.3)

where $N\{Z\}$ is the normal ogive function. Figures 7.2.1 and 7.2.2 show families of normal ogive item characteristic curves. In the first, the parameter μ_j of the set varies whereas σ_j is fixed, while in the second μ_j is fixed and σ_j varies. (We must bear in mind that the latent trait is in standard measure and, if normally distributed, most subjects' values lie between -3 and $+3$.) Just from inspection of these curves, we can recognize that the larger the value of μ_j, the more *difficult* the item is, in the sense that a larger value of the latent trait corresponds to a given probability of passing the item. We may, indeed, think of μ_j as a parameter measuring item difficulty. We can also recognize that the σ_j value orders the items in respect of the maximum rate of change of probability of passing the item as a function of ability, and this may be crudely identified with a notion of the discriminating power of the item. An item whose $p_j|x$ changes rapidly with x discriminates well between subjects of different abilities.[4]

Birnbaum[5] showed that there are mathematical advantages to the use of the *logistic* model, whose item characteristic curve is given by

$$P\{y_j = 1 | x = X\} = L\left\{\frac{D(X - \mu_j)}{\sigma_j}\right\}$$ (7.2.4)

where

$$L(Z) = \frac{1}{1 + e^{-Z}}$$ (7.2.5)

is the logistic function. This curve is virtually indistinguishable from the normal ogive with a choice of the constant $D = 1.71$. In the ensuing discussion the two models will generally be treated as though they are interchangeable. Most applications of the normal ogive and logistic models are to cognitive tests, and it is

---

[4]See Lord and Novick (1968) for further discussion of the normal ogive model.
[5]See Lord and Novick (1968).

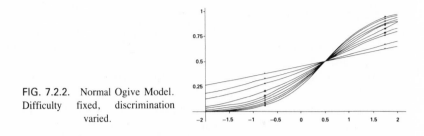

FIG. 7.2.2. Normal Ogive Model. Difficulty fixed, discrimination varied.

reasonable in such applications to follow the convention that describes the latent trait as an *ability*.

There are alternative sets of parameters that have been used to describe the normal ogive and logistic models. Writing $N(Z)$ or $L(Z)$ for the respective characteristic curves, we can have, alternatively,

$$Z_j = \frac{X - \mu_j}{\sigma_j} \tag{7.2.6}$$

$$Z_j = a_j X + d_j \tag{7.2.7}$$

$$Z_j = a_j(X - \mu_j) \tag{7.2.8}$$

and

$$Z_j = \frac{f_j X + t_j}{\sqrt{1 - f_j^2}} \tag{7.2.9}$$

All four of these representations have been used. By elementary algebra we can express any pair of parameters (μ_j, σ_j), (μ_j, a_j), (b_j, a_j), (t_j, f_j) as functions of any other pair by writing

$$a_j = \frac{1}{\sigma_j} \tag{7.2.10}$$

$$f_j = \frac{a_j}{\sqrt{1 - f_j^2}} = \frac{1}{\sqrt{1 + \sigma_j^2}} \tag{7.2.11}$$

$$d_j = -\mu_j a_j = \frac{-\mu_j}{\sigma_j} \tag{7.2.12}$$

and

$$t_j = \frac{d_j}{\sqrt{1 + a_j^2}} = \frac{-\mu_j}{\sqrt{1 + \sigma_j^2}} \tag{7.2.13}$$

So, given the parameters in one form of the model, we can easily derive the corresponding values in another form. In the form (7.2.6) the parameters μ_j and σ_j correspond, respectively, to the mean and standard deviation of the normal ogive or logistic distribution. Both (7.2.7) and (7.2.9) show clearly that these two models can be thought of as nonlinear transformations, suitable for binary data, of the Spearman single-factor model for measured variables. One way to derive this relationship is to suppose that underlying the n binary variables there are n hypothetical variables z_j^* (not themselves common factors) that fit the common factor model,

$$z_j^* = f_j x + \delta_j \qquad\qquad (7.2.14)$$

where δ_j is a unique variable, and that if an item's hypothetical score z_j^* exceeds t_j, which is the item's *threshold value* for a positive response, then a positive response is emitted by the examinee. The normal or logistic distribution enters the model to determine the probability that the unique variable δ_j takes a large enough value to make the hypothetical score exceed the threshold. The advantage, therefore, of the representation (7.2.9) resides in the fact that the loadings f_j literally represent the regression coefficients of the hypothetical item scores z_j^* on the common factor x (and also represent the correlation between them and the factor). They are contained within the range -1 to $+1$ and can be interpreted by the usual standards of the common factor model. If, in particular, we obtain a value of unity for f_j, the data are warning us that we have a Heywood case. In contrast, the quantities σ_j and a_j theoretically range from minus to plus infinity and do not possess a direct factor-analytic interpretation.

There are two general approaches available to the estimation of the parameters of these models from a sample of examinees. The first, the random traits approach, treats the ability of the examinees as a random variable and does not try to estimate its values in the sample. The second, the fixed traits approach, treats the abilities $X = X_1, \ldots , X_N$ of the examinees as parameters to be estimated simultaneously with the $2n$ item parameters.

The first method of estimation rests on classical results in the theory of the normal distribution for two variables. Either by analyzing the item characteristic curve into a sum of polynomials or by integration methods, it is possible to derive a method of fitting the item parameters that virtually consists of a restricted common factor analysis of a matrix of item covariances, in which the factor loadings are restricted to be (nonlinear) functions of the item parameters.[6]

---

[6]McDonald (1967) showed that we may approximate the curve itself by a polynomial series, using harmonic analysis. Christofferson (1975) obtained an equivalent result by evaluating integrals connected with the normal bivariate distribution. Both mathematical analyses yield an expression for the factor loadings of the item covariance matrices as functions of the item parameters. Table 7.2.1 was obtained by McDonald's harmonic analysis, using a program derived from work with program COSAN. See McDonald [1983; in press].

Table 7.2.1 shows the results of a study applying such a method to artificial data. Such studies show that reasonable estimates of the item parameters can be recovered from samples of more than 500 examinees provided that the true item difficulty parameters and discrimination parameters do not go outside certain limits, perhaps not beyond a range from -2.5 to $+2.5$ in terms of μ_j and a range from 0.5 to 4.0 in terms of σ_j, with ability in standard measure. (These suggestions are based on inspection of results in an unpublished Monte Carlo study and are merely tentative guidelines.) Intuitively we can see that the parameters may be poorly estimated outside these ranges because an item with an extreme

TABLE 7.2.1
Artificial Data: 50 Items by 3000 Examinees,
with Normal Distribution of Latent Trait

μ_j Estimates (N = 3000)

True μ_j	True σ_j				
	2.27	2.00	1.72	1.52	1.35
-1.00	-1.042	-0.997	-1.056	-1.056	-1.033
-0.80	-0.800	-0.865	-0.756	-0.756	-0.757
-0.60	-0.584	-0.525	-0.529	-0.595	-0.541
-0.40	-0.456	-0.358	-0.398	-0.366	-0.381
-0.20	-0.316	-0.236	-0.207	-0.277	-0.245
0.00	0.050	0.040	-0.038	0.013	-0.040
0.20	0.207	0.236	0.180	0.239	0.252
0.40	0.378	0.478	0.405	0.319	0.484
0.60	0.489	0.631	0.596	0.593	0.605
0.80	0.830	0.759	0.847	0.879	0.817

σ_j Estimates (N = 3000)

True μ_j	True σ_j				
	2.27	2.00	1.72	1.52	1.33
-1.00	2.257	2.062	1.768	1.598	1.315
-0.80	2.289	2.057	1.680	1.569	1.348
-0.60	2.332	2.059	1.606	1.471	1.316
-0.40	2.231	1.845	1.818	1.585	1.321
-0.20	2.504	2.050	1.687	1.747	1.348
0.00	2.620	1.903	1.995	1.452	1.338
0.20	2.123	2.141	1.617	1.579	1.458
0.40	2.078	1.990	1.954	1.534	1.502
0.60	2.241	2.405	1.668	1.589	1.339
0.80	2.419	1.928	1.793	1.652	1.539

value of μ_j and a low value of σ_j will give an item characteristic curve that is practically flat on the part of the range of ability where the examinees are concentrated. Even an extraordinarily large sample will then not contain enough information in the right range to determine even remotely where the curve turns or how sharply it does so.

Like most of the analyses treated in this book, the random traits analysis yields residual covariances of the items that measure the departure in the sample from conditional independence, as measured by covariance. That is, the residual covariances measure the misfit of the data to the principle of local independence, under the assumed regression model, in its weak, correlational sense. If the residual covariances are too large, we would reject the single-latent-trait model in favor of a more general one. (We would not, however, reject the principle of local independence itself. This principle defines the entire family of latent trait models, of which the single-trait normal ogive and logistic models are very simple and restrictive members. A sufficiently general latent trait model must fit any data set, just as with sufficient factors the common factor model must fit any data set.)

The main advantages of the random traits methods of estimation are (1) they easily generalize to give equivalents for binary data of most of the models discussed in Chapter 3, 4, and 6; and (2) they can be applied with reasonable numerical efficiency to data sets of unlimited sample size and to reasonably large numbers of items (a hundred or more on typical computer systems). Their main disadvantages are that (a) they do not directly yield estimates of the abilities of the examinees in the sample to which they are fitted; and (b) they make the strong assumption that the distribution of the ability is normal. It can be claimed that in practice we seldom wish to know the abilities of the examinees in the sample used to fit the model. Generally we are interested only in estimating the item parameters to modify the test, or to *calibrate* the items (as it is sometimes expressed) in order to use them to score future examinees. If we do wish to score the examinees in the calibration sample, we can do so immediately after estimating the item parameters. It can also be claimed that the assumption of normality is not more unreasonable here than elsewhere, as, for example, in factor analysis and path analysis with latent variables. Also these estimation methods appear reasonably robust against violation of the assumption of normality.

The second approach to estimation, the fixed traits method, is usually applied to yield maximum likelihood estimates jointly of the n difficulty parameters, the n discrimination parameters, and the N abilities of the examinees in the calibration sample. It does not, however, yield a likelihood ratio test of fit of the model, and unfortunately most programs written to implement this group of methods do not give residual covariances or any other suitable measures of misfit of the model to the data, so it is virtually impossible to tell whether or not the model is appropriate to the data to which it is being fitted. Sometimes the investigator performs a crude linear factor analysis of the items before fitting the latent trait model in order to determine if the data fit a single-factor model, in which case the latent trait model is guessed to be appropriate without further testing. It seems more appropriate to examine the residual covariances after fitting the actual latent trait model. The advantage of the fixed traits approach is that obviously it does not require us to assume a normal distribution for the ability. Its disadvantage is that it is limited in the sample size that can be treated by typical computer systems, and the required arithmetic is very demanding of computer time.[7]

A model for item responses independently developed by Georg Rasch has been recognized, in one formulation of it, to be a special case of the logistic model in which all the items have the same value of the discrimination parameter, σ_j or f_j in (7.2.6) or (7.2.9). From a factor-analytic point of view the *Rasch model* is a nonlinear transformation of the special case of the Spearman single-factor model in which the factor loadings are required to be all the same. It is as though we assume that if n items measure just one attribute in common, they must all measure it equally well. This is a very strong assumption, quite unlikely to be true in applications. We can make it a requirement in test construction rather than an assumption, throwing out items if their discrimination parameters are too low or if they are too high, until we have a subset with approximately equal discrimination parameters.

Advantages claimed for the Rasch model over models with both difficulty and discrimination parameters are that (1) the total score on the n items for each examinee contains all the information from the data needed to estimate his or her ability, whereas the total number of examinees passing each item contains all the information from the data needed to estimate the difficulty of the item; (2) the estimates of the item parameters are independent of the abilities of the examinees in the sample, whereas the estimates of the abilities are independent of the difficulties of the items chosen to measure the ability in question. The first of these advantages holds only in the unusual case where we wish to know the abilities of the examinees in the sample used to calibrate the items. More commonly we would be satisfied to calibrate the set of items by estimating just the item parameters and then using the resulting calibrated test to score future examinees. In such a case, the two-parameter model yields sufficient information for estimating an examinee's ability from a weighted item-sum score in which the items are differentially weighted by multiplying each response by the discrimination parameter [in the form a_j from (7.2.7) or (7.2.8)]. The second advantage is not really a special property of the Rasch model. It seems to be a general property of all common factor or latent trait models. It follows from Pearson's selection theorem that item parameters, being coefficients of a regression function, should be invariant except for rescaling of the latent traits under choices of populations of examinees, provided that the choice is not related to the responses to the

---

[7]See Lord (1980).

items. It follows also from behavior domain theory that subsets of items or tests fitting a given latent trait or common factor model should consistently estimate the latent traits or common factors defined in the domain.[8]

The misfit of the Rasch model to a data set can (as with the other models in this book) be measured by the size of the item residual covariances. Unfortunately, some computer programs for fitting the Rasch model do not give any information about these. It has also been conjectured that the sizes of the residuals themselves, possibly standardized, yield information about the misfit of the model, but the logical foundation of this conjecture does not seem to have been published. It is mathematically possible to find parameter values such that a data set fitting the Rasch model has larger residuals (but smaller residual covariances) than another data set that does not fit the Rasch model.

A choice consistent with the general framework of this book would be to fit the Rasch model by a random traits method and examine the covariance matrix of the item residuals, not the sizes of the residuals themselves, to see if the items are indeed conditionally uncorrelated, as required by the principle of local independence.

We have gone from consideration of two-parameter models for item responses to a one-parameter model for which special properties have been claimed. Now we go in the opposite direction briefly. A special problem arises in fitting a latent trait model to cognitive items in the multiple-choice format, with a choice of answers of which one is keyed correct and the others are distractors. An examinee who possesses no knowledge relevant to the question nevertheless chooses some answer, and the answer chosen may be the correct one. It follows that in a multiple-choice item there is a nonzero probability that the correct answer will be chosen at every level of ability. We may not wish to say that the probability that examinees at the lowest value of ability (conventionally, minus infinity) get the right answer is the probability of one examinee being correct "by guessing," and we generally cannot assume that this probability is the reciprocal of the number of response options, as though all options are equally attractive to such an examinee. Nevertheless, it is reasonable in fitting the normal ogive or logistic model to multiple-choice items to introduce a third parameter, the height of the lower asymptote of the item characteristic curve, which we may loosely refer to as a *guessing parameter*. Each item characteristic curve is then described by three parameters: one for difficulty, one for discrimination, and one for guessing, that is, for the height of the lower asymptote.

Attempts to fit the three-parameter model seem to indicate that even with quite unusually large sample sizes—say over 100,000—the estimates may be subject to unacceptable sampling error. Instead of attempting to estimate all three parameters, one might prefer either to take the reciprocal of the number of response options as an estimate of the lower asymptote that is at least an im-

---

[8]For an alternative view, see Wright and Stone (1979).

provement on zero, or to estimate it as the proportion passing the item in the lowest fractile of a large enough sample, divided on the basis of total test score. We would then fit the remaining parameters of the model by a random traits or fixed traits procedure with the guessing parameters treated as fixed and known. This method works well in studies of artificial data when the assumptions about the guessing parameters are correct.

It is possible to modify the Rasch model also by introducing a guessing parameter while keeping discrimination equal for all items. It is not appropriate to refer to the resulting model as a "Rasch model with guessing" as it no longer possesses the main properties that define the Rasch model. If we fit the Rasch model to multiple-choice data, estimates of the difficulty parameters can be poor in the presence of nonzero lower asymptotes.

An early development in theory for items, mentioned previously as scalogram analysis, can be regarded as a limiting special case of the Rasch model. Binet's early work on developing a test of intelligence rested on the principle of finding items that are ordered in difficulty so that only typical children of a specific age typically pass them. Walker (1931) described as an *ideal answer pattern* the situation in which the items are ordered in difficulty in such a way that if a subject passes a given item, he passes all easier items. Thus, out of what are 2^n possible patterns of (right/wrong) response to the n items, actually only $n + 1$ "answer patterns" occur.

Guttman (1950) gave a penetrating analysis of Walker's ideal answer pattern, which he renamed the *perfect scale*, and described methods and devices (mechanical contrivances) for selecting items that in a given sample yield only $n + 1$ response patterns. Such methods collectively comprise *scalogram analysis*, and a set of items yielding only the ideal answer patterns is said to be scalable. In the latent trait model that represents such a set of items, each item characteristic curve may be represented as a step or jump function. That is, up to a certain latent trait value x_j, there is zero probability of $y_j = 1$, and above that value there is unit probability. Rather strong claims have been made for scalogram analysis as perhaps the best way to obtain a set of *homogeneous* items (i.e., items measuring just one thing). McDonald (1967) gave reasons for considering scalability as too strong a demand to place on items to achieve homogeneity. Theoretically, any set of items whose response patterns are explained by one latent trait, via the principle of local independence, is *homogeneous*. Whether the item characteristic curves are (1) linear; (2) nonlinear as in the normal ogive model; or (3) extreme jump functions as in the perfect scale affects, we might say, how the discriminating power of the item varies along the latent trait dimension. Birnbaum (in Lord & Novick, 1968) examines this question very precisely. Here, for brevity, we shall just note that if discriminating power were simply assessed by the rate of change of probability of passing the items as ability increases, then a linear item (i.e., an item with a linear characteristic curve) possesses uniform discriminating power at all points of the latent trait line, whereas in contrast a scalable item would discriminate "infinitely well" at one point on the line and not at all elsewhere. A normal ogive item would have a normal distribution of discriminating power. Any set of items accounted for by one latent trait is homogeneous. The shapes of the item characteristic curves determine the distribution of discriminating power. The point distribution of the perfect scale is not obviously better than the other alternatives.

In practice, it seems to be very difficult to find items in any area of social science research that are scalable or even approximately scalable. Those that do scale seem to do so at a price, because one typically finds in a scalable set of more than four or five items that the items are slight variations on a single stem, with the variants designed to have the effect of ordered categories such as "very much" to "very little" or "very often" to "seldom." It seems very difficult to capture rich psychological content in a scalogram.

7.3.   FACTOR ANALYSIS AND TEST THEORY

The object of this section is to make a brief examination of some of the key concepts of classical test theory from a factor-analytic perspective. The advantage of this perspective is that it provides a very definite, unified treatment of the concepts considered. The correlative disadvantage is that it is necessarily narrow and does not provide a general account of these topics. The concepts to be dealt with are *reliability, unidimensionality, homogeneity, internal consistency, validity,* and *generalizability* as psychometric properties of a test. Some prior acquaintance with these terms would be helpful to the reader of this section.

In the same year, 1904, Spearman laid the foundations of common factor analysis and of true-score theory, and it is interesting to note that the two theories were alternative interpretations of the same set of data. That is, at first Spearman wanted to think of the school tests listed in Table 1.4.1 as measuring the same true score and differing only by errors of measurement. But within months he reinterpreted them as measuring an attribute in common and differing by having stable specific properties as well as errors of measurement.

Some 80 years later, it is still theoretically and empirically hard to make and verify a distinction between the partitioning of a test score into a common part and a unique part on the one hand and into a true score and an error of measurement on the other. It is possible to make an arbitrary choice between these partitionings without noticing that a choice has been made. The classical true-score model can be written as

$$y_j = t + e_j \quad j = 1, \ldots, n \tag{7.3.1}$$

where $y_1, \ldots, y_n$ are n tests that are assumed to be measuring the same true-score t and differing by uncorrelated errors $e_1, \ldots, e_n$. This model is a rescaling of a special Spearman common factor model

$$y_j = fx + e_j \quad j = 1, \ldots, n \tag{7.3.2}$$

where $y_1, \ldots, y_n$ are n tests dependent on a single common factor x (with unit variance), having equal factor loadings and differing by uncorrelated unique (specific plus error) components $e_1, \ldots, e_n$. If the residual (error or unique) variances in (7.3.1) or (7.3.2) are equal, the n tests are said to be *parallel forms*. If the residual variances are unequal, they are said to be *tau equivalent* (true-score equivalent) tests.

We can check the fit of a sample to the hypothesis of parallelism for two or more tests and to the hypothesis of tau equivalence for three or more tests by confirmatory factor analysis of their covariance matrix. (It is inappropriate to analyze the correlation matrix, as the hypothesis of equal factor loadings makes the model dependent on scale.) Under the hypothesis of parallelism there are just two parameters to estimate, namely the factor loading and unique variance that are the same for every test, so even two tests (with two variances and one covariance) yield an overidentified, restrictive model with one degree of freedom for the chi-square test. Under the hypothesis of tau equivalence we have one factor loading and n unique variances to estimate, so the model is just-identified with two tests and becomes a restrictive hypothesis with three or more. Of course, the test itself does not distinguish between errors and specific components.

It is axiomatic that unique variance includes error variance (however error might be defined) so it is axiomatic that error variance cannot be greater than unique variance. If we were to identify errors of measurement with errors of replication, we might attempt to estimate error variance from a repeated-measures design. However, it is logically and empirically possible for a trait to be unstable over time, to such an extent that retest error variance exceeds unique variance, seemingly contradicting the axiomatic assertion that unique variance includes error. It thus appears that the error variance of a test, unlike its unique variance, cannot be given a general definition whereby it becomes an identifiable, estimable parameter in the context of any research design we might try to develop for the purpose of estimating it. In most applications, we can at best obtain a bound on this not-well-defined quantity (i.e., a statement that the error variance does not exceed such and such an amount).

One of the central objects of classical test theory was to obtain an estimate of the error variance of a test, typically from the product of the *reliability coefficient* of the test, defined as the ratio of its true-score variance to its total variance and the total variance of the test score, however it happens to be scaled. Given the error variance, we can then put confidence bounds on the true score of an examinee. In theory and in applications, attention has tended to become focused on the reliability coefficient itself rather than on the error variance that is the proper goal of any study of reliability. It is therefore important to recognize that under mild assumptions the error variance of a test will be independent of the population on which the test is calibrated, provided that it is measured in units, such as raw score units, that are themselves independent of the calibrating population. In contrast, the reliability coefficient directly depends on the true-score variance of the calibrating population and is therefore a quantity of doubtful utility except possibly in the context of a *normed* test, calibrated on a large-scale, representative group whose mean and standard deviation supply the origin and unit for the measurement of future examinees. For most research purposes it will usually be appropriate to seek to estimate or place a bound on the error variance of a test, in units independent of the sample or samples studied. This last statement would be true also of *criterion-referenced* tests, in which the intention is to evaluate the mastery or nonmastery of a given set of items by an examinee, with no concern to compare the obtained score with those of other examinees.

Two of the oldest approximations to reliability are the *retest reliability coefficient* and the *parallel-forms reliability coefficient*. The first of these is the correlation between repeated measures on the test, with a carefully chosen time interval between the two occasions of testing. The second is the correlation between the test and another test that is deemed by the investigator to be parallel to it. The first of these methods seeks to treat error of measurement as error of replication but with uncertainties arising from the fact that what is measured may itself not be stable over time. Retest methods do not seem to be in common use, perhaps for reasons of cost and inconvenience. The second method has undergone extensive theoretical developments, beginning with the recognition that a test of $2n$ items could be split into halves, and the correlation between scores on the two resulting sets of n items could be made to yield an estimate, the *split-half reliability*, of the correlation of the entire test with a hypothetical parallel form. This notion was carried further with the derivation of Kuder and Richardson's formula 20 (KR20). Their work, as slightly generalized by Cronbach, yields a quantity, commonly known as *coefficient alpha*, defined as the expression

$$\alpha = \frac{n}{n-1} \; \frac{\sum\limits_{\substack{j \neq k}}^{n} \mathrm{Cov}\,\{y_j, y_k\}}{\sum\limits_{\substack{j \neq k}}^{n} \mathrm{Cov}\,\{y_j, y_k\} + \sum\limits_{j=1}^{n} \mathrm{Var}\,\{y_j\}} \tag{7.3.3}$$

where the sum of covariances is over the $n(n-1)$ distinct covariances of n subtest or item scores y_j, making up a total test score

$$s = \sum_{j=1}^{n} y_j \tag{7.3.4}$$

If the n items fit the restricted common factor model (7.3.2) that corresponds to tau-equivalent tests, with equal factor loadings f and possibly unequal uniquenesses, then (7.3.3) reduces to the simple expression

$$\alpha = \frac{nf^2}{nf^2 + \overline{u^2}} \tag{7.3.5}$$

where $\overline{u^2}$ is the average of the n uniquenesses. This expression can also be written as

$$\alpha = \frac{nc}{(n-1)c + \overline{v^2}} \tag{7.3.6}$$

where $c = f^2$ is the covariance between any two items y_j and y_k, and $\overline{v^2}$ is the average variance of the n items. The condition that the items are tau equivalent is a necessary and sufficient condition that coefficient alpha, in the form (7.3.5) or (7.3.6), is a measure of reliability of the total test score. If the item covariance matrix is described by the more general Spearman model with unequal factor loadings, coefficient alpha is then given by the expression

$$\alpha = \frac{n}{n-1}\left[\frac{n(\overline{f})^2 - \overline{f^2}}{n(\overline{f})^2 + \overline{u^2}}\right] \tag{7.3.7}$$

where $\overline{f}$ is the average of the n factor loadings and $\overline{f^2}$ is the average of the squares of the n factor loadings. The reliability of the total score is then necessarily greater than alpha, and we should properly take alpha only as a lower bound, possibly a very poor lower bound, to reliability. (This is true also if the covariance matrix requires more than one factor to account for it, and then an even more complex function of factor loadings would be needed as the expression for alpha.) In these more general cases, factor analysis provides a better lower bound than alpha to the reliability of the total test score. If the Spearman model fits the items, the quantity omega (ω) given by

$$\omega = \frac{n(\overline{f})^2}{n(\overline{f})^2 + \overline{u^2}} \tag{7.3.8}$$

is equal to the reliability of the total score, if we are willing to assume that each unique variance consists entirely of error and is less than it to the extent that the unique parts of the items contain specific components. It may be proved that omega is greater than or equal to alpha and is equal to it if and only if the factor loadings in the Spearman model are equal. The expression (7.3.8) can also be written as

$$\omega = 1 - \frac{\overline{u^2}}{\text{Var}\,\{s\}} \tag{7.3.9}$$

which may be computed in a case where the items fit a multiple-factor model, and it still has the property of being a better lower bound than alpha to the reliability of the total test score. However it is then questionable whether such a test score should be formed, being a sum of heterogeneous parts. If, on the other hand, the items fit the parallel-forms case of the Spearman model, then every item has the same value, u^2, of its uniqueness as well as the same value, f, of its common factor loading, so

$$\alpha = \frac{nf^2}{nf^2 + u^2} \tag{7.3.10}$$

which may be written as

$$\alpha = \frac{nr}{(n - 1)r + 1} \tag{7.3.11}$$

where r is the correlation between every pair of items y_j and y_k. Equation (7.3.11) is the classical Spearman–Brown formula for the reliability of a test consisting of n parallel items.

The obvious implication of the factor-analytic perspective on reliability theory then is that a confirmatory factor analysis of a set of n items or subtests yields at the same time both the basic test as to whether the items are parallel, tau equivalent, single factor or multifactor, and the basic information in the form of factor loadings and uniquenesses from which a good lower bound to reliability can be computed, namely omega given by (7.3.8) or (7.3.9).

At the same time as a factor analysis of its items yields information about the reliability of the total test score, the factor analysis also yields information relevant to the *unidimensionality* or *homogeneity* of the test, as already indicated in Section 7.2. Although both terms have been used in the literature as though they lack a clear denotation, it is natural to claim, within the framework of common factor analysis and (more generally) latent trait theory, that there is one clear conceptualization of a unidimensional test, a conceptualization that also seems reasonably consistent with the general history of the term. That is, a unidimensional test is a test whose items fit a latent trait or common factor model, possibly nonlinear, with just one latent trait or common factor. The best check on unidimensionality is then the traditional factor-analytic one, verifying that the partial covariances become small when just one latent trait is fitted. A test that is unidimensional in this sense can also be said to be *homogeneous*, having parts of the same kind (*homos* = same, *genos* = kind), because the items then measure just one attribute in common. On this interpretation *homogeneous* is a synonym for unidimensional, and because a test is either unidimensional or multidimensional, a test is either homogeneous or heterogeneous. That is, we cannot regard the homogeneity of a test as having a measurable degree, from more to less homogeneous, without doing violence to language.

Another term in psychometric usage that seems to have a somewhat vague denotation is *internal consistency*. The basic notion seems to have been that a test is internally consistent to the extent that its items measure the same attribute. This would be a virtual synonym for *homogeneous* or *unidimensional,* but a belief seems to have grown up through the historical development of test theory that internal consistency is a quantitative property of tests that may be indexed in some way by the covariances of the items. Indeed, there seems such a widespread belief that the bound to reliability, alpha, given by (7.3.3) is a measure of internal consistency that one might be tempted to turn logic upside down and say that internal consistency is what alpha measures, whatever that may one day be discovered to be. It can be said that the higher the intercorrelations of the items in a unidimensional test, the higher will be their multiple correlation with the single factor that they measure in common. We could take just such a multiple correlation as a measure of how well the items measure their common attribute, though there would seem no reason to label it as an index of internal consistency. It is possible to invent examples in which unidimensional tests have low values of alpha and multidimensional tests have high values, so there are no good reasons to think of alpha as in any way giving information about the unidimensionality or homogeneity of a test.

Another notion in test theory that has a somewhat confused history is that of the *validity* of a test. Many writers seem to reject as too imprecise the old, commonplace assertion that a test is valid if it measures the attribute it is designed to measure or, quantifying this notion, that the validity of a test is the extent to which it measures the attribute it is designed to measure. The objection to this definition seems to rest on the once-dominant logical positivist conception of meaning as verification, according to which the validity of a test would actually be the operation by which we seek to verify that the test is valid. A number of such operations can be and have been invented, so a number of "validities" of a test have been defined.

If in the opinion of "authorities" a test measures the attribute it was designed to measure, it is said to have *content validity*. If this opinion is held only by "laymen," the test is said to have *face validity*. In order to escape from what has seemed to them an intolerable subjectivity in these "opinions," test theorists have sought alternative definitions that will at least appear to avoid "subjective" opinions about test content.

The extreme alternative is to declare that a test has as many validities as there are variables with which its total sum score has a nonzero correlation. It is certainly true that tests are used for prediction, and without doing violence to English usage we could choose to describe a test as a valid predictor of a given dependent variable if the correlation between them is nonzero. But generally the investigator cannot avoid subjectivity of opinion or, rather, the responsibility for choosing items that are examplars of the attribute that the test is intended to measure by choosing some dependent variable as a *criterion* and calling the correlation of the test with the criterion a validity or possibly *the* validity of the test, for the choice of criterion itself involves an understanding of the concepts that are embodied in both the test and the criterion. It is true that occasionally quite heterogeneous batteries of items, subtests, or tests are assembled to yield a composite score that optimally correlates with some other performance, concurrent or future, of the examinees as in vocational or academic selection. Such a test battery is, by construction, a good predictor of the specified predictand, but it seems to add little to language, except the possibility of semantic confusion, to say that the test battery has *concurrent validity* or *predictive validity* but not *content validity*.

A variant on the view that the validities of a test are its correlations with other tests includes the notion that a test may not only have *empirical validities* indexed by its correlations with observable variables but also have *theoretical validities* indexed by its correlations with hypothetical, unobservable variables with which it should be correlated according to theory. If, in particular, we say that the *construct validity* of a test is "the degree to which a test measures the construct it was intended to measure," then we return to the point where this discussion of validity started. The term *hypothetical construct* is a positivist label for an attribute. (The term was chosen by the logical positivists in order to express the extreme view that the theorist freely invents constructs rather than forming concepts about the world. It does not seem an appropriate label for the terms of worthwhile theories.)

Even when we confine our attention to the notion that has been labeled the construct validity of a test (i.e., the extent to which it measures the intended attribute), we still find no generally accepted explication and methodology for this notion. But there is at least some agreement that the construct validity of a test is supported by evidence that (1) it correlates well with tests with which theory implies it should correlate well; and (2) it correlates less well or not at all with tests with which theory implies it should not correlate well. Campbell and Fiske (1959) have called condition 1 *convergent validity* and condition 2 *discriminant validity*.

A natural explication, though perhaps not the only one, of the combined notions of convergent and discriminant validity is provided by the independent-clusters case of the common factor model. It is illustrated by the oblique confirmatory factor analysis of the Thurstone data in Table 2.2.2 as analyzed in Table 3.2.2. The "constructs" are the attributes, factors, or latent traits, labeled *verbal ability, word fluency,* and *reasoning*. The three tests of each show (1) convergent validity by their high correlations with each other; and (2) divergent validity by their lower correlations with tests from other groups. Underlying these two properties are the facts that (1) each group of tests defines a common factor and (2) the common factors are correlated, but the correlations are low enough for the factors to be regarded as distinct "constructs."

Occasionally it is feasible to assess each of a number of traits by each of a number of methods, equally applicable to all the traits, as when N persons are rated on n defined personality traits by m judges or under m conditions of observation. Such a data set yields what Campbell and Fiske (1959) called a *multitrait–multimethod* covariance matrix, which is an example of multimode data as discussed in Section 6.3. The independent-clusters factor model would still appear to be an appropriate test of convergent and discriminant validity, that is, of the hypothesis that the m methods are measuring just n distinct traits. But in such a case we might be prepared to suppose in addition that the m ratings should have the same factor loadings on each of the n traits. This assumption results in a more restricted version of the independent-clusters model with equality constraints. Such a model is not scale-free and would have to be fitted to the covariance matrix. A less restrictive model, with multiple factors for a trait or a method, would seem to contradict the basic hypothesis of convergent and discriminant validity. From this point of view, the points deserving emphasis are that (1) the notion of convergent and discriminant validity has a very natural explication in the independent-clusters model of common factor analysis, with the common factors as the "hypothetical constructs"; and (2) it is not necessary, and perhaps not even desirable, to associate this notion of validation with multitrait–multimethod data, a form of data that appears to be of extremely limited scope, within the field of test construction.

If we carry this line of thought two steps further, we reach some very curious conclusions. Suppose now that we wish to have a numerical index of the construct validity of the total score on a homogeneous test. (Indeed, we might suppose also that only a homogeneous test can be said to have a construct validity.) If the construct is the common factor of the n items or subtests of the test, then the natural choice for a validity coefficient would be the correlation between the total test score and the common factor. This correlation is easily obtained from the algebra of the Spearman model, and it turns out to be the square root of the quantity omega given in (7.3.8) and (7.3.9) as a good lower bound (better than alpha) to the reliability of a test. So we are led to conclude that the square of the construct validity of a test is less than or equal to its reliability, with equality attained if the parts of the test contain no specific components, in which case the construct is the same as the true score.

As the second step, we ostensibly turn to a distinct topic. The notion of a behavior domain has already been introduced (Section 2.3 and Section 5.3). Implicit in a number of discussions of the notion of *generalizability* is the idea that we should be able to measure the extent to which the results obtained by testing on a limited number of items generalize to the behavior domain from which the items were drawn. A natural measure would be the correlation between the total test score and a sum score based on the other items in the behavior domain. Suppose, then, that we have a homogeneous test whose n items fit the Spearman model along with infinitely many more items in what is thus taken to be a homogeneous behavior domain. It is then possible, by applying some limit theory to the Spearman model, to show that the square of the correlation between the sum of the scores on the n given items and the sum of the scores in the behavior domain is, again, given by omega in (7.3.8). That is, coefficient omega, computed from a Spearman factor analysis of the items of a test, is (1) a best lower bound to the reliability of the test; (2) a measure of its construct validity; and (3) a measure of its generalizability. As explicated in terms of the common factor model, there is no reason to distinguish between validity and generalizability and very little basis for a distinction between these and reliability. The reader is once again advised that this treatment of the topics is one-sided and does not begin to do justice to their breadth and complexity.[9]

---

[9]For a discussion of reliability theory and, in particular, coefficient alpha as a lower bound to reliability, see Lord and Novick (1968). McDonald (1970) gave coefficient omega (there called *theta*) as a better lower bound to reliability than alpha. For further discussion of unidimensionality, homogeneity, and internal consistency, see McDonald (1981). The proof that coefficient omega measures generalizability was given by McDonald (1978a).

General Note: Further reading for this chapter would include Lord and Novick (1968) and Lord (1980).

8 Summary

8.1. INTRODUCTION

8.1.1 Factor analysis comprises a set of techniques for data processing that include falsifiable statistical hypotheses and techniques for the reduction of data. 8.1.2 We may distinguish between the experimental mode of inquiry in the prototype of which subjects are randomly assigned to contrasted groups and the survey mode in which observations are made on subjects randomly drawn from a single population. The objectives of experiments seem clearer than the research objectives of multivariate surveys. A number of kinds of explanation can be offered for the fact that two variables are correlated. In particular, one may be said to *cause* the other, or both may be effects of a common cause, or the two variables may be said to be measures of the same thing. The theory of linear structural relations rests on the first two of these explanations, whereas factor analysis rests on the third.

We can recognize a crude classification of the observable properties of subjects as measurable observations and multicategory observations. Binary data can be treated as measurable data or multicategory data. Generally we are free to choose the origin and unit of measurement of measurable observations as suits our theoretical or practical convenience. In particular, we can choose deviation measure with the origin at the mean or standard measure with the origin at the mean and the standard deviation as the unit in either a sample or the population (but not both).

In regression theory, a dependent variable is expressed as a sum of two uncorrelated parts, the part due to the regression on one or more independent variables (the conditional mean) and a residual. This yields an analysis of variance of the dependent variable as a sum of the variance due to the independent variables and the residual variance. We "explain" the variance of the dependent variable by its covariation with the independent variable(s).

8.1.3 The multiple regression of a dependent variable on two or more independent variables is a weighted combination of the independent variables chosen to maximize its correlation with the dependent variable or to minimize the residual variance. The correlation between the dependent variable and this weighted combination is the multiple correlation of the dependent variable with the independent variables. The partial correlation of two (dependent) variables is the correlation of their residuals about their regressions on a set of independent variables. If a partial correlation of two (dependent) variables is zero, the independent variables "explain" the correlation between the dependent variables.

8.1.4 Useful multivariate statistical tests include a test that n variables are mutually uncorrelated, a test that two groups of variables are uncorrelated, and a test that n variables have all zero partial correlations. These hypotheses are conveniently described as hypotheses that the variables have a diagonal or a diagonal block correlation matrix.

8.1.5 Common factor theory began with Spearman's observation that certain correlation matrices of cognitive tests can be explained by the assumption that there exists an additional, unobserved, independent variable that, if held constant, would reduce all the partial correlations of the variables to zero and thus explain their mutual relations by their individual relations with the unobserved *common factor*. The common factor is a generic property that the tests measure in common. Each test also possesses a unique part, which may consist of a "stable" specific property and an "unstable" error of measurement. The theory yields a restrictive, testable statistical hypothesis with parameters that are not difficult to estimate, namely the correlations of the tests with the one common factor, and their unique variances.

Failure to confirm Spearman's single-factor hypothesis on all correlation matrices of cognitive tests led to the development of a multiple-common-factor model in which the correlations of observed test scores are explained by the regressions of the tests on two or more common factors, sufficient in number to reduce all the partial correlations of the tests to zero when the factors are held constant. If we postulate only the number of common factors needed to explain the correlations, we do not fix enough conditions to make the parameters in the model unique quantities to be estimated. From any set of factor loadings (regression weights of the tests on two or more factors) we may obtain alternative sets of numbers that equally explain the correlations by a process that is equivalent to rotating the axes of graphical plots of loadings on one factor upon loadings on another. If the common factors are chosen to be uncorrelated, we have an *orthogonal* factor analysis. If the common factors are allowed to be correlated, we have an *oblique* factor analysis. Thurstone has recommended the principle of simple structure to determine a preferred solution. We first explain all the correlations in the matrix with the smallest number of common factors possible, and we then choose a solution in which any one correlation is explained by as few of these factors as possible.

In exploratory factor analysis we fit a number of factors and then transform ("rotate") an obtained set of common factor loadings to approximate the condition of simple structure. In confirmatory factor analysis we postulate both the number of factors and the exact form of the simple structure.

The problem of exploratory factor analysis is to fit m factors to n variables, estimating nm common factor loadings and n unique variances, and then transform the factor loadings to yield approximate simple structure with either uncorrelated factors (an orthogonal approximate simple structure) or correlated factors (an oblique approximate simple structure) yielding also the resulting correlations of the factors. The problem of confirmatory factor analysis is to postulate a simple structure as a pattern of zero loadings in an $n \times m$ matrix of factor loadings and to estimate the nonzero parameters in the matrix, the n unique variances, and (almost always) the factor correlations.

8.2. EXPLORATORY COMMON FACTOR ANALYSIS

8.2.1 The hypothesis that the correlations of n variables are explained by their regressions on m common factors is not sufficiently definite to identify the common factor loadings (i.e., to make them fixed unknown quantities to be estimated). We estimate an *unrotated* factor pattern and then transform it to approximate simple structure.

8.2.2 One good estimation procedure is the method of least squares by which we choose parameters to minimize the n^2 discrepancies between the sample correlations (including the diagonal unities) and the correlations reproduced from the factor loadings and the unique variances. Another good estimation procedure is the method of maximum likelihood by which we choose parameters to maximize the probability of our sample observations. Arithmetic algorithms for minimizing such functions are built into modern factor analysis computer programs. With least-squares estimation, we can judge the misfit of the model with the chosen number of factors by the sizes of the residual covariances. Maximum likelihood estimation also yields a chi-square test in large samples. The chi-square test and the residuals are best used together, also taking account of the interpretation of the analysis, the object being to find enough interpretable factors to approximate the correlations with no overfitting of factors resulting from chance.

8.2.3 The principal components of a set of n variables are weighted combinations of the variables chosen to be mutually uncorrelated and such that each in turn has a maximum sum of squares of its correlations with the n variables. Having obtained n principal components, we can write each test score as a weighted combination of component scores and can approximate them by the m

of those that have the largest sums of squares of correlations. Each maximized sum of squares of correlations is also the total variance of the tests explained by the components when the tests are in standard measure. Because of their mathematical history they are known also as eigenvalues, latent roots, and characteristic roots. By definition, principal components optimally explain the variance of the variables, and a few of them do this better than the same number of common factors. The common factors, by definition, optimally explain the covariation of the variables, and they do this better than the same number of principal components. Principal components yield commonly used approximations to common factors.

The partial image of a variable is its regression on the $n - 1$ other variables in a finite set of n variables. The total image of a variable is its regression on infinitely many other variables in a universe of content or behavior domain. In certain circumstances, common factor theory and image theory coincide in the limit in an infinite behavior domain. In a finite set of tests drawn from such a domain, image theory gives useful inequalities and approximations for factor theory.

Approximate methods of factor analysis, based on principal components or image theory, are useful (1) to save computer costs in exploratory work; (2) for large data sets, if they must be analyzed; (3) as starting points for arithmetic for least-squares or maximum-likelihood methods. They have also been recommended to avoid Heywood cases.

Heywood cases, or improper solutions, yielding negative estimates of unique variances occur quite commonly in practice. The most common cause of Heywood cases seems to be failure on the part of the investigator to represent each factor by at least three tests with large loadings on it.

8.2.4 There are four main approaches to obtaining approximate simple structure, namely graphical methods, counting methods, simplicity function methods, and target methods. Graphical methods require a human operator to move axes on a graph and are rarely used. In counting methods, we try to make the computer optimize the number of points near hyperplanes. Simplicity functions are functions of the factor loadings that are chosen so that their optimum values will tend to coincide with an approximation to simple structure. It does not seem possible to define a simplicity function that is best for all data sets. In target methods we postulate the locations of zeros in the pattern and transform it to make the corresponding loadings as small as possible.

8.2.5 Inverse factor analysis is a term for the notion of factoring correlations between persons over tests. It does not seem possible to develop a rigorous inverse counterpart of the common factor model, and one may question whether the notion has any useful applications. Optimal scaling is one name for a collection of techniques for weighting qualitative data to obtain optimal scores. In a number of optimal scaling problems the optimal weights are arbitrary. The converse regression of the qualitative variables on the optimal scores gives invariant results that can be interpreted like a factor analysis.

Multidimensional scaling is a collection of techniques for representing dissimilarities of a set of objects as distances or functions of distances in a space of reduced dimensionality. Nonmetric multidimensional scaling has been applied to functions of correlation coefficients as measures of dissimilarity and a nonmetric counterpart of principal component analysis has been developed. A nonmetric counterpart of common factor analysis would be very difficult to develop.

8.3.   THE ANALYSIS OF COVARIANCE STRUCTURES

8.3.1 The analysis of covariance structures is a general class of procedures for fitting restrictive hypotheses in which the covariances and variances of a set of variables are functions of some number of parameters.

8.3.2 In confirmatory factor analysis we employ the analysis of covariance structures to fit a common factor model in which the matrix of factor loadings of n tests on m common factors has fixed zeros in prescribed locations. Generally we would choose an oblique factor model, but we are free to prescribe that one or more of the correlations between the common factors is zero. (1) The most common hypothesis is that of prescribed simple structure, satisfying the classical rules recommended by Thurstone. (2) It is also possible to prescribe a higher-order common factor model, in which the (first-order) factor model for the observed tests is supplemented by a (second-order) factor model explaining the correlations between the (first-order) common factors. Although it is possible in theory to fit a higher-order model by successive applications of exploratory factor analysis with rotation to approximate oblique simple structure, confirmatory methods would seem preferable. (3) An alternative to the higher-order common factor model is the hierarchical solution in which we depart from Thurstone's simple-structure principle to admit a general factor in place of a higher-order factor. It is possible to set up quite complex hierarchical structures reflecting various degrees of specificity of classification.

8.3.3 Hypotheses of equality of correlations, covariances, variances, or factor loadings provide the means to check for partial or total equivalence between tests, as in certain models of classical true-score theory.

8.4.   MODELS FOR LINEAR STRUCTURAL RELATIONS

8.4.1 The concept of causal relations remains a controversial one in the philosophy of science. We commonly make statements of the form "C applied to S causes E," either as a general law or as a description of a particular sequence of events, and we intend the statement to be understood asymmetrically and not just as an assertion of co-occurrence.

Accounts of the causal relation as (1) quasi-logical implication of E by C; (2) as a function $E = f(C)$; (3) as resting on temporal order (i.e., E follows C in time) seem inadequate. The treatment of it as a counterfactual conditional assertion, "if C had not occurred, E would not have occurred," which is asymmetric, goes some way toward capturing the concept and leads to the paradigm of inquiry into causal relations by observing that event E occurs in an isolated system S if event C is arbitrarily applied to S, and not otherwise.

This paradigm yields in turn the strict experimental design with randomized treatments. If both C and E are measurable changes, classical experiments yielding analyses of variance with manipulation of levels of causal variables in randomized balanced designs, keep the effects of distinct causal variables unconfounded. Under linear assumptions the unstandardized regression coefficients of the dependent variable on the independent variables then literally give the amount of change of the dependent variable (the effect) resulting from changes in each independent variable (causes). Under reasonable assumptions, these regression coefficients are the scientific invariants obtained from the experiment.

If a survey is substituted for the experiment, there is uncontrolled variation and covariation of the independent variables; hence the effects of the causal variables are confounded, and the obtained regression coefficients are not invariant under addition of further causal variables. Hence nonexperimental causal modeling rests on the strong assumption that all causal variables omitted from a study are uncorrelated with those that are included (though the latter may be, and usually are, mutually correlated). Causal analysis (path analysis) usually proceeds by fitting regressions, and under this strong assumption the fitted regression coefficients estimate the path coefficients (rates of change of the effect variable with each causal variable).

In models for causal analysis we postulate causal chains or sequences of variables or groups of variables, described by a network of causal paths with directed paths from a causal variable to its effect variable, and undirected paths representing residual covariation of variables. A causal model is recursive if no circuit exists whereby one variable affects another and also conversely. Otherwise it is nonrecursive. The causal model is expressed in the pattern of nonzero path coefficients postulated and in expectations about the residual covariances that follow from the basic assumption of causal modeling that the residual of a variable (the disturbance term) is uncorrelated with all causally prior variables. The traditional treatment of path analysis has been to fit all the individual regressions specified by the model and examine the results in a piecemeal fashion for fit to the postulated restrictions. The modern approach uses analysis of covariance structures to fit the postulated regressions and the postulated nonzero residual covariances (and variances).

8.4.2 The simplest known model, and apparently the simplest possible model, for path analysis, causal analysis, or the analysis of linear structural relations is the reticular action model (RAM). A RAM model is specified by three steps. (1) We write down a complete set of regression equations in which every variable is regressed on all the other variables (with zero coefficients prescribed for omitted relationships). (2) We specify the pattern of the residual covariances. (3) We label each variable as observable or unobservable. The model can be fitted by a standard program for the analysis of covariance structures, such as LISREL or COSAN, with output including the matrix of regression coefficients, which we interpret as path coefficients, and the fitted residual covariance matrix. Depending on the number of parameters in relation to the size of the covariance matrix of the observable variables, the parameters may be underidentified, just-identified, or overidentified. In the latter case the model is restrictive and yields a chi-square test of fit. Common cases in the analysis of linear structural relations include (1) univariate regression, of one variable on one or more independent variables; (2) partial covariance, of two or more dependent variables regressed on one or more independent variables; (3) a causal chain, of three or more variables in a causal sequence; (4) multivariate regression, of two or more dependent variables on one or more independent variables; (5) block recursive models, in which two or more variables intermediate as a group between one or more dependent variables and one or more independent variables; (6) causal models with latent variables, in which the common factor of a group of variables is placed in a causal network. Most recursive models for path analysis will consist of, or combine, one or more of these six. For any such model, given a pattern of zero and nonzero regression weights, we prescribe the corresponding residual covariance matrix by (1) the recursive priority rule, which states that a residual covariance of two variables is zero if one causally precedes the other; and (2) the latent variable rule, which states that a residual covariance of two variables is zero if they are both regressed on one or more of the same group of latent variables (factors).

The LISREL model consists of two measurement models, relating two sets of observed variables to corresponding sets of latent variables, and a structural model, regressing one set of latent variables on the other. COSAN is a block recursive model, regressing blocks of variables on each other and on preceding blocks of variables.

8.5. THE PROBLEM OF FACTOR SCORES

8.5.1 A common outcome of a factor analysis is the construction of homogeneous tests whose total scores are intended to measure the traits identified in the factor-analytic investigation. In such a case, the test score substitutes for any factor score that we might seek to approximate or estimate.

8.5.2 The regressions of the factors on the tests follow from classical regression theory, yielding regression estimators of the factor scores from the known correlations of the tests and their known correlations with the unknown factor scores. Maximum likelihood estimators of factor scores can also be obtained from the factor loadings and unique variances. Both of these estimators are mutually correlated when the factors are uncorrelated. The former are also biased and correlated with factors other than the one each estimates, whereas the latter are not.

8.5.3 The common factor scores of a finite number of tests are mathematically indeterminate and can be said to be undefined. It is theoretically possible for two investigators to augment a given set of tests with further tests (independently) subject only to the condition that they continue to fit the common factor model with the same factor loadings for the initial set and in the limit of this process obtain determinate common factor scores that are unrelated to each other. If each draws tests from a common, clearly denoted behavior domain, their factor scores will coincide in the limit. Thus the problem of factor score indeterminacy seems to be the problem of finding a good approach to the specification and sampling of a behavior domain. The substitution of component scores or image scores from a finite number of tests for factor score estimates does not yield better approximations to the scores in a behavior domain.

8.6. PROBLEMS OF RELATIONSHIP BETWEEN FACTOR ANALYSES

8.6.1 The problem of identifying factors from different investigations is a difficult one in its general form and offers no general principles. By Pearson's selection theorem, under mild regularity conditions we can expect unstandardized factor loadings to remain invariant under selection of populations. The resemblance between factors is sometimes measured by a coefficient of congruence, the normalized raw product moment of their factor loadings. Transformations can be applied to maximize congruence of a factor pattern to a target pattern or of two or more factor patterns to each other.

8.6.2 Jöreskog has described a general model for simultaneous factor analysis in several populations. Within the model one can test hypotheses that the factor loadings are the same, whereas the factor correlations are possibly different, and other hypotheses, more or less restrictive.

8.6.3 Repeated-measures designs yield multimode data consisting of tests × occasions or conditions of testing × examinees. A very general model for such data has been given by Tucker. The general model is subject to severe problems of underidentifiability. It perhaps can never be used in an exploratory fashion, and it seems difficult to find general principles governing its use and interpretation. A simpler model given by Harshman embodies Cattell's principle of parallel proportional profiles that factor loadings should change proportionately from condition to condition. The model in effect assumes that factor scores may change their variance from condition to condition but not their correlations. The invariant factors model carries over the condition of invariant factor loadings from independent populations to repeated measures, assuming that the effect of conditions is at most to change means, variances, and covariances of factor scores.

8.7. ITEM RESPONSE THEORY

8.7.1 It has commonly been believed that the factor analysis of binary items yields factors due to item difficulty. It turns out that difficulty factors, if they occur, are due to the curvilinearity of the regressions of binary items on a factor. The regression of a binary item (scored unity or zero) on a factor is the curve of conditional probability of the response to the item that is scored unity and is also known in the literature as an item characteristic curve or trace line. It is not unreasonable to fit the common factor model to a covariance matrix of binary items, but it is generally better to apply one of the models of latent trait theory.

8.7.2 Latent trait theory or item response theory yields a class of models, mainly for binary data, based on the principle of local independence. This principle postulates that, conditional on a fixed set of values of the latent traits, the item responses are mutually statistically independent. This includes the weaker defining principle of common factor analysis that conditional on fixed values of the common factors or latent traits the item responses are mutually uncorrelated. Although other models, such as the latent class model, have been explored, the best-known latent trait models are the virtually indistinguishable normal ogive and logistic models. These are single-trait models with a monotone regression function in the form of a cumulative probability distribution function, with lower and upper asymptotes. The models can be described by two parameters per item, namely the position of the point of inflexion, which governs item difficulty, and the slope at that point, which governs item discriminating power. A third parameter, controlling the lower asymptote, can be introduced to account for "guessing" in multiple-choice cognitive items. By setting a common value of the parameter controlling discrimination, we obtain a version of the Rasch model. By a technique that essentially reduces to approximating these models by polynomial series, it is possible to fit the item parameters, treating the latent trait as a normally distributed random variable, with reasonably efficient arithmetic. It is also possible to estimate the item parameters and the latent trait values of the examinees simultaneously, by maximum likelihood. In principle, we can always check the fit of such models by inspecting the item residual covariances. Most computer programs for fitting them do not supply this information, and investigators have tended to substitute prior tests that have been conjectured to relate to unidimensionality, for a test of fit of the model itself.

8.7.3 A number of concepts from classical test theory lend themselves to explication and measurement on the basis of common factor analysis. Coefficient omega, a function of the uniquenesses of a set of items and of the variance of their sum, provides a better lower bound to the reliability of the sum score than does the well-known coefficient alpha. Coefficient omega also measures the construct validity of the test and its generalizability to the behavior domain from which its items are drawn. At the same time, the factor analysis yields evidence that the test is homogeneous (unidimensional).

Appendix
Some Matrix Algebra

A.1. MATRICES, VECTORS, SCALARS

From the point of view of the mathematician, who prefers on principle not to know what he is talking about, a matrix is an unidentified mathematical object whose definition consists solely in the rules (of addition, multiplication, and the like) that it obeys. From the point of view of practical persons, who usually like to believe that they know what they are talking about, a matrix is primarily a rectangular array of numbers. We can have the best of both worlds if we say that a matrix is an array of numbers that is subject to the fundamental operations, given in the following, of matrix algebra.

A rectangular array of mn numbers, written so as to have m rows and n columns, is said to be an $(m \times n)$ matrix or, in other words, a matrix of *order* $(m \times n)$. [We read $(m \times n)$ as "m by n," not as "m times n," and carefully distinguish this from mn, as when we say "there are mn numbers altogether, arranged to form the $m \times n$ matrix.") If in particular $m = n$, the matrix is said to be *square of order n*. We follow the conventions of *lexical* (reading) order and count *rows* of the matrix from the top down and *columns* of the matrix from left to right. The number in the jth row and the kth column is the (j, k)th *element* of the matrix. Collectively, one or more of the numbers in the matrix are called *elements* of the matrix. We shall follow the convention of denoting a matrix by a boldface uppercase letter.

We indicate a matrix by writing its elements inside square brackets. Where there is no ambiguity, we may denote an entire matrix by writing its general element inside square brackets. For example, the six numbers $a_{11}, a_{12}, a_{13}, a_{21}, a_{22}, a_{23}$ are elements of the (2×3) matrix:

$$\mathbf{A} = [a_{jk}] = \begin{bmatrix} a_{11} & a_{12} & a_{13} \\ a_{21} & a_{22} & a_{23} \end{bmatrix} \qquad (A.1.1)$$

By convention, the first subscript is the row index and the second subscript is the column index.

TABLE A.1.1			
Subject	Test 1	Test 2	Test 3
Snug	113	56	29
Quince	98	47	20
Bottom	110	52	23
Starveling	87	40	17
Flute	65	38	12
Snout	53	37	13

TABLE A.1.2			
	Weight		
Rat	First Week	Second Week	Third Week
1	520	540	556
2	532	532	548
3	486	506	522
4	551	571	538

The ordinary tabular representation of data immediately invites matrix definition and matrix treatment. Tables A1.1.1 and A1.1.2 are interpretable as matrices as soon as they are shorn of the marginal information (which may be recovered from the defined order of the rows and columns when it matters) and thereby prepared for matrix operations. That is, they become, respectively, the data matrices

$$\begin{bmatrix} 113 & 56 & 29 \\ 98 & 47 & 20 \\ 110 & 52 & 23 \\ 87 & 40 & 17 \\ 65 & 38 & 12 \\ 53 & 37 & 13 \end{bmatrix} \text{ and } \begin{bmatrix} 520 & 540 & 556 \\ 532 & 532 & 548 \\ 486 & 506 & 522 \\ 551 & 571 & 538 \end{bmatrix}$$

The *transpose* of a matrix $\mathbf{A} = [a_{jk}]$ of order $(m \times n)$ is the matrix $\mathbf{A}' = [a_{kj}]$. For example, the transpose of the matrix in (A.1.1) is the matrix

$$\mathbf{A}' = \begin{bmatrix} a_{11} & a_{21} \\ a_{12} & a_{22} \\ a_{13} & a_{23} \end{bmatrix}$$

(In this book we use a superscript prime to denote a transpose. Another common convention is the use of a superscript T, as in $\mathbf{A}^T$.) The element in the jth row and kth column of the given matrix is the element in the kth row and the jth column of the transpose of the matrix. The *operation* of obtaining the transpose of a given matrix is referred to as *transposition*.

A *vector* is an ordered set of numbers. Each number in the vector is referred to as a *component* of the vector. By convention, we denote a vector by a boldface lowercase letter. Also by convention it is usually written as a column of numbers when presented in full rather than as a row. The ordered set of numbers

$$\mathbf{a} = \begin{bmatrix} a_1 \\ \cdot \\ \cdot \\ \cdot \\ a_m \end{bmatrix}$$

is an m-component vector. If we wish to write a vector in full as a row (for example, out of kindness to the printer), we indicate this by a prime, writing for example

$$\mathbf{b}' = [b_1 \ \ldots \ b_n]$$

a row vector of n components. Thereby we have introduced or defined the column vector $\mathbf{b}$. From one point of view the column vector $\mathbf{a}$ is an $(m \times 1)$ matrix, and the row vector $\mathbf{b}'$ is a $(1 \times n)$ matrix. Sometimes, therefore, we say, redundantly, that $\mathbf{a}$ is an $(m \times 1)$ vector and $\mathbf{b}'$ is a $(1 \times n)$ vector. Also, obviously, the prime on $\mathbf{b}$ signifies that $\mathbf{b}'$ is thought of as a column vector that has been transposed. It is an accident of history that we customarily speak of the *elements* of a matrix and the *components* of a vector.

A *scalar,* from one point of view, is a single number, in contrast to vectors and matrices that are arrays of numbers. From another point of view, a scalar is a quantity that obeys simpler algebraic rules than the rules obeyed by matrix and vector quantities.

A.2. MATRIX EQUALITIES, SUMS AND DIFFERENCES

We write

$$\mathbf{A} = \mathbf{B}$$

if and only if

$$[a_{jk}] = [b_{jk}].$$

That is, two matrices are equal if and only if the (j, k)th element of $\mathbf{A}$ is equal to the (j, k)th element of $\mathbf{B},$ for all j and k. This implies that matrices can be equal only if they are of the same order.

The matrix $\mathbf{C}$ is the *sum* of two matrices, $\mathbf{A}$ and $\mathbf{B}$; that is,

$$\mathbf{C} = \mathbf{A} + \mathbf{B} \tag{A.2.1}$$

if and only if

$$[a_{jk}] = [a_{jk} + b_{jk}].$$ (A.2.2)

Thus, if

$$A = \begin{bmatrix} 1 & 2 & 0 \\ 3 & 0 & -1 \end{bmatrix} \quad \text{and} \quad B = \begin{bmatrix} -1 & 1 & 1 \\ -4 & -1 & 2 \end{bmatrix}$$

then

$$C = A + B = \begin{bmatrix} 0 & 3 & 1 \\ -1 & -1 & 1 \end{bmatrix}$$

The *null matrix* or *zero* matrix has every element equal to zero. If A is a matrix of order $(m \times n)$ and O is a null matrix of order $(m \times n)$, then

$$A + O = A.$$ (A.2.3)

A.3. MULTIPLICATION—LENGTH OF A VECTOR

The definition of a product of matrices arises naturally out of the applications of matrix theory. At first sight, it is not the most compelling definition. We shall approach it in stages.

The *scalar product* of two $(n \times 1)$ vectors is defined as the sum of the products of the n corresponding components. That is, if $a' = [a_1, \ldots, a_n]$ and $b' = [b_1, \ldots, b_n]$, then their scalar product

$$s = a'b = \sum_{j=1}^{n} a_j b_j$$ (A.3.1)

Suppose, for example, that we have the first row of Table A.1.1 as a vector $[113 \quad 56 \quad 29]$ of scores on three tests, and we decide to *weight* the tests according to some prior notion of their relative importance, say that Test 2 is 3 times as important as Test 1, and Test 3 is $1\frac{1}{2}$ times as important as Test 1. We want to form a combined score consisting of the weighted sum of the three scores. This quantity,

$$s = 1.0 \times 113 + 3 \times 56 + 1.5 \times 29 = 324.5$$

can be rewritten as

$$s = w'x$$ (A.3.2)

where

$$\mathbf{w}' = [1.0 \quad 3.0 \quad 1.5] \quad \text{and} \quad \mathbf{x}' = [113 \quad 56 \quad 29]$$

We notice from the form of (A.3.1) that

$$\mathbf{a}'\mathbf{b} = \mathbf{b}'\mathbf{a} \tag{A.3.3}$$

A special case of a scalar product is the scalar product of a vector with itself. Instead of a sum of products, we then of course have a sum of squares; that is,

$$\mathbf{a}'\mathbf{a} = \sum_{j=1}^{n} a_j^2 \tag{A.3.4}$$

In Fig. A.3.1, we have a point whose coordinates in a two-dimensional graph are $\mathbf{a}' = [a_1 \ a_2]$. By Pythagoras' theorem, the quantity $\mathbf{a}'\mathbf{a}$ is the square of the distance of the point from the origin. More generally, in the undrawable and unimaginable geometry of n-dimensional space, the sum of squares $\mathbf{a}'\mathbf{a}$ is the square of the distance of the point $\mathbf{a}$ from the origin; hence

$$l = \sqrt{\mathbf{a}'\mathbf{a}} \tag{A.3.5}$$

is the *length* of the line (i.e., the length of the vector $\mathbf{a}$). We notice that $\mathbf{a}'\mathbf{a} = 0$ if and only if $\mathbf{a} = \mathbf{0}$. (A sum of squares is zero if and only if every term in the sum is zero.) That is, the length of a vector is zero if and only if every one of its n components is zero. The vector is different from a null vector to the extent that one or more of its components are different (positively or negatively) from zero, and the length of the vector tries to capture in one number the extent of this difference in terms of a sum of squares.

The *product* of two matrices $\mathbf{A}$ and $\mathbf{B}$, denoted by $\mathbf{AB}$, is defined if and only if matrix $\mathbf{A}$ has column order equal to the row order of matrix $\mathbf{B}$ [i.e., if $\mathbf{A}$ is $(m \times n)$ and $\mathbf{B}$ is $(n \times p)$, say]. The product is then of order $(m \times p)$. We write

$$\mathbf{C} = \mathbf{AB} \tag{A.3.6}$$

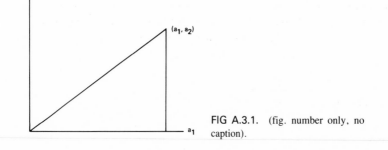

FIG A.3.1. (fig. number only, no caption).

where

$$\mathbf{C} = [c_{jk}] = \left[\sum_{i=1}^{n} a_{ji} b_{ik} \right] \tag{A.3.7}$$

If we regard the $(m \times n)$ matrix $\mathbf{A}$ as a collection of m row vectors $\mathbf{a}_1' \ldots,$ $\mathbf{a}_m'$, each having n components, and the $(n \times p)$ matrix $\mathbf{B}$ as a collection of p column vectors $\mathbf{b}_1', \ldots, \mathbf{b}_p'$, each also having n components, then the (j, k)th element of the product matrix $\mathbf{C} = \mathbf{AB}$ is the scalar product of the jth row vector of $\mathbf{A}$ and the kth column vector of $\mathbf{B}$. That is,

$$\mathbf{A} = \begin{bmatrix} \mathbf{a}_1' \\ \cdot \\ \cdot \\ \cdot \\ \mathbf{a}_m' \end{bmatrix} \qquad \mathbf{B} = [\mathbf{b}_1, \ldots, \mathbf{b}_p] \tag{A.3.8}$$

so that

$$\mathbf{C} = \mathbf{AB} = [c_{jk}] = [\mathbf{a}_j' \mathbf{b}_k]. \tag{A.3.9}$$

For example, if

$$\mathbf{A} = \begin{bmatrix} 1 & 2 & 0 \\ 3 & 0 & -1 \end{bmatrix} \qquad \mathbf{B} = \begin{bmatrix} 1 & 2 & 1 & 1 \\ 2 & 3 & 3 & 1 \\ 3 & 1 & 2 & 1 \end{bmatrix}$$

then

$$\begin{aligned} \mathbf{a}_1' &= [1 \quad 2 \quad 0] \\ \mathbf{a}_2' &= [3 \quad 0 \quad 1] \end{aligned} \qquad \mathbf{b}_1 = \begin{bmatrix} 1 \\ 2 \\ 3 \end{bmatrix} \qquad \mathbf{b}_2 = \begin{bmatrix} 2 \\ 3 \\ 1 \end{bmatrix} \qquad \mathbf{b}_3 = \begin{bmatrix} 1 \\ 3 \\ 2 \end{bmatrix} \qquad \mathbf{b}_4 = \begin{bmatrix} 1 \\ 1 \\ 1 \end{bmatrix}$$

and

$$\begin{aligned} \mathbf{a}_1' \mathbf{b}_1 &= 5 & \mathbf{a}_1' \mathbf{b}_2 &= 8 & \mathbf{a}_1' \mathbf{b}_3 &= 7 & \mathbf{a}_1' \mathbf{b}_4 &= 3 \\ \mathbf{a}_2' \mathbf{b}_1 &= 0 & \mathbf{a}_2' \mathbf{b}_2 &= 5 & \mathbf{a}_2' \mathbf{b}_3 &= 1 & \mathbf{a}_2' \mathbf{b}_4 &= 2 \end{aligned}$$

which, collected together, yields

$$\mathbf{C} = \begin{bmatrix} 5 & 8 & 7 & 3 \\ 0 & 5 & 1 & 2 \end{bmatrix}.$$

Returning now to the expression (A.3.7), we note that in general if the product $\mathbf{AB}$ is defined, it need not be true that the product $\mathbf{BA}$ is defined, because it may not be true that $m = p$. If $\mathbf{A}$ is $(m \times n)$ and $\mathbf{B}$ is $(n \times m)$, so that both the column order of $\mathbf{A}$ equals the row order of $\mathbf{B}$, and the row order of $\mathbf{A}$ equals the column order of $\mathbf{B}$, then both $\mathbf{AB}$ and $\mathbf{BA}$ are defined, but in general they are of different orders, $(m \times m)$ and $(n \times n)$. Even if $m = n$, in general $\mathbf{AB}$ and $\mathbf{BA}$ are unequal. For example, if

$$\mathbf{A} = \begin{bmatrix} 2 & 3 \\ 1 & 4 \end{bmatrix} \quad \text{and} \quad \mathbf{B} = \begin{bmatrix} 1 & 0 \\ 2 & 5 \end{bmatrix}$$

then

$$\mathbf{AB} = \begin{bmatrix} 8 & 15 \\ 9 & 20 \end{bmatrix} \quad \text{and} \quad \mathbf{BA} = \begin{bmatrix} 2 & 3 \\ 9 & 26 \end{bmatrix}.$$

Notice also that in general $\mathbf{A}'\mathbf{A}$ and $\mathbf{AA}'$ are not equal. For example, here

$$\mathbf{AA}' = \begin{bmatrix} 13 & 14 \\ 14 & 17 \end{bmatrix} \quad \text{and} \quad \mathbf{A}'\mathbf{A} = \begin{bmatrix} 5 & 10 \\ 10 & 25 \end{bmatrix}.$$

We sometimes say that $\mathbf{AB}$ is obtained by "premultiplying $\mathbf{B}$ by $\mathbf{A}$" or by "postmultiplying $\mathbf{A}$ by $\mathbf{B}$," to avoid ambiguities in speaking of the *operation* whereby the product is obtained.

We repeatedly use a rule that states that the transpose of a product of matrices is equal to the product of their transposes in reverse order. That is, if

$$\mathbf{C} = \mathbf{AB} \tag{A.3.10}$$

then

$$\mathbf{C}' = \mathbf{B}'\mathbf{A}' \tag{A.3.11}$$

A.4. THE TRACE OF A MATRIX

If a matrix $\mathbf{A}$ is square of order n, its n elements $a_{11}, a_{22}, \ldots, a_{nn}$ are referred to as its *diagonal* elements. They are said to constitute, or to lie on, the *principal diagonal* of $\mathbf{A}$. For example, if $n = 4$, and

$$\mathbf{A} = \begin{bmatrix} \underline{a}_{11} & a_{12} & a_{13} & a_{14} \\ a_{21} & \underline{a}_{22} & a_{23} & a_{24} \\ a_{31} & a_{32} & \underline{a}_{33} & a_{34} \\ a_{41} & a_{42} & a_{43} & \underline{a}_{44} \end{bmatrix}$$

the underscored elements constitute the principal diagonal. (There is also a secondary diagonal, consisting, in the example, of a_{41}, a_{32}, a_{23}, a_{14}. This is rarely of interest.)

The sum of the diagonal elements of a square matrix is known as its *trace*, and we represent this number by

$$\text{Tr } \{\mathbf{A}\} = \sum_{j=1}^{n} a_{jj} \tag{A.4.1}$$

In the last example of Section A.3, we have two matrix products **AB** and **BA** to demonstrate that in general $\mathbf{AB} \neq \mathbf{BA}$. We note, however, that both have a trace equal to 28. In general, when both products are defined, they are both square, so both traces are defined, and

$$\text{Tr } \{\mathbf{AB}\} = \text{Tr } \{\mathbf{BA}\}. \tag{A.4.2}$$

This is because

$$\text{Tr } \{\mathbf{AB}\} = \sum_{j=1}^{n} \sum_{i=1}^{m} a_{ji} b_{ij}$$

and

$$\text{Tr } \{\mathbf{BA}\} = \sum_{i=1}^{m} \sum_{j=1}^{n} b_{ij} a_{ji}.$$

In particular,

$$\text{Tr } \{\mathbf{AA}'\} = \text{Tr } \{\mathbf{A}'\mathbf{A}\}. \tag{A.4.3}$$

In terms of the elements of **A**, of order $(m \times n)$,

$$\text{Tr } \{\mathbf{AA}'\} = \text{Tr } \{\mathbf{A}'\mathbf{A}\} = \sum_{j=1}^{m} \sum_{k=1}^{n} a_{jk}^2. \tag{A.4.4}$$

That is, $\text{Tr}\{\mathbf{AA}'\}$ is the sum of the squares of the mn elements of **A**. The expression (A.4.4) suggests that $\text{Tr}\{\mathbf{AA}'\}$ is a good single measure of the difference between **A** and the null matrix. Comparing (A.4.4) with (A.3.5), we might willingly think of (A.4.4) as measuring the square of the "distance" of **A** from the null matrix.

More generally, the difference between two $(m \times n)$ matrices **A** and **X**, which consists in reality of mn differences in corresponding terms, can be summarized in the quantity

$$d^2 = \text{Tr}\ \{(\mathbf{A} - \mathbf{X})(\mathbf{A} - \mathbf{X})'\} = \sum_{j=1}^{m} \sum_{k=1}^{n} (a_{jk} - x_{jk})^2 \qquad (A.4.5)$$

If, as the notation already hints, $\mathbf{A}$ were a matrix of fixed and known numbers and $\mathbf{X}$ were a matrix of variables (perhaps functions of other quantities), a choice of $\mathbf{X}$ to minimize d^2 would amount to minimizing the sum of the squares of the mn discrepancies between a_{jk} and x_{jk}, as in the general principle of fitting by least squares, and we would say that the *matrix* $\mathbf{X}$ is the least-squares best-fitting matrix to matrix $\mathbf{A}$. Note also that $\mathbf{A} = \mathbf{X}$ if and only if $d^2 = 0$; hence knowing that $d^2 = 0$ is equivalent to knowing mn equalities, $a_{jk} = x_{jk}$.

A.5 SPECIAL MATRICES

As mentioned already, a square matrix has the same number of rows as it has columns, and it suffices to describe the order of an $(n \times n)$ matrix by saying that it is *square of order n*. The elements $a_{11}, a_{22}, \ldots, a_{nn}$ of a square matrix $\mathbf{A}$ are its diagonal elements, and the remainder are its nondiagonal or off-diagonal elements.

A *lower triangular* matrix is a square matrix all of whose off-diagonal elements above the principal diagonal are zero. (Conversely, an *upper triangular* matrix has all off-diagonal elements below the diagonal equal to zero.) Consider the examples

$$\mathbf{T}_l = \begin{bmatrix} t_{11} & & \\ t_{21} & t_{22} & \\ t_{31} & t_{32} & t_{33} \end{bmatrix} \qquad \mathbf{T}_l = \begin{bmatrix} 1 & 0 & 0 \\ 2 & 3 & 0 \\ 0 & 1 & 4 \end{bmatrix} \qquad \mathbf{T}_u = \begin{bmatrix} 1 & 2 & 0 \\ 0 & 3 & 1 \\ 0 & 0 & 4 \end{bmatrix}$$

with self-explanatory notation.

A *diagonal* matrix is a matrix all of whose off-diagonal elements are zero. We sometimes form a diagonal matrix from a given square matrix $\mathbf{A}$ by the operation of replacing its off-diagonal elements by zeros. We symbolize the result of this operation by Diag $\{\mathbf{A}\}$, so that if

$$\mathbf{A} = \begin{bmatrix} 1 & 1 & 2 \\ 2 & 3 & 9 \\ 0 & 1 & 4 \end{bmatrix} \qquad \text{Diag}\ \{\mathbf{A}\} = \begin{bmatrix} 1 & & \\ & 3 & \\ & & 4 \end{bmatrix}.$$

(It is common practice to replace zeros by blanks in special matrices such as these.) Sometimes we form an $(n \times n)$ diagonal matrix, using n given elements as its diagonal elements. From, for example, $d_1, \ldots, d_n$, given, we might define, using the same notation,

$$\mathbf{D} = \text{Diag}\,\{d_1, \ldots, d_n\} = \begin{bmatrix} d_1 & & & & \\ & d_2 & & & \\ & & \cdot & & \\ & & & \cdot & \\ & & & & \cdot \\ & & & & & d_n \end{bmatrix}$$

A *scalar* matrix is a diagonal matrix all of whose diagonal elements are equal. It may be verified that multiplying a given matrix by a scalar matrix multiplies each of its elements by the common scalar, so if

$$\mathbf{K} = \begin{bmatrix} k & & & & \\ & k & & & \\ & & \cdot & & \\ & & & \cdot & \\ & & & & \cdot \\ & & & & & k \end{bmatrix}$$

then

$$\mathbf{KA} = \mathbf{AK} = k\mathbf{A} = \mathbf{A}k. \tag{A.5.1}$$

The *identity matrix* of order n is a scalar matrix each of whose diagonal elements is unity. We follow the convention of denoting the identity matrix by $\mathbf{I}$, usually subscripted by its order, writing, for example,

$$\mathbf{I}_2 = \begin{bmatrix} 1 & \\ & 1 \end{bmatrix} \qquad \mathbf{I}_3 = \begin{bmatrix} 1 & & \\ & 1 & \\ & & 1 \end{bmatrix}$$

It is easily seen that for any $(m \times n)$ matrix $\mathbf{A}$,

$$\mathbf{AI}_n = \mathbf{A} \qquad \mathbf{I}_m\mathbf{A} = \mathbf{A} \tag{A.5.2}$$

so that the identity matrix is indeed the identity operator under multiplication, as it leaves $\mathbf{A}$ unaltered. We note that an $(n \times n)$ scalar matrix can be conveniently written as $k\mathbf{I}_n$, where k is its repeated diagonal element.

A *symmetric matrix* is formally defined as a matrix that is equal to its own transpose (i.e., $\mathbf{A}$ is symmetric if and only if $\mathbf{A} = \mathbf{A}'$). This means that the general element $a_{jk} = a_{kj}$. In performing algebra on matrices we test for symmetry by testing whether $\mathbf{A} = \mathbf{A}'$. In actual arrays, we recognize symmetry by inspection, reading down and to the right from each diagonal term, to find matching elements.

The special matrices introduced so far—triangular, diagonal, scalar, identity, and symmetric matrices—are all recognizable by inspection. The remaining type requires to be tested by a multiplication operation.

An *orthogonal* matrix $\mathbf{Q}$ is a square matrix such that

$$\mathbf{QQ}' = \mathbf{Q}'\mathbf{Q} = \mathbf{I}_n. \tag{A.5.3}$$

We can dissect this definition into parts by regarding $\mathbf{Q}$ as a set of column vectors; that is,

$$\mathbf{Q} = [\mathbf{q}_1, \ldots, \mathbf{q}_n]$$

so that $\mathbf{Q}'\mathbf{Q} = \mathbf{I}_n$ implies

$$\mathbf{q}'_j\mathbf{q}_j = 1 \qquad j = 1, \ldots, n$$

and

$$\mathbf{q}'_j\mathbf{q}_k = 0 \qquad \text{for all } j \neq k.$$

Thus, the columns of $\mathbf{Q}$ are of unit length, and distinct columns have zero scalar products. Two vectors whose scalar product is zero are said to be *orthogonal*. If we plot them as points in space, we find that the lines joining them to the origin are indeed at right angles (*ortho* = right, *gonia* = angle).

For example, the matrix

$$\mathbf{Q} = \begin{bmatrix} \dfrac{1}{\sqrt{2}} & \dfrac{1}{\sqrt{2}} \\ \dfrac{-1}{\sqrt{2}} & \dfrac{1}{\sqrt{2}} \end{bmatrix} \tag{A.5.4}$$

is easily seen to satisfy these conditions. More generally, if x is any number between -1 and $+1$,

$$\mathbf{Q} = \begin{bmatrix} x & \sqrt{1 - x^2} \\ -\sqrt{1 - x^2} & x \end{bmatrix} \tag{A.5.5}$$

is orthogonal. Orthogonal matrices of higher order can be built up by multiplying together matrices of the type

$$\begin{bmatrix} 1 & & & & & \\ \cdot & 1 & & & & \\ \cdot & \cdot & x & & \sqrt{1 - x^2} & \\ \cdot & \cdot & \cdot & 1 & & \\ \cdot & \cdot & -\sqrt{1 - x^2} & & x & \\ \cdot & \cdot & & \cdot & & 1 \end{bmatrix}$$

A.6.   THE INVERSE OF A MATRIX

In scalar algebra, we may divide a given number by any number except zero. In the case of division by zero, we say that the quotient "does not exist." The counterpart division in matrix algebra involves more subtle considerations.

If for a given square $(n \times n)$ matrix $\mathbf{A}$ there exists a matrix to be denoted by $\mathbf{A}^{-1}$ (we read this as "A-inverse"), such that

$$\mathbf{AA}^{-1} = \mathbf{I}_n$$

then $\mathbf{A}^{-1}$ is the *inverse* of $\mathbf{A}$. It can be shown that if such a matrix exists, it is unique, and it is also true that

$$\mathbf{A}^{-1}\mathbf{A} = \mathbf{I}_n.$$

If $\mathbf{A}$ has an inverse, we say that it is *nonsingular;* whereas if $\mathbf{A}$ does not have an inverse, we say that it is *singular.* For example, if

$$\mathbf{A} = \begin{bmatrix} 1 & \frac{1}{2} \\ \frac{1}{2} & 1 \end{bmatrix} \quad \text{then} \quad \mathbf{A}^{-1} = \begin{bmatrix} \frac{4}{3} & -\frac{2}{3} \\ -\frac{2}{3} & \frac{4}{3} \end{bmatrix}$$

as may be verified by multiplication. On the other hand, the matrices

$$\begin{bmatrix} \frac{1}{2} & \frac{1}{2} \\ \frac{1}{2} & \frac{1}{2} \end{bmatrix} \quad \text{and} \quad \begin{bmatrix} 1 & 2 \\ 2 & 4 \end{bmatrix}$$

do not have an inverse.

The actual arithmetic whereby we obtain the inverse of a given matrix (if an inverse exists) is equivalent to a systematic approach to solving a system of linear equations. The system of equations

$$
\begin{aligned}
a_{11}x_1 + \cdots + a_{1n}x_n &= b_1 \\
a_{21}x_1 + \cdots + a_{2n}x_n &= b_2 \\
\cdot \quad \cdot \qquad \cdot \quad \cdot \quad \cdot \\
a_{n1}x_1 + \cdots + a_{nn}x_n &= b_n
\end{aligned}
\tag{A.6.1}
$$

can be written as a single matrix equation

$$\mathbf{Ax} = \mathbf{b} \tag{A.6.2}$$

where $\mathbf{A} = [a_{jk}]$, $\mathbf{x}' = [x_1 . . . x_n]$, $\mathbf{b}' = [b_1 . . . b_n]$. For a system that is not too large, we usually learn to obtain its solution by a process of elimination of variables and back substitution of the solution for each variable. The basic operations of forward elimination and back substitution are, essentially, multiplying an equation by a constant and subtracting one equation from another. Formally, if a unique solution to (A.6.2), hence to (A.6.1), exists, we may write it as

$$\mathbf{x} = \mathbf{A}^{-1}\mathbf{A}\mathbf{x} = \mathbf{A}^{-1}\mathbf{b} \tag{A.6.3}$$

but in practice the arithmetic computation of the inverse involves equivalent arithmetic to the tedious process of solving (A.6.1). However, the process can safely be left to a computer subroutine. Therefore the reader new to matrix methods is advised that if he or she acquires facility in matrix multiplication, and hence can verify by multiplication that he or she indeed has an inverse if one is supplied, he or she need not learn an algorithm for matrix inversion. It is sufficient to be familiar with the concept, and acquaintance with a computing algorithm does not seem to improve this familiarity much.

A.7.   DETERMINANTS

The determinant of a square matrix $\mathbf{A}$ is a scalar function of all its elements, denoted by $|\mathbf{A}|$ or occasionally by Det $\{\mathbf{A}\}$. For an extraordinarily large number of purposes, it is sufficient to know just the following principles:

1. The determinant of the product of two square matrices is equal to the product of their determinants. That is, if $\mathbf{A}$ and $\mathbf{B}$ are square of order n, then

$$|\mathbf{AB}| = |\mathbf{A}||\mathbf{B}|.$$

2. The determinant of a triangular matrix is equal to the product of its n diagonal elements. That is, if $\mathbf{T}$ is a triangular matrix of order n, then

$$|\mathbf{T}| = \prod_{j=1}^{n} t_{jj}$$

3. Any square matrix can be factored into the product of a lower triangular matrix and an upper triangular matrix. That is, given $\mathbf{A}$ of order n, we can always find $\mathbf{L}$ lower triangular, and $\mathbf{U}$ upper triangular, such that

$$\mathbf{A} = \mathbf{LU}. \tag{A.7.1}$$

It then follows that

$$|\mathbf{A}| = |\mathbf{L}|\,|\mathbf{U}| = \left\{ \prod_{j=1}^{n} l_{jj} \right\} \left\{ \prod_{j=1}^{n} u_{jj} \right\}. \tag{A.7.2}$$

For example,

$$\mathbf{A} = \begin{bmatrix} 3 & 2 & 1 \\ 3 & 6 & 3 \\ 3 & 6 & 6 \end{bmatrix} = \begin{bmatrix} 1 & & \\ 1 & 2 & \\ 1 & 2 & 3 \end{bmatrix} \begin{bmatrix} 3 & 2 & 1 \\ & 2 & 1 \\ & & 1 \end{bmatrix}$$

hence

$$|\mathbf{A}| = (1 \times 2 \times 3)(3 \times 2 \times 1).$$

The arithmetic for the factorization (A.7.2) is equivalent to the (forward) elimination of variables in solving a system of linear equations. We leave this arithmetic to a computer subroutine.

We note:

4. The determinant of a null matrix is zero.

5. The determinant of a diagonal matrix is the product of its diagonal elements.

6. The determinant of the identity matrix is unity.

A.8. PARTITIONED MATRICES

Sometimes we have reason either to express a given matrix as the *adjoined* combination of a number of matrices or to adjoin a given set of matrices to form one entire matrix. In practice, we never create such jigsaw puzzles as would be represented by

$$\mathbf{A}_{11} = \begin{bmatrix} a_{11} & a_{12} \\ a_{21} & a_{22} \end{bmatrix} \quad \mathbf{A}_{12} = \begin{bmatrix} a_{13} \\ a_{23} \end{bmatrix} \quad \mathbf{A}_{13} = \begin{bmatrix} a_{14} & a_{15} \\ a_{24} & a_{25} \\ a_{34} & a_{35} \end{bmatrix}$$

$$\mathbf{A}_{21} = \begin{bmatrix} a_{31} & a_{32} & a_{33} \\ a_{41} & a_{42} & a_{43} \\ a_{51} & a_{52} & a_{53} \end{bmatrix} \quad \mathbf{A}_{22} = \begin{bmatrix} a_{44} & a_{45} \\ a_{54} & a_{55} \end{bmatrix}$$

from a (5×5) matrix $\mathbf{A}$, but rather we always adjoin or divide in such a way that one can indicate partitions of rows and columns in the matrix such as

$$\mathbf{A} = \begin{bmatrix} \mathbf{A}_{11} & \mathbf{A}_{12} \\ \mathbf{A}_{21} & \mathbf{A}_{22} \end{bmatrix} = \left[\begin{array}{cc:ccc} a_{11} & a_{12} & a_{13} & a_{14} & a_{15} \\ a_{21} & a_{22} & a_{23} & a_{24} & a_{25} \\ \hdashline a_{31} & a_{32} & a_{33} & a_{34} & a_{35} \\ a_{41} & a_{42} & a_{43} & a_{44} & a_{45} \\ a_{51} & a_{52} & a_{53} & a_{54} & a_{55} \end{array} \right].$$

When a sequence of matrices of the same number of rows are adjoined from left to right, and a sequence of matrices of the same number of columns are adjoined one below the previous, as in the example, or when we label the adjoined matrices obtained by partitioning a given matrix by rows and/or columns as indicated, we say we have a *partitioned matrix* and refer to the adjoined component matrices as *submatrices* of the entire matrix. (Some writers make a distinction between partitioning a given matrix into submatrices and adjoining given matrices to form a *supermatrix*. The distinction carries no mathematical significance and seems rather superfluous.)

A property of partitioned matrices that might seem almost remarkable is that the basic rule of matrix multiplication in terms of the elements of the matrix applies, with appropriate partitioning, to submatrices. Thus, if

$$\mathbf{A} = \begin{bmatrix} \mathbf{A}_{11} & \mathbf{A}_{12} \\ \mathbf{A}_{21} & \mathbf{A}_{22} \end{bmatrix} \qquad \mathbf{B} = \begin{bmatrix} \mathbf{B}_{11} & \mathbf{B}_{12} \\ \mathbf{B}_{21} & \mathbf{B}_{22} \end{bmatrix}$$

then

$$\mathbf{AB} = \begin{bmatrix} \mathbf{A}_{11}\mathbf{B}_{11} + \mathbf{A}_{12}\mathbf{B}_{21} & \mathbf{A}_{11}\mathbf{B}_{12} + \mathbf{A}_{12}\mathbf{B}_{22} \\ \mathbf{A}_{21}\mathbf{B}_{11} + \mathbf{A}_{22}\mathbf{B}_{21} & \mathbf{A}_{21}\mathbf{B}_{12} + \mathbf{A}_{22}\mathbf{B}_{22} \end{bmatrix}.$$

(The reader might wish to verify the truth and meaning of this statement by constructing a small numerical example and computing the product as an ordinary matrix product and as a product of the partitioned matrices.)

A.9. EXPECTED VALUES

For the purposes of this book, we define the *expected value* of a variable as the arithmetic mean of the variable in the population. (Mathematicians would require a deeper definition.) If x is a measure on subjects drawn from a population, we write $E\{x\}$ for the expected value of x (i.e., for the mean of x in the population). We apply the same operation to squares and products (and conceivably other functions) of measures, writing, for example, $E\{x^2\}$ for the mean square of x, and $E\{xy\}$ for the mean product of two measures x and y.

If a variable x is in deviation measure in the population, then its variance is given by

$$\sigma_x^2 = E\{x^2\}. \tag{A.9.1}$$

If two measures x and y are in deviation measure in the population then their covariance is given by

$$c_{xy} = E\{xy\} \tag{A.9.2}$$

and if they are in standard measure, this becomes their correlation

$$r_{xy} = E\{xy\}. \tag{A.9.3}$$

If $x_1, \ldots, x_n$ are n measures on an individual randomly drawn from a population, and we define the vector $\mathbf{x}' = [x_1, \ldots, x_n]$, then it is natural to define the $(n \times 1)$ vector $\boldsymbol{\mu}' = [\mu_1, \ldots, \mu_n]$ of expected values of the n components of $\mathbf{x}$ by

$$\boldsymbol{\mu} = E\{\mathbf{x}\} \tag{A.9.4}$$

to express the fact that $\mu_j = E\{x_j\}$, $j = 1, \ldots, n$.

Suppose that $\mathbf{x}$ is in deviation measure, and write

$$\mathbf{A} = \mathbf{xx}' \tag{A.9.5}$$

an $(n \times n)$ matrix, whose (j, k)th element is given by

$$[a_{jk}] = [x_j x_k]. \tag{A.9.6}$$

If we accept that

$$E\{\mathbf{A}\} = [E\{x_j x_k\}] \tag{A.9.7}$$

that is, that the expected value of the matrix $\mathbf{A}$ is the matrix of expected values of its elements, then we see that the covariance matrix of $\mathbf{x}$ is given by

$$\mathbf{C} = E\{\mathbf{xx}'\} \tag{A.9.8}$$

because $E\{x_j x_k\}$ is the covariance of x_j and x_k, by (A.9.2), and $E\{x_j^2\}$ is the variance of x_j by (A.9.1). If, further, $\mathbf{x}$ is in standard measure in the population, then the correlation matrix of $\mathbf{x}$ is given by

$$\mathbf{R} = E\{\mathbf{xx}'\}. \tag{A.9.9}$$

A basic rule that we shall take for granted in operating with expected values of matrices and vectors is that if $\mathbf{Z}$ is a matrix that has an expected value and $\mathbf{A}, \mathbf{B}, \mathbf{C}$ are matrices of constants, then

$$E\{\mathbf{AXB} + \mathbf{C}\} = \mathbf{A}E\{\mathbf{X}\}\mathbf{B} + \mathbf{C} \tag{A.9.10}$$

We note immediately that if $\mathbf{x}$ is an $(n \times 1)$ vector of deviation measures and $\mathbf{w}$ is an $(n \times 1)$ vector of weights, then the variance of the weighted combination

$$s = \mathbf{w}'\mathbf{x} \tag{A.9.11}$$

is given by

$$\sigma_s^2 = E\{\mathbf{w}'\mathbf{x}\cdot\mathbf{x}'\mathbf{w}\}$$
$$= \mathbf{w}'E\{\mathbf{xx}'\}\mathbf{w}$$
$$= \mathbf{w}'\mathbf{Cw} \tag{A.9.12}$$

where C is the covariance matrix of x. If

$$z = Bx \tag{A.9.13}$$

is an $(m \times 1)$ vector of linear combinations of the n variables $x_1, \ldots, x_n$, then the $(m \times m)$ covariance matrix of z is given by

$$E\{zz'\} = E\{Bxx'B'\}$$
$$= BE\{xx'\}B'$$
$$= BCB'. \tag{A.9.14}$$

[Note the use of (A.3.12) here.]

References

*Bentler, P. M., & Weeks, D. G. (1980). Linear structural equations with latent variables. *Psychometrika, 45,* 289–308.

*Blalock, H. M. (1964). *Causal inference in nonexperimental research.* University of North Carolina Press: Chapel Hill.

Burt, C. (1948). The factorial study of temperamental traits. *British Journal of Psychology, Statistical Section, 1,* 178–203.

Campbell, N. J. (1957). *Foundations of science: the philosophy of theory and experiment.* Dover, New York.

Campbell, D. T., & Fiske, D. W. (1959). Convergent and discriminant validation by the multitrait–multimethod matrix. *Psychological Bulletin, 56,* 81–105.

Carroll, J. B. (1953). An analytic solution for approximating simple structure in factor analysis. *Psychometrika, 18,* 23–38.

Carroll, J. B. (1957). Biquartimin criterion for rotation to oblique simple structure in factor analysis. *Science, 126,* 1114–1115.

Cattell, R. B. (1944). Parallel proportional profiles and other principles for determining the choice of factors by rotation. *Psychometrika, 9,* 267–83.

Cattell, R. B., & Muerle, J. L. (1960). The "maxplane" program for factor rotation to oblique simple structure. *Educational and psychological Measurement, 20,* 269–290.

Christofferson, A. (1975). Factor analysis of dichotomized variables. *Psychometrika, 40,* 5–22.

*Duncan, O. D. (1975). *Introduction to structural equation models.* New York: Academic Press.

*Evans, G. T.(1971). Transformation of factor matrices to achieve congruence. *British Journal of mathematical and statistical Psychology, 24,* 22–48.

*Gorsuch, R. L. (1974). *Factor analysis,* Philadelphia: Saunders.

Guttman, L. (1950). The principal components of scale analysis. In S. S. Stouffer et al. (Eds.), *Measurement and Prediction.* Princeton, NJ: Princeton University Press.

Guttman, L. (1955). The determinacy of factor score matrices with implications for five other basic problems of common-factor theory. *British Journal of statistical Psychology, 8,* 65–81.

---

*Recommended for further reading.

Hakstian, A. R. (1971). A comparative evaluation of several prominent methods of oblique factor transformation. *Psychometrika, 36,* 175–193.

Hakstian, A. R., & Abel, R. A. (1974). A further comparison of oblique factor transformation methods. *Psychometrika, 39,* 429–444.

Harman, H. H., & Fukuda, Y. (1966). Resolution of the Heywood case in the minres solution. *Psychometrika, 31,* 563–571.

Harris, C. W. (Ed.) (1962). *Problems in measuring change.* Madison: University of Wisconsin Press.

Harris, C. W., & Kaiser, H. F. (1964). Oblique factor analytic solutions by orthogonal transformations. *Psychometrika, 29,* 347–362.

Harshman, R. A. (1970). Foundations of the PARAFAC procedure: Models and conditions for an "explanatory" multimodal factor analysis. *UCLA Working Papers in Phonetics 16.*

Hendrickson, A. E., & White, P. O. (1964). PROMAX: A quick method for rotation to oblique simple structure. *British Journal of statistical Psychology, 17,* 65–70.

Heywood, H. B.(1931). On finite sequences of real numbers. *Proceedings of the Royal Society, Series A, 134,* 486–501.

Hotelling, H. (1933). Analysis of a complex of statistical variables into principal components. *Journal of educational Psychology, 24,* 417–441, 498–520.

*James, L. R., & Mulaik, S. A. (1982). *Causal analysis: Assumptions, models and data: Studying organizations: Innovations in methodology.* Beverly Hills, CA: Sage.

Jennrich, R. I., & Sampson, P. F. (1966). Rotation for simple loadings. *Psychometrika, 31,* 313–323.

Jöreskog, K. G. (1962). On the statistical treatment of residuals in factor analysis. *Psychometrika, 27,* 335–354.

Jöreskog, K. G. (1971). Simultaneous factor analysis in several populations. *Psychometrika, 36,* 409–426.

*Jöreskog, K. G. (1973). A general method for estimating a linear structural equation system. In A. S. Goldberger & O. D. Duncan (Eds.), *Structural equation models in the social sciences.* New York: Seminar Press.

Kaiser, H. F. (1958). The varimax criterion for analytic rotation in factor analysis. *Psychometrika, 23,* 187–200.

Kaiser, H. F. (1970). A second-generation Little Jiffy. *Psychometrika, 35,* 401–415.

Kruskal, J. B., & Shepard, R. N. (1974). A nonmetric variety of linear factor analysis. *Psychometrika, 39,* 123–157.

*Kruskal, J. B., & Wish, M. (1978). *Multidimensional Scaling.* Beverly Hills, CA: Sage.

*Law, H. G., Snyder, C. W., Hattie, J. A., & McDonald, R. P. (Eds.) (in press). *Research methods for multimode data analysis.*

Lawley, D. N. (1940). The estimation of factor loadings by the method of maximum likelihood. *Proceedings of the Royal Society of Edinburgh, 60,* 64–82.

Lazarsfeld, P. F. (1950). The logical and mathematical foundation of latent structure analysis. In S. A. Stouffer et al. (Eds.), *Measurement and Prediction.* NJ: Princeton University Press.

Lazarsfeld, P. F., & Henry, N. W. (1968). *Latent structure analysis.* Boston, MA: Houghton Mifflin.

*Lord, F. M. (1980). *Applications of item response theory to practical testing problems.* Hillsdale, NJ: Lawrence Erlbaum Associates.

*Lord, F. M., & Novick, M. R. (1968). *Statistical theories of mental test scores: with contributions by Alan Birnbaum.* Reading, MA: Addison-Wesley.

Martin, J. K., & McDonald, R. P. (1975). Bayesian estimation in unrestricted factor analysis: a treatment for Heywood cases. *Psychometrika, 40,* 505–517.

McArdle, J. J. (1978). *A structural view of structural models.* Paper presented at Winter Workshop on Latent Structure Models Applied to Development Data. University of Denver, December.

McArdle, J. J., & McDonald, R. P. (in press). Some algebraic properties of the RAM logic for structural equation model specification. *British Journal of mathematical and statistical Psychology.*

McDonald, R. P. (1962). A note on the derivation of the general latent class model. *Psychometrika, 27*, 203–206.

McDonald, R. P. (1967). Nonlinear factor analysis. *Psychometric Monograph No. 15.*

McDonald, R. P. (1970). The theoretical foundations of principal factor analysis, canonical factor analysis, and alpha factor analysis. *British Journal of mathematical and statistical Psychology, 23*, 1–21.

McDonald, R. P. (1977). The indeterminacy of components and the definition of common factors. *British Journal of mathematical and statistical Psychology, 30*, 165–176.

McDonald, R. P. (1978a). Generalizability in factorable domains: "Domain validity and generalizability." *Educational and psychological Measurement, 38*, 75–79.

McDonald, R. P. (1978b). A simple comprehensive model for the analysis of covariance structures. *British Journal of mathematical and statistical Psychology, 31*, 59–72.

*McDonald, R. P. (1980). A simple comprehensive model for the analysis of covariance structures: Some remarks on applications, *British Journal of mathematical and statistical Psychology, 33*, 161–183.

*McDonald, R. P. (1981). The dimensionality of tests and items. *British Journal of mathematical and statistical Psychology, 34*, 100–117.

McDonald, R. P. (1983a). Alternative weights and invariant parameters in optimal scaling. *Psychometrika, 48*, 377–391.

*McDonald, R. P. (1983b). Linear versus nonlinear models in item response theory. *Applied psychological Measurement, 6*, 379–396.

McDonald, R. P. (in press). *Unidimensional and multidimensional models for item response theory.* Transactions of Conference on Item Response Theory and Computerized Adaptive Testing, Minneapolis, July 1982.

McDonald, R. P., & Ahlawat, K. S. (1974). Difficulty factors in binary data. *British Journal of mathematical and statistical Psychology, 27*, 82–99.

McDonald, R. P., & Burr, E. J. (1967). A comparison of four methods of constructing factor scores. *Psychometrika, 32*, 381–401.

*McDonald, R. P., & Mulaik, S. A. (1979). Determinacy of common factors: a nontechnical review. *Psychological Bulletin, 86*, 297–306.

McNemar, Q. (1964). Lost: Our intelligence? Why? *American Psychologist, 19*, 871–882.

Meredith, W. (1964). Notes on factorial invariance. *Psychometrika, 29*, 177–185.

Meyer, W. J., & Bendig, A. W. (1961). A longitudinal study of the Primary Mental Abilities Test. *Journal of educational Psychology, 52*, 50–60.

Miller, C. R., Sabagh, G., & Dingman, H. F. (1962). Latent class analysis and differential mortality. *Journal of the American statistical Association, 57*, 430–438.

*Mulaik, S. A. (1972). *The foundations of factor analysis,* New York: McGraw-Hill.

Mulaik, S. A., & McDonald, R. P. (1978). The effect of additional variables on factor indeterminacy in models with a single common factor. *Psychometrika, 43*, 177–192.

*Nishisato, S. (1980). *Analysis of categorical data: dual scaling and its applications.* Toronto: University of Toronto Press.

*Rummel, R. J. (1970). *Applied factor analysis.* Evanston, Il.: Northwestern University Press.

Saunders, D. R. (1961). The rationale for an "oblimax" method of transformation in factor analysis. *Psychometrika, 26*, 317–324.

Saunders, D. R. (1962). *Trans-varimax: Some properties of the ratiomax and equimax criteria for blind orthogonal rotation.* Paper presented at the meeting of the American Psychological Association, St. Louis.

Schlesinger, I. M., & Guttman, L. (1969). Smallest space analysis of intelligence and achievement tests. *Psychological Bulletin, 71*, 95–100.

Spearman, C. (1904). General intelligence, objectively determined and measured. *American Journal of Psychology, 15*, 201–293.

Thomson, G. H. (1934). Hotelling's method modified to give Spearman's *g. Journal of educational Psychology, 25*, 366–374.

Thomson, G. H. (1950). *The factorial analysis of human ability.* London: University of London Press.

Thurstone, L. L. (1947). *Multiple factor analysis.* Chicago, Il.: University of Chicago Press.

Tucker, L. R. (1951). *A method for synthesis of factor analysis studies.* PRS Report No. 984, Educational Testing Service.

Tucker, L. R. (1964). The extension of factor analysis to three-dimensional matrices. In N. Fredriksen & H. Gulliksen (Eds.), *Contributions to mathematical Psychology.* New York: Holt, Rinehart & Winston.

Walker, D. A. (1931). Answer pattern and score scatter in tests and examinations. *British Journal of Psychology, 22*, 73–86.

Wright, B. D., & Stone, M. H. (1979). *Best test design.* Chicago: Mesa Press.

Author Index

Numbers in *italics* indicate pages with complete bibliographic information.

253

Subject Index